You, _____,

will find the help, hope, and encouragement in this book

that will serve as a reminder that if man can take

moldy bread and make penicillin out of it,

just think what a loving God can make

out of you.

Zig

Zig

THE AUTOBIOGRAPHY
OF ZIG ZIGLAR

DOUBLEDAY
New York   London   Toronto
Sydney   Auckland

WATERBROOK PRESS
Colorado Springs

Published by Doubleday
a division of Random House, Inc.
1540 Broadway, New York, New York 10036

Doubleday and the portrayal of an anchor with a dolphin are
trademarks of Doubleday, a division of Random House, Inc.
WaterBrook and its deer design logo are registered trademarks of
WaterBrook Press, a division of Random House, Inc.

This book is copublished with WaterBrook Press,
2375 Telstar Drive, Suite 160, Colorado Springs, Colorado 80920,
a division of Random House, Inc.

BOOK DESIGN BY JENNIFER ANN DADDIO

Library of Congress Cataloging-in-Publication Data
Ziglar, Zig.
Zig : the autobiography of Zig Ziglar.—1st ed.
1. Motivation (Psychology) 2. Ziglar, Zig. 3. Motivational
speakers—United States—Biography. I. Title.
BF503 .Z54 2002
158'092—dc21
[B]
2002022454

ISBN 0-385-50296-6 (Doubleday)
ISBN 1-57856-502-2 (WaterBrook)

PRINTED IN THE UNITED STATES OF AMERICA

August 2002

First Edition

1   3   5   7   9   10   8   6   4   2

Dedicated to my mother,

Lila Wescott Ziglar.

Kind—gentle—wise

pillar of strength and shining

example for all who knew her.

Contents

Foreword

Autobiographies often flaunt, exaggerate, rationalize, and end up on bookstore bargain tables. But not this one! Zig Ziglar invites you to travel a road filled with colorful characters, humorous stories, and hope.

Zig is a man with a story. More important, he is a man with a message for you. His faith-based, high-performance system has created a new way of thinking for men and women worldwide. The principles he shares are distinct and grounded in enthusiastic discipline.

The measure of a public man is taken in the private moments. Gimmickry and hype rarely survive the heat of real life. As someone Zig calls mentor and friend, I know the man who inspires thousands. I also know the man who grieves, yet "not like those without hope." Zig's gift is not optimism but the clear understanding of the power of gratitude. His methods work because they are born of profound appreciation and awe. In his life he demonstrates that the light of gratitude dispels the darkness of discouragement.

His life's foundation is commitment: to God, to family and friends, and to all those his life touches. You hear him say, "If you help enough people get what they want, you will get what you want." Those closest to him know that he walks the talk. In reading his story you will be encouraged to take the next step in your plan and keep on stepping until you've reached the goal. The benefit of reading the life stories of our heroes is to understand and apply, take a thought and make it an action—then you will truly have understood Zig's story.

Fred Smith
Businessman, Author, Lecturer,
Consultant, and Mentor to many

Thank You

There are so many who meant so much to me in my life that identifying them all would be impossible. However, as always, there are some who played bigger roles than others and that's particularly true of this effort.

In apportioning our thanks, we begin with this book's editor, my daughter, Julie Norman. The countless hours she spent, her love for me, and her knowledge of my life, along with her marvelous insights, made her an invaluable asset in getting this story down and getting it straight. She has a unique talent in connecting the links, and since she is of a different generation and a different gender, she brings balance to our work together.

Laurie Magers, my faithful executive assistant for the last twenty-five years, as always did yeomanlike work in transcribing my dictation, recalling events and details that had slipped from my memory bank, and working in tandem with Julie. She contributed mightily to the effort this book represents.

Bruce Barbour, our friend and agent, was more than generous with his time and his thoughtful suggestions. He made the book better balanced and stronger, and he enhanced the message.

Margaret Langstaff, for stepping in and smoothing out the rough edges. Her ability to tweak the text in just the right places contributed significantly to the quality of this work.

Of course, I must here recognize the person to whom I refer throughout all of my books and talks, the one who gives my life special meaning and brings joy and delight to me on a daily basis, and who after more than fifty-five years of marriage is still the light of my life (my crush on her is obviously permanent). I'm talking about my wife Jean (the Redhead). Her support and love during the writing of this book, as well as her candid advice, have meant a great deal to me and to the outcome of this project.

The twenty-six people whose pictures occupy my Wall of Gratitude and to whom I refer throughout the book played huge roles in my life, and I want to recognize them individually: Lila Wescott Ziglar, Jean Abernathy Ziglar, Sister Jessie, Suzan Ziglar Witmeyer, Mrs. Dement Warren, John R. Anderson, Walton Haining, Mrs. Margaret Worley, Mrs. J. W. Parker, Jobie Harris, W. P. (Bill) Cranford, P. C. Merrell, Bob Bales, Dr. Norman Vincent Peale, Dr. Emol Fails, Hal Krause, Harry Lemmons, Frank Grubbs, Bernie Lofchick, Cavett Robert, Dr. and Mrs. W. A. Criswell, Fred Smith, Mary Kay Ash, Mary Crowley, Dr. Kenneth Cooper.

In addition, I owe a special thanks to the seminar leaders who over the years made it possible for my name to be spread in the marketplace when I spoke at their seminars.

Then, of course, there are the other members of my family. My son, Tom, who is our president and CEO, and Richard Oates, my son-in-law, who is our chief operating officer, kept things going in our organization during extraordinarily busy times. As I frequently tell people, although I am in on the major decisions, my primary function is to make speeches and write books. My family and staff are critical to my efforts because they free me to do "my thing" while not having to get involved in the day-to-day responsibilities necessary to keep the ship afloat. That's critical as we work together to fulfill *our mission,* which is *to be the difference makers in the personal, family, and professional lives of enough people to make a positive difference in the world.*

I especially want to recognize my niece, Virginia Everett, for helping me keep the facts straight. She has spent countless hours working on the genealogy of the Ziglar family, and her resources were a tremendous help.

I am forever indebted to my late sister, Turah Ziglar Allen, the family matriarch, who helped me reconstruct some of my early childhood memories and other incidents that had an impact on my life. She was a "little mother" as much as a big sister to me.

To the countless other people who have played roles in my life, who were the unseen friends and helping hands that over the years have been difference makers in my life, thank you. Your letters, words of appreciation, and support have all been extremely meaningful.

My publisher, Doubleday and Waterbrook Press, and their editors have been gracious and very helpful in every way possible. Eric Major led the editing effort and worked diligently with my staff and me to achieve the best possible end result. I am sincerely grateful to all of them.

This work has been a real labor of love, and vitally dependent on the involvement of both the obvious persons as well as anonymous contributors to my life. Without all of them this book would never have been written or published. I'm truly grateful to all of you. May God bless you.

Sincerely,
Zig Ziglar

Introduction

When I was born, the doctor handed me to my mother and said, "Mrs. Ziglar, you have a perfectly fine, healthy baby boy." Nine days later he picked me up and sadly shook his head, indicating that I was dead. Yes, I died when I was nine days old. However, my family has told me that my grandmother walked to me, picked me up, held me in her hands, and started talking to me. Of course, we all know that she was not really talking to *me* . . . and in a matter of seconds breath came back into my body; at age seventy-five it's obvious I lived.

My friends, it's been like that ever since.

If my life has had a theme, I suppose it has been a typical American theme in that, for most of it, I have been looking for happiness and success. Like the Horatio Alger stories that were popular in the nineteenth century, mine has been a tale of rags to riches. As I write this the story isn't over yet. I honestly feel more excited about the future today than I did even ten years ago. There is no way I can know what's actually in store for me, but I have set my goals and fully expect to reach them. I've made it through the first three-quarters of a century of living in a fashion I am pleased with, and I feel confident that the lessons I've learned so far have equipped me for whatever my future holds.

I was born in the rural South in very modest circumstances, number ten in a family of twelve children. My papa died when I was five years old, leaving my mama to raise us alone. All of her best efforts could not protect us from the general pain and suffering loose in the land during the Depression years, nor could it shield her children from the petty injustices and hurts normal to childhood. By the standards of the small town, Yazoo City, Mississippi, in which we lived, our family was "poor." Somehow, with every one of us pulling together and working hard, we always had enough to eat. Yes, we children did wear hand-me-down clothes, but our clothes were always neat and clean. My siblings and I didn't have much time for the idylls of childhood if "idleness" had anything to do with it.

But my mother, Lila Ziglar, was a remarkable woman. The more life rained on her, the stronger she seemed to grow. There is a saying that some people thrive on adversity. Lila Ziglar was one of them. Her self-discipline and moral decency were greater than the challenges she faced. Her faith in God was unswerving, something she felt accounted for every success and good thing that came into her life. She reared her children "right," according to the old-fashioned sense of the word. The Golden Rule prevailed in her home. Her children respected authority and did what she told them to do. By example she taught us the importance of putting God first in your life so everything else could fall into place, a lesson I knew rationally as a child but not "by heart" until many years later.

I was the first of her children to graduate from high school, not a small thing to her or the rest of us in those days and circumstances. I suppose all of us children were industrious and more or less ambitious, but without her encouragement and faith we would not have amounted to much. Certainly everything else around us, including the social customs of small town life, denied that we could achieve anything worthwhile.

In my pursuit of the American Dream I've jumped more than my share of fences looking for greener pastures. Initially I pursued a career in sales and, after a lot of hard work, experienced significant professional and financial success. But my blindness to the larger questions and issues in life led to my making serious errors in judgment, which in turn resulted in major setbacks for me and my own growing family. After a good deal of longing and effort, I was able to establish a career as a speaker and author—for me, a dream come true. It is no mean accomplishment for a small boy from a small town with few advantages to have thousands of people come to listen to what he has to say. Throughout my speaking career, I have met and worked with titans of industry, American presidents, and world leaders. I've written a number of best-selling books. I've started companies that have done well and endured through time. I've found joy in my home and family, and special blessings in my wife. In a sense, I reached the summit, the top, inching my way up from very small unspectacular beginnings, initially with two steps forward, one step back.

Over the years, I've been asked many times to expand on stories I've told about my life in my books and talks. It truly amazes me that people are interested. I hope that this work will satisfy the people who want to know how life has played out for this "too small, poor boy from Yazoo City, Mississippi."

Since this is the story of my life, some of it will be recognizable to those who have read my books or heard me speak, but I have made it my objective to fill in the blanks, tell the good with the bad, and share hard-won knowledge along with God-given blessings.

I have very few personal memories before the age of five, so the best information I can give you about my family and me from that time period has been gathered over the years from older sisters and brothers, extended family, and friends. My mother shared some of the stories mentioned here with me. I have done my best to verify the truth and accuracy of what is written here, but as everyone knows, family stories have a way of "glorifying themselves" over the years. I apologize for any unintentional inaccuracies that take place within this work. In my heart of hearts, I can honestly tell you that I've written the truth, as I know it.

My story is proof that you can start anywhere and get to where you want to go. I hope you see through my story that life is a great teacher, that failure is only an event, and that regardless of what happens to you along the way, you will eventually come to understand that everything that occurs teaches and prepares you for the next stage of life. Nothing is lost. It is my hope, prayer, and belief that this book will benefit, entertain, surprise, and possibly even delight you. I know you'll pick up nuggets of the wisdom my mother taught me, and I hope that the people who influenced me for the better will have a similar effect on you.

If you were to come to our corporate headquarters today, you would notice the pictures of twenty-six men and women prominently displayed on what I call my Wall of Gratitude. I honor each one of them because they had a strong impact on my life, and their influence shaped my beliefs, my values, and my choices over the years. I will talk about all of these mentors and the part they played in my life as we progress through the book. So that you can put faces to the names, let me encourage you to turn to the center of the book and review the pictures of my mentors, as well as pictures of myself and my family from the early years to the present. My favorite pictures are of my wife. Take a look for yourself, and you'll see how beautiful she is. As you read through the book you'll notice that I lovingly refer to her as the Redhead, but her given name is Jean. When I'm speaking to her, I call her Sugar Baby.

If you enjoy reading this book just half as much as I've enjoyed living my life—well, then, we'll both be winners! And, just as I said in my very first book, I really will see you "at the Top!"

PART ONE

The Early Years

Mama Married Papa

When my mother, Lila Hannifew Wescott, was fifteen years old, she married my father, eighteen-year-old, John Silas "Judge" Ziglar. Their wedding date was December 18, 1902. They lived with Mama's parents, Ephram and Emily Wescott, for six months before they settled in south Alabama near what is currently the town of New Hope.

I'm told Mama was different from many young women of her time largely because of the influence of her mother—a successful merchant of sewing materials, sewing machines, and sewing machine parts. In the 1880s few women were independent or enterprising enough to have their own businesses—my grandmother was a true exception. Apparently she instilled her strong-willed personality arising out of her Irish background in Mama, because I never knew Mama to be at a loss over any circumstance.

It seems my mama's unusual background perfectly suited her for my entrepreneurial father. Papa farmed, owned a sawmill, operated and managed a shingle mill, and juggled several businesses simultaneously. He was a forebear of the successful work ethic later associated so closely with the 1940s and '50s in this country. My papa, John Silas Ziglar, was a man of action, who balanced family life well with his work.

As a family provider, Papa had few peers. He was never wealthy, but his energy and common sense guaranteed that our family never went without. Papa bartered his farmed goods with the people in our community; he drained and sold resin from pine trees; he took the excess syrup from his brother Oscar's cane mill, made cane juice, and developed a "route" where he put cans of cane juice in mailboxes early in the week and collected his money from the mailboxes later in the week. Papa often rode across the Alabama state line to Florida and bought (or traded for) fish, which he placed in iced barrels and delivered to people who had purchased them in advance. In those days no one had refrigerators and very few had ice boxes, so fresh fish had a special appeal. On more than one occasion Mama had to remind Papa to "stop at our house first," since his fresh Florida fish were in such demand.

The Judge

Papa earned his nickname, the Judge, for his ability to quickly differentiate right from wrong. In addition, he was not shy about sharing his opinion. He was umpire for the community weekend baseball games, and when the Judge spoke, there was no rebuttal.

As the story goes, on one occasion the home team traveled several miles for a game that erupted into a loud and prolonged argument over a disputed call by the local umpire. Both teams mounted horses or wagons or set out on foot to travel the distance between the field and our home. You can well imagine my mother's surprise when she answered the front door to find forty to fifty disgruntled baseball players and spectators demanding to see the Judge.

The competitors explained the situation. My father rendered his decision, and everyone left satisfied. Debating or questioning the Judge's decision never occurred to anyone. He was a thoughtful man possessed of great confidence. Everyone respected his intelligence, fairness, and judgment.

The Love of a Father

Our family was full of affection as Mama and Papa were both "huggers." When anyone visited our home, they were engulfed in hugs and surrounded by laughter and love. While Mama was known for the gravity of the few words she spoke, Papa was noted for being quite the talker. His quick wit and fun-loving ways created a joyful atmosphere.

I'm told that we used to pile on top of him when he'd arrive home from a "fishing expedition," demanding stories of his most recent adventures in Florida. The stories were always funny yet demonstrated the time-honored "southern traditions" of honesty, character, integrity, faith, loyalty, and love. Papa never missed an opportunity to teach his children the basics of moral living.

One of our family rituals was to ask Papa what day it was when he'd arrive home especially late. He'd always respond with, "Thursday, what's left of it," or "Wednesday, but not for long!," and all the children would smile and sometimes giggle with delight. On the rare occasions when Papa was going to be home for an entire day, he'd get up early, and when we asked him why he was getting up so early on his "day off," he would say, "If I'm not gonna do anything, I'm sure gonna get started early!"

I never wondered if my father loved me or my brothers and sisters. When any of us would ask to spend the night with a friend, he'd always say, "Invite them here! When I get home, I need my children to be here with me." His message was clear—not only did he cherish and love his children—he wanted them around him.

The Love of a Heavenly Father

In our home, the weekend activities revolved around the church. When the doors of the church opened, my mama and her children were there. Whenever possible, Papa was there, too, but his work and travel schedule often interfered.

One of the few (if not the only) disagreements that Mama and Papa ever had was about Sundays. It seems Papa umpired baseball games between Sunday morning and Sunday evening church services—an activity that Mama strongly felt was a distraction from God's day. The two of them often discussed the pros and cons of Papa continuing to umpire on Sunday, but God had the final word in the matter!

One Sunday afternoon, Papa called off a game in the late innings because the weather had become intolerable. As the players were leaving the field, lightning struck a tree near the center-field area, knocking three men to the ground. No one was injured, but Papa got the message. He went home and admitted to Mama that she was exactly right and there would be no more Sunday umpiring. Papa was willing to listen to a Higher Authority!

Brothers and Sisters

On May 4, 1906, my oldest sister, Amanda Lera Ziglar was born. The local doctor delivered her and all the children who followed, which was a significant fact because most children of that time came into the world with the aid of a midwife. My father wanted the best he could provide for Mama and his children, so he made sure there was enough fish, resin, cane juice, crops, or dollars to compensate the doctor fairly.

Two years later, on May 29, 1908, Lola Ziglar was born. On August 27, 1910, twin brothers, Willie Hubert and James Huie Ziglar arrived. Silas Houston Ziglar joined them on May 16, 1913.

On September 9, 1915, Emily Turah brought the count to three boys and three girls. Three years later, on March 15, 1918, Huel G. Ziglar (the G. was taken from Dr. E. G. Bragg, the physician who delivered most of the Ziglar children) put the boys in the lead until July 7, 1920, when Evia Jane Ziglar made the count four boys and four girls. Howard Huglar Ziglar put the boys in the lead for good on October 16, 1922.

Number Ten

On November 6, 1926, I arrived five weeks early—making me my mother's only premature baby. Dr. Bragg asked my parents if they had ever thought about how God had blessed them, pointing out that I was their tenth "perfect" child. I was named Hilary Hinton Ziglar, and now you know why I go by the name Zig.

When I was only nine days old, my oldest sister, Lera, gave birth to my mother's first grandchild, Lucille. Mama was extremely nervous about the whole situation and breathed a huge sigh of relief when she found out baby and mother were both doing well. It was shortly after that—just a matter of a few hours, I'm told—that Mama's feelings of joy about Lucille turned to stark terror over the fear of losing me. Apparently I had turned blue while Mama held me. She screamed for my sister Turah to get my grandmother. Maw, my papa's mother, was visiting to help with the children and chores while Mama recovered from having me.

Papa heard the commotion, and when he saw Mama's face and my skin tone, he ran the hundred yards across the road to fetch the doctor, who was still at Lera's house. When they got back to the house, I'm told, Mama was quietly crying, big tears pouring down her cheeks. The doctor, very concerned, picked me up and held my tiny body to his ear in an effort to hear breathing or a heartbeat. After a few silent moments he handed me back to

Mama. He didn't utter a word, but I'm told his slumped shoulders and the look on his face plainly said that I was gone. The doctor looked at my father and slowly began to shake his head from side to side.

My grandmother understood that everyone thought I was dead, but she walked to my mother's bedside and said, "Please give me that baby."

She lifted me up and gently blew into my discolored face. Then she cradled me close to her body and began walking around the room, patting and rubbing my back. My sister Turah said the whole time you could hear her praying fervently, and even though you couldn't make out the words, you could tell she was in direct contact with my Maker. Then Turah said Maw stopped, blew in my face, and started the process over again. After what seemed an eternity, Maw stopped her primitive CPR and handed me back to Mama—all pink and breathing normally. It's said in the family that Maw's love and God's grace brought me back to life.

Since I had been born prematurely I was suffering from cyanosis, a malady that in my case was the result of incomplete lung expansion. The condition is often called "blue baby," because the baby looks blue due to the lack of oxygen in the blood. I've been told the story of my birth, death, and revival many times, and it has never failed to overwhelm me.

I well remember March 25, 1929, the day my little brother, Horace Judge Ziglar, was born. The winds had become so strong the chimney and fireplace in the room where Mama had Horace blew down. Luckily, they blew away from the house so no one was hurt, but the cold March winds came blowing in through the house and chilled everyone and everything. When I was twelve years old I told Turah how scared I was that day, and that during the worst of the storm, I remembered seeing someone carry Mama across the hall to the other, safer bedroom with a fireplace. Turah told me that that someone was my papa. This is one of the very few memories I have of Papa.

The Move to Mississippi

Shortly after Horace was born, Papa was offered and accepted a job managing a large farm for Mr. Pierce in the Mississippi Delta. His new duties required him to focus on farming, reduce his travel schedule, and manage the families that worked the land. After nearly twenty-eight years of marriage and eleven children, "settling down" seemed like a good thing to do, so in 1930 we made the move that created one of my earliest memories.

When we moved from Coffee County, Alabama, to the Mississippi Delta farm eight miles outside of Yazoo City, I was four years old. We had a flatbed truck with sides on it, and we loaded our furniture and the family on the truck. The roads were primarily mud and gravel, and it was a two-day trip. We made a sight right out of a WPA photo of those tough years in America. Nearly a dozen dusty children piled on top of everything we owned in the world moving on to what we hoped were greener pastures.

The first night we found an abandoned farmhouse along the side of the road, and moved in to spend the night and get something to eat. My mother had baked biscuits before we left and had brought some "salt meat," eggs, and milk. The old home had a fireplace, and we found some logs that had been cut to fit it stacked by the side of the house. Mama had her old iron skillet with her, so she fried the "salt meat" to go with the biscuits and eggs, and we had a fine meal.

My two older brothers, Hubert and Houston, both hunted during the trip, primarily for rabbits and squirrels, and neither indulged in target practice because every shell was important and represented a financial investment. They did not shoot unless they had an excellent chance of making it count. They referred to squirrels as "limb bacon," and "limb bacon" was a regular staple in our diet.

I also recall that the house we lived in when we got to Mississippi was on a lake outside of Yazoo City, although "swamp" would be a more appropriate description. My brother, Houston, set out some trotlines, and the night he hooked two large catfish was a happy occasion for us. As a child, I thought they looked huge, and I suspect they did weigh eight or ten pounds each. For our family that represented fried fish for two or three days, and catfish stew on at least one occasion.

Soon I discovered that lake was good for more than just fishing. Its uses were limited only by the extent of a small boy's active imagination. Shortly after we moved to the farm we went to one of the local churches on a Sunday evening. Since we've always been Baptist, I assume it was a Baptist church. At any rate, there were several baptisms that night. As best I can remember, the preacher was pretty loud, and as he baptized each person he said, "I now baptize you in the name of the Father, the Son, and the Holy Ghost!"

As a four-year-old, I was mighty impressed by this scene, and it gave me some ideas of my own. Since we lived out in the country, there were always a number of cats around the barns and grounds to control the mouse and rat populations. There were unsuspecting small kittens on the scene at this particular time, and some of them were handy. I proceeded, along with one of my buddies whose name has long ago been forgotten, to baptize those kittens in the same way we had seen the people baptized at church: "I now baptize you in the name of the Father, the Son, and the Holy Ghost," and *bang!* we would just throw them into the lake.

We had done this four or five times when my older sister Turah caught wind of what we were doing and put a stop to it pronto! I have forgotten exactly what happened after that, but I do know that was the one and only time cat baptisms were held at our place. Given our early age, it never occurred to us that we were abusing those kittens. But it is an instance that demonstrates something that I believe to this day. Kids will do what they see their parents and other adults doing. They are natural mimics. Obviously, as a four-year-old, I was in no position to baptize adults, so the kittens fell victim to my childhood shenanigans.

As an aside, one of the things I also remember is that with the exception of Sunday-morning services, much of the church activity took place at night; farmers, particularly in those difficult times, often worked from sunup to sundown. In those days, parents traditionally brought quilts to church services and placed them on the floor, most of the time next to the pews in which they were seated, or in the aisles of the church, or between the pulpit and the first row of pews. As the little ones went to sleep in their parents' arms, Mom or Dad would place them on the quilts on the floor with a pillow, where they would sleep for the rest of the church service. Those worship experiences built a certain unity, sense of community, and interdependence among the families in attendance.

An Even Dozen

When Winnie Beth Ziglar was born on that farm, September 25, 1931, the number of Ziglar children rounded out to an even dozen. Mama had her hands full with all of us, so she was grateful for the help when my eleven-year-old sister Evia Jane all but adopted Winnie Beth. Growing up, I always thought a dozen was an awful lot of children, so I asked my mother one time why she had so many, and she in turn asked me, "Well, son, where do you think I should have stopped?" Since I was the tenth child born, I certainly didn't think she should have stopped after number nine!

Bearing Life's Burdens

Winnie Beth was barely a year old when Papa started having headaches and dizzy spells. On several occasions he actually blacked out, losing consciousness for several seconds. Back in those times people thought little of problems like that, but on Monday, October 31, Papa told Mama that something was wrong. He had been working the fields that morning, and the weather was cold and wet, setting up a chill in him that he just couldn't shake. Mama sent him to bed, covered him with a wool blanket, and surrounded him with bricks that she had heated in the fireplace. She warmed up the "smoothing iron" (normally used for smoothing wrinkles out of clothing) on the potbellied stove and placed it with the bricks, but no amount of heat would break Papa's chill.

By nightfall Papa was unable to talk. One of the older children was sent to get the doctor. When the doctor arrived, he summoned an ambulance to take Papa to the hospital in Yazoo City. It was clear the situation was grave. In those days an ambulance was used only under the most dire of circumstances.

At the small hospital in Yazoo City, on Wednesday, November 2, 1932, at approximately five A.M., with my oldest brother Hubert and Mama at his side, Papa looked into Mama's eyes and spoke his final words, "I love you, Lila." A cerebral hemorrhage brought on by a malarial infection claimed my papa's life. He was only forty-eight years old.

I have no real personal recollection of his death because of my age at the time, but the results of his death, the aching absence we felt as a family, became one of the chief realities of my childhood.

I'm told that shortly after Papa died, other family members arrived at the hospital to look after Mama. Several were in the room when our family doctor, W. D. McCaleb, asked to speak with my brother Hubert alone. The look on the doctor's face told Hubert that this was to be an important private conversation. They stepped into another room, and the doctor's conversation with my brother went something like this:

*"Hubert, as the oldest male member of the Ziglar family, you and I
need to have a talk. Your father was a fine man, and an excellent
provider for your family. No one loved your mother more than Judge
Ziglar. No one worked harder to provide for his family than Judge Ziglar.
And now, Hubert," he continued, "you are going to have to be the man
of the family. I wish planning your father's funeral was all we needed to
discuss, but as important as that is, there is something even more
important for us to discuss.*

*"Hubert, as you know, Winnie Beth has struggled for the last six
months with everything from measles to whooping cough. Last week I
found out why she has been so susceptible to these problems. Hubert,
Winnie Beth has a disease known as leukemia. Those who get leukemia
have problems with their blood that eventually lead to death. Hubert . . .
Winnie Beth isn't going to be with us much longer."*

I can only imagine what my twenty-two-year-old brother felt, but I suspect he and the doctor held each other and wept at the weight of it all before Hubert returned to our father's deathbed to comfort our mother. In the
wisdom God granted my brother to deal with his new knowledge, Hubert
decided that grieving one death at a time was enough for our family. He determined to bear the additional burden alone until after our father's funeral.
Dr. McCaleb had told him that Winnie Beth was already getting the medicine and tonics she needed to be comfortable. There was nothing more
medical science could do for her at that time.

Papa's Funeral

For two days Papa's body lay at the farmhouse, and on the third day after
his death he was buried about ten miles from Yazoo City, near Lake City,
Mississippi. The beautiful, white-framed Baptist church, which stands to
this day, was filled with mourners for the service. So many people came to
pay their respects to Papa—he was admired and loved greatly. Even some
of the black families Papa had worked with on the farm came to the funeral.
It was 1932, and in that day and time, especially in the South, blacks and
whites didn't mix. The black men and women who came to the funeral
wept openly and chose to remain standing as a tribute to the respect my

papa had earned in the black community. Their children—our playmates—
knew the love of my father and mourned the loss of him with us.

Two days later Winnie Beth died.

Winnie Beth's Funeral

We buried Papa November 5; I had my sixth birthday November 6, and
Winnie Beth died November 7. As an adult writing this, I can't imagine the
magnitude of what my mother was dealing with. I know what it is to lose a
child. My mind can't couple that indescribable grief with the simultaneous
loss of my wife. I can tell you that circumstances don't create character,
they reveal character, and what was revealed in my mother was truly a godly
character. The circumstances she faced would have overwhelmed many,
but as several of us children have said over the years, "Mama never took
anything into her own hands."

November 10, 1932, was icy cold. The whole family gathered near the
big fireplace in the bedroom when we returned from Winnie Beth's grave-
side funeral service. Mama was sitting upright at the head of the bed, and
the rest of us were settling in when Turah noticed that twelve-year-old Evia
Jane, Winnie Beth's devoted little caregiver, was not in the room. Turah has
told me that her first thought was, Oh, no! Not another tragedy! She
searched the house and couldn't find Evia Jane, so all of us started looking
frantically. After more than a few anxious moments, Turah found Winnie
Beth's self-appointed guardian curled up in an exhausted sleep under her
bed. Tear streaks stained Evia Jane's face as Turah bundled her up and carried her into the big, warm bedroom to join the rest of the family.

Family Counsel

It was an exhausting, emotionally draining time, and being together at that
sorrowful time in that one room united us into something stronger than any
one of us could have been individually. Our unified grief seemed to bind
our family even more tightly together. Mama began by stating the obvious.
"I'm in charge now, children, and you will listen to me. We all know what
we have been through. We all know how difficult this time is. Yet God is
with us and will see us through! He has promised to be with us, and now
we will call upon His promises."

Hubert, the oldest of us, jumped in, saying, "When Mother says to do something, we will do it! I am here to see to it that we all support our mother."

Right there in that bedroom the habit of unquestioned trust with which we had invested Papa was passed on to Mama. Mama always knew what was best. And if we tested her, the pencil-thin peach-tree switch she could readily acquire with a few fast steps down the back stairs was a reminder that her burdens required obedience and cooperation from us. Rarely did any of us go against her instructions, and, while being switched was painful and embarrassing, not once did we ever feel that we had been unfairly treated, abused, or severely punished.

She closed our family meeting that day by saying, "Children, some people will say to you that they are sorry for our 'loss.' You are to say, 'thank you.' But I want you to understand something very important. Your father and your sister are not lost. When someone is lost, that means we don't know where he or she is. Your father and sister are with Jesus in heaven right now. Someday we will all be there together."

It was comforting for all of us to hear the conviction, love, and faith in Mama's voice as she instructed us in what was to come. It was obvious that she was counting on God to help her raise the eight children who still lived under her roof.

A New Way of Life in Yazoo City

Just a few days after Winnie Beth's funeral Dr. Webb Brame and Mrs. Koonce from First Baptist Church of Yazoo City called on our family. Family tradition has it that they gave me the once-over when I opened the door to let them in, and that Mrs. Koonce commented how remarkable it was that even under our circumstances Mama had managed to keep her children in clean clothes and her house spotless.

Dr. Brame told Mama that they had heard about our losing Papa and Winnie Beth so close together. They felt the Lord wanted them to come visit us and express their sympathies. Mama invited them into the kitchen for a pot of coffee, and much discussion commenced.

Dr. Brame told Mama that he had heard that her family loved the Lord and that she was a godly woman. He pointed out that the older children would be an enormous help with chores and farmwork, but that with eight children still at home she would require even more help than they could provide.

Mama sat up a little taller and let him know she was not a charity case. The preacher let her know that they were just following the instructions in the Bible about taking care of widows. Mama backed off a bit with that revelation and told them she'd appreciate anything they felt called to do.

On hearing that, Mrs. Koonce told Mama that several church members had donated items they thought would be useful to us. Out in the automobile, she said, were several sets of warm clothing—jackets, sweaters, and wool shirts, as well as a box of groceries—mostly staples and basics.

Dr. Brame added that he had heard Mama was planning to move into town. He had taken the liberty of locating a suitable house for her to rent. It was on a large lot that would be perfect for gardening. An anonymous donor from the church had already paid the first month's rent of ten dollars. Not only that, church members were going to help with the physical aspects of the move.

Mama was overwhelmed by what they were trying to do. She always had difficulty accepting help. She admitted to them that she would soon have to give up the "caretaker's" home on the farm so the new farm manager and his family could move in, but she wasn't at all sure about moving to the city. According to her way of thinking, city folk had their days and nights mixed up. They stayed up 'til all hours and they drove their big cars fast on the smooth city streets—it would be dangerous for the children.

Dr. Brame tried to put Mama at ease by promising to help her adjust to city life. He also promised to help my two oldest brothers find jobs. Mama was so touched by the kindnesses they were offering her and her children, she wept. Dr. Webb and Mrs. Koonce shed a few tears of their own with her.

During Thanksgiving week, with the help of the church members, we moved into the house on Grand Avenue. Just as Dr. Brame had promised, the white, wood-framed city house had over an acre of land for gardening, something that would be very valuable to us in the years to come.

The Big City

The "big city" Mama was so concerned about is a topic in many of the speeches I make before the public. My roots in that small, Mississippi Delta town run deep, and the things I remember from my time there are still as fresh as yesterday. Smells, sounds, sights, even certain phrases bring Yazoo City back to me in a flash.

When people ask me if I was born in Yazoo City, I jokingly tell them that actually, I was born in L.A.—that is, Lower Alabama. I keep up the kidding by telling them that I know a lot of folks go around the country trying to impress people by claiming to be from Yazoo City, Mississippi, but I really am! I wouldn't say that Yazoo City is a small place, but our Avon lady also doubles as the church bell. Yes, Yazoo City is an exciting place—about once a month a train comes through town—which might not sound like excitement to you, but when you understand we don't have tracks there, that changes the picture. Main Street runs through the car wash, and we've hung a huge mirror at the end of Main Street to make the town look bigger. We don't even have a village drunk. We share one with the little community next to us.

All kidding aside, people often ask me if I offend Yazoo City folks by teasing about our town. I always say no because the residents clearly understand just how significant Yazoo City really is. Many outstanding people got their start there. A former president of the American Bar Association, a former president of the Mississippi Medical Association, a former chairman of the Republican National Committee, a former editor of *Harper's* magazine, a former president of the Southern Baptist Convention, a former Secretary of Agriculture, a former vice president of the Southern Baptist Convention, and comedian Jerry Clower are all from Yazoo City. I'm not sure what the other two people did.

In 1985 I was honored to receive the Mississippian of the Year award from the Mississippi Broadcasters Association. I don't think they would have given it to me if people were offended at the little funnies I make about Mississippi and Yazoo City. The award was deeply meaningful to me because I am so grateful for my Mississippi heritage. To be candid, it's just really nice to be recognized by those who watched you grow up and followed your career thereafter.

I'm often asked how is it that Yazoo City has produced so many outstanding people, and I always respond there are two basic reasons: We've had some outstanding preachers there and some outstanding superintendents of education, and when you combine faith and education, you're going to produce some remarkable people.

One of the outstanding educators Yazoo City had to offer was my first-grade teacher, Mrs. Dement Warren. When we moved into town after my father's death, I missed four months of school because of childhood illnesses. I would undoubtedly have failed the first grade had it not been for Mrs. Warren's extra efforts. Twice each week for those four months she came to our home and spent an hour with me, bringing me up to speed and giving me my assignments. Had she not done that I would have had to repeat the first grade. Had I repeated first grade, I would have been drafted out of high school in World War II and probably would never have seen the inside of a college. As it happened, I was able to graduate with my class, qualify for the Naval V5 Program, and get started in college. Without that training, my entire life would have been dramatically different. The message is clear: You never know when a helping hand will change another person's entire life.

Sometimes Mrs. Warren's hand helped in ways I didn't particularly like! When Mrs. Warren discovered that I could learn but just wouldn't, she spanked me. My mother said, "Thank you, Mrs. Warren. Do it again." Those readers who oppose corporal punishment might react to this with horror, but in my particular case, it was one of those necessities of life. When my mother encouraged Mrs. Warren to "do it again," she made it crystal clear to me that she approved of discipline if it made me a better student. Mrs. Warren quickly learned that she had the cooperation of my mother. I believe that if parents today would cooperate like this with educators, our students would be much better prepared for life. I'm not advocating abuse or punishment: discipline is what you do *for* someone; punishment is what you do *to* someone.

Just in case this picture is starting to sound a little too quaint and cozy, I should point out here that growing up in the 1930s and '40s in Yazoo City was in no way similar to Norman Rockwell's version of American life in those days. Nothing came to us without hard work of the kind young people today probably can't even imagine. But we did feel reasonably safe. After supper every evening, weather permitting, we played in the streets until dark, darting in and out of our neighbors' homes and yards as if they were our own. No one locked their doors back then, and we knew who our neighbors were. If a neighbor saw one of us do something wrong, he or she was as likely to reprimand us as our parents were!

Since Papa had set up the family tradition of his children being home when he got home, we were in the habit of having our friends come to our house rather than stopping our play. Our move to the city didn't alter that tradition, and our house was soon full of new friends. In 1934, Dr. C. L. Wallace, a dentist, moved his family into a house on Grand Avenue a few blocks from our home. His eight-year-old son, Clinton ("Red") Wallace, and I became fast friends. Another boy I got along with especially well was Louie Russell Williams. He lived just down the street from me.

It didn't take long for Red to grow real fond of my mama as well. She had a knack for making children feel comfortable, almost as if she were just an older friend. Mama wasn't overtly affectionate, but she was always ready with a hug and a kind word when it was needed. She would listen intently, hanging on every word the child at hand had to say. Her practical application of God's word gave her advice to children an uncommon depth of wisdom—and young ones came back to her time and again for help.

Well, one day long after I had learned that cows don't "give" milk, I was out fighting the cows for every drop of milk I could get when Red wandered up on the porch to spend some time with Mama. It had become a ritual between the two of them that they both seemed to enjoy. This particular day Red had a big question on his mind, and Mama sensed that something was up. She asked Red to churn the butter she'd been working on so that she could snap peas while they talked. When they were settled into their respective chores, Red let his thoughts spill out.

"Mrs. Ziglar, my momma don't understand money. I've been selling peanuts on Saturdays, and I get up early, go downtown, and sell 'til noon. At noon, when it gets real hot, I go to the movie with the money I've earned. Usually by then I got thirty or forty cents, so eleven cents to get in sure don't seem like much.

"After the movie, I come out and sell some more. I walk up and down the streets and even go into the stores callin' out 'Hot Peanuts for Sale!,' and business is good. Why Mrs. Ziglar, I make between eighty cents and a dollar every Saturday!"

Mama asked him what that long story had to do with his momma not understanding money. He went off again: "Momma wants me to quit sell-ing peanuts and go to work at the Jitney Jungle for just sixty-five cents—for all day Saturday!"

They sat together in silence for a while and then it was Mama's turn. "Son," she said, "in Exodus, chapter twenty, verse twelve, the Good Book says to 'honor your father and mother.' And in Proverbs, chapter six, verse twenty, it says, 'My son, keep thy father's commandment, and forsake not the law of thy mother.' Now if your mother wants you to go to work at the grocery store, you need to do it for those reasons alone. And you need to do it with a smile and a joyful spirit."

Red was a little disappointed. This was not what he had hoped to hear. Mama continued, expanding on the lesson (I may have taken a little liter-ary license here, but if Mama didn't say it she should have), "Obedience, Red, is one of the things that all of us need to learn, and the earlier we learn it, the better off we will be. So obey your mother because it sets the tone for what will happen later in life. Since you will have been obedient to your mother, it will follow that you consider obedience important as you move into whatever area of life you choose. By working in a structured, organized store you will learn how business operates, how to get along with other peo-ple, and how to make friends, not only with young people your own age, but with adults as well. It will be very helpful to you, Red, throughout your life. You will also learn that when you are obedient and become a leader your-self, your expectations of others being cooperative and obedient will stand you in good stead. So take the job in the grocery store, Red, and you will be better prepared for your future."

My friend Red Wallace resigned himself to the truth of what Mama had said. As he continued to churn the butter in silence, he more contentedly contemplated the new job ahead of him. Mama had a gift for relating to children. She had scored again.

A Lifetime Education

I speak often of my mother's wisdom in spite of the fact that she had very little formal education. She only went through "six books" in the one-room schoolhouse of her day (the equivalent of a fifth- or sixth-grade education), but she was an avid reader all of her life. Most of her reading was done in

"One Book—God's Book." She was also fond of proclaiming that if you knew the spelling and the definitions of all the words in the old blue book speller, you'd have the same thing as a college education. She was always hungry for knowledge, and she sought the wisdom of the Lord her whole life.

My mother taught me the importance of absolute integrity, faith, hard work, responsibility, love, and commitment. She was my first and greatest role model. Her life-shaping sayings remain so fresh in my mind that I can recall them in the sound of her very voice. I can still hear her saying: "Beauty is as beauty does." "Your children more attention pay, / to what you do than what you say." "What you are speaks so loudly that I can't hear what you're saying." "When a task is once begun, / you leave it not until it's done." "Be a matter great or small, / do it well or not at all." "Tell the truth and tell it ever, costeth what it will; / for he who hides the wrong he did, does the wrong thing still." These are time-honored truths every generation needs to hear.

She taught her children about life by her example of her own living. In this regard, all of us had "complete" educations. One of the most amazing examples of Mama's character I witnessed as a child had to do with Aunt Mandy, an elderly black lady whom my mother came to know and love. Aunt Mandy sold used clothing to people who had even less than we did, particularly those in the black community. She picked up our used cloth-ing—and it was really used, frequently by two or three of us before we out-grew it—to sell to others even less fortunate. Sometimes we wouldn't hear from her for weeks, but if anybody dared suggest that maybe Aunt Mandy had disappeared with our money, my mother would always staunchly de-fend her and say, "No, Aunt Mandy will be back. She will have sold the clothes and she will bring our part." And my mother was always right be-cause she knew Aunt Mandy's word was as good as gold. I vividly remem-ber how much Mother trusted her and that Aunt Mandy never let her down. I'm sure that's why I always try to trust people who have proven themselves trustworthy—even, and *especially*, when others attack their reputations.

The High Cost of Living

Before I start telling you about all the jobs I had as a child, I want you to know that my mother often lamented the fact that her children had missed much of their childhood because they had to work to help make money for the family. The hard work of our early years was a part of our education she wished we had not had. Yet, without exception, each of us, even as children, felt we had gotten a head start on other children by having to work and be responsible at an early age. None of us saw our childhood lifestyle as unfair or burdensome. We were happy for the most part and managed to conceive of our hardships as blessings in disguise.

You will notice throughout this book that I speak a great deal about the "cost" of things, especially during my penny-pinching early years. I can't help but compare the relative poverty I lived in as a child with the lifestyle I'm blessed to have today. The contrast is so stark it is impossible for me to ignore. When I was growing up, money—the lack or the abundance of it— was the ruler everyone used to measure material success. Moreover, during the Depression and the war years, money was a scarce commodity for most people in our country and even more so for people in Mississippi. I learned as a child that if you had "enough" money to eat and put a roof over your head, you were doing just fine. If you had enough money to own a business, a car, or a house of your own, you were doing really great and everyone *respected* you. You were important. You counted. You had worked hard and it showed. You had made something of yourself. In thinking back, I believe it was the respect that I truly desired, but my childish mind couldn't conceive of that concept independent of money. Money was the universally accepted method of "keeping score." I spent the majority of my years before age forty-five trying to acquire plenty of it—and not doing a very good job.

The Ziglar Work Ethic

Ours was a busy, hardworking, but overall very joy-filled and loving home. Many times I saw my mother on our back porch churning cream she'd skimmed off the milk to make butter to sell. The butter churn Mama had was a large container called a "stomper" churn. There was a hole in the cover big enough for a broom handle–size pole (which, incidentally, usually came from a worn-out broom) and two small, thick boards were nailed crossways from each other to form a "dasher" at the end of the broom handle. You simply moved the pole up and down, and that churned the cream, making butter. The liquid remaining in the churn after the butter was formed was buttermilk. I can't count the times I watched my mother churning as she sang her favorite gospel songs, "Sweet Hour of Prayer" and "The Old Rugged Cross." Just the memory of it gives me a sense of contentment and peace, and it often brings tears to my eyes in a mixture of grief and gratitude.

Many times late at night I would awaken to cross the back porch to our lone bathroom, glance through the hallway door, and see my mother quilting away by the light of a kerosene lamp. She sewed together patch after patch of cloth to make something warm, useful, and lovely. I was always amazed because I had been asleep for a long time when I awoke and saw her quilting. Even as a child I never understood quite how she managed to do all she did, because when she awakened us in the morning it was always to the smell of cooking breakfast—biscuits, scrambled eggs, bacon and/or "salt meat." She had to have gotten up at least an hour before we did to build the fire and get it hot enough to bake the biscuits. The image of my godly mother working night and day to provide for us made an indelible impression on my mind, as it did on my brothers' and sisters'. We saw that our mother worked hard out of necessity. All of us have worked hard because we had such a marvelous role model to follow.

My First Real Job

Until September 1935, I was fully employed after school and on weekends by my mother. Our family survived the Depression because of her faith and her ability to work incredibly hard and organize her children to do what we could. A big part of what we could do was work in the garden and tend to the cows. In addition, even though we were in the city limits, we also raised hogs, which we killed and preserved with the aid of salt. By the time I was seven years old, I was selling vegetables and milk (remember, sanitation laws were nonexistent in those days) to our neighbors.

Early on, Mama had me working in the capacity of a gardener, milkman, yard worker, and salesman. Eventually, I went to part-time status with

Mama so that I could work the other part of my time with Mr. John R. Anderson at the Piggly Wiggly store, which Mr. Anderson owned. Later, I also worked under Walton Haining, Mr. Anderson's meat-market manager and fill-in store manager. I was all of nine years old when I started working in the grocery store and twelve years old when I started working in the meat market.

When I first started working at the store, most of the customers believed that Mr. Anderson had given me the job not because of any work I was going to do but because he had no children and wanted a "surrogate son" and possibly a playmate. My mother knew he had given me the job because he was a compassionate man who understood that with six small children too young to do any significant work and no husband, every dime made a difference in our family's fight for dignity and survival.

Mr. Anderson took me under his wing and in many ways became the father I had lost so early in my life. Just what impact did Mr. John Anderson have on my life? It was huge. As a matter of fact, we named our son John Thomas Ziglar after him. The Thomas is from the Redhead's dad—the John is from John Anderson.

My brothers Huel and Howard had previously done good work for Mr. Anderson, so even though there wasn't a great deal for a child my age to do in a grocery store, Mr. Anderson took me on. I earned forty cents for inserting circulars inside every screen door in Yazoo City two afternoons a week. Eventually, I trained my brother Horace Judge to distribute the grocery-store circulars, which Mr. Anderson called "dodgers." The more I proved myself able to handle responsibility, the more Mama let me take on. Selling peanuts also soon became one of my after-school jobs.

I want to jump ahead in this story to an afternoon not too many years before my daughter Suzan died. I was telling her about the week I sold eighty-seven bags of peanuts, and she was so moved she wrote a beautiful account of my story. Her sensitive retelling will give you an accurate glimpse of what my nine-year-old world was like. She titled the story "The New Jacket," and I included it in my book about losing Suzan, *Confessions of a Grieving Christian,* because I wanted my readers to know Suzan better. I am republishing it here for two reasons: because I'm extremely proud of Suzan's writing ability and so that you can get to know me better.

THE NEW JACKET

By Suzan Ziglar Witmeyer

It was a brisk, late fall afternoon in Mississippi. The year was 1936 and the Depression raged. Hilary Ziglar shifted his weight to his right foot and then back again as he counted his money. He stood on a street corner in downtown Yazoo City. It had been an unusually good week for him in the peanut business. He had sold 87 bags of peanuts at a profit of a penny a bag.

A gust of wind sent Hilary's hands diving for the pockets of his overalls as a shiver ran the length of his frail, nine-year-old body. Mississippi weather in late October got very uncomfortable for a boy dressed only in well-worn cotton.

"87 cents," he thought, "in one week. I'm going to do it, I'm going to Warrens' now!" With that he stood a little straighter, squared his shoulders, tucked in his chin and began a little march-jog step down Main Street in the direction of Dement Warren's Haberdashery.

Hilary's father, Silas, had been a plantation overseer until his death, three years earlier. The family had been in desperate straits ever since. That's why Hilary was downtown working while his school friends played sandlot ball.

Young Hilary Hinton was as fully employed as a nine year old could be and still go to school. He sold peanuts on the streets of Yazoo City for Uncle Joe's Peanuts every day after school, and on Saturdays he worked in Mr. John Anderson's grocery store.

Inside Warrens', Hilary carefully counted out his 87 cents and pointed to the window where a tan, button-down jacket was displayed. "That's the one I want, ma'am," he said to the sales clerk. Glancing quickly at the price tag the clerk said, "That's right Hilary, 87 cents, right on the money!" "Yes, ma'am!" he said proudly.

The clerk removed the jacket from its hanger and carefully folded it. She then wrapped it in a large piece of brown paper and tied it with string. The wrapping completed, she handed the package to the shyly beaming boy who then headed for the door.

Outside again, Hilary set out for the Black and White store to see

*his sister, Turah. As he entered the store he was greeted with a warm, "Hi
there, Short Boy!" He grimaced slightly at his nickname but smiled as
his brown eyes met the identical eyes of his lovely sister. "Hi, Sis," he
said, "guess what I've got here?" "Well I don't rightly know, boy. Did you
pick up somethin' for Mama?" she asked. "Nope, I did not pick up
anything for Mama, I bought this for my own self with my own money
that I made THIS week!" "And you only nine years old, Short Boy. Let
me see!" Turah begged. "Oh no you don't, Sis, nobody's gonna see this
before Mama and that's that!" Hilary said. "Well I just don't know what
the world is coming to when a nine-year-old boy can go out and buy
goodness knows what brand spankin' new!"*

*Glancing at the clock Hilary saw that it was almost suppertime.
"Gotta go, Sis," he said, "almost time to eat." With that he walked out into
the brisk evening air, the precious package tucked firmly under his right
arm. Turah watched sadly from the window as the slender form of her little
brother faded into the night. "Take care, Short Boy," she whispered.*

*Traveling through the neat streets of Yazoo City, young Hilary started
to jog. It wasn't that he was in a hurry; he simply was getting very cold.
His thin cotton shirt was no match for the moist, cold, late October
weather. He would not consider opening his package and wearing his
new jacket. On and on he jogged, crossing the bayou and heading for
the railroad tracks and home. The mile and a half journey seemed
endless. His ears began to tingle and his toes were going numb but still
he jogged, coatless, his paper bundle safe under his arm.*

*Lila Wescott Ziglar moved with great economy around her simple
kitchen. Mother of eleven living children, widow, she had no steps to
waste. Life was a grueling round of work and more work. She lived for
Sundays, a time to worship her God and to rest. Today was Friday, one
more day to go, now where was Hilary?*

*Oh, how she worried about her children, especially her younger
ones. These last three years without Silas had been brutal. She
remembered so clearly the move into town after his death. Her sad
farewell at the graves of her husband and baby, graves made only five
days apart. She didn't pretend to know the mind of God, she accepted*

what was handed to her, trusting in Him completely. Oh but she hated sending her little ones out to work!

"Now where is Hilary?" Lila muttered as she shoved another pan of biscuits into the oven. A layer of flour coated her long, slim fingers while her left cheek sported a grainy, Florida-shaped configuration of the white powder.

Just then she heard the familiar thud of the front door and knew Hilary was home at last. "Boy," she called, "where have you been? You know how I worry." At the sound of heavy breathing she realized he had entered the room. She looked up and was startled by the intensity of his smile. "Why, Hilary," she said, "what have you done? Why are you smiling like that?" "Look Mama," he said, "look what I bought with my own money." A package wrapped in brown paper and tied with string materialized in front of her.

Her fingers trembled slightly as she freed the jacket from its bonds. Little bits of flour floated towards the linoleum as the paper fell away and the jacket came into full view. "Why, boy," she said with a tone of wonder, "you've gone and bought yourself a coat, a new coat, all by yourself. I don't know what to say, Hilary. I'm proud of you, son."

The proud boy trying on his new jacket for the first time did not notice the unnatural brightness of his mother's eyes as she fought to hold back her tears.

Fifty years after my father bought his first jacket he told me this story. When he got to the part where he showed my grandmother the jacket, he was overcome with emotion. His respect for his mother was so great, his need to help his family in some concrete way was so enormous, that a half-century could not dim the feelings. My heart ached as I saw the little, too thin Delta boy with tears in his eyes. I was reminded once again that my father would always remain that little fatherless boy from Yazoo City in some significant ways.

Life's Lessons Selling Peanuts

Selling peanuts allowed me to buy that jacket, but the selling of those peanuts also established two things in my mind quite clearly. First of all, there was a direct correlation between what I did and what I received.

Second, I acquired an important habit from the man who gave me the job selling the peanuts, "Uncle Joe." His little coffee shop and peanut stand were in the block next door to the Piggly Wiggly store where I worked for Mr. Anderson. Uncle Joe had a strange but useful habit. When he finished roasting his peanuts with his hand-turned, wood-burning roaster, which was out behind his shop, he would dump the peanuts in a large box then fill the bags. After filling the bags he would remove two peanuts from each bag and place them in a smaller box. By the time he finished bagging all the peanuts, he had enough left over in the small box for several more bags. From Uncle Joe I learned that if I were to lay aside little things, over a period of time they would grow bigger and add significantly to my well-being. I can't say with certainty, but I believe that's one of the reasons that to this day, even when I leave hotel rooms, my natural inclination is to turn off the lights and save that cost and energy.

I'm certain that more of that line of thinking came from my mother's influence than my peanut-selling experience, but the combination of the two of them surely taught me to be frugal. I heard my mother say many times as she carefully managed every penny out of sheer necessity for survival that "willful waste makes woeful want."

As an adult I continued the tradition of thrift with my children. A number of years ago when our son was a teenager, he walked into the bathroom where I was preparing to shave and shampoo. I had just poured the shampoo from a large, economical gallon container into a smaller bottle, and I had spilled some of the shampoo onto the sink. I reached down, scooped it up and smeared it onto my head; obviously, my hair was then a mess. Tom walked in and said, "Dad, what happened?" I explained that I didn't want to waste the shampoo that had spilled, and he laughed and said, "Dad, I don't think anybody will ever accuse you of being wasteful." I looked at my son and said, "Son, let me tell you something. It was only by saving the little things that we were able to buy you that used Thunderbird you've got sitting in the driveway."

I know the circumstances of my childhood created my lifelong habit of being conservative with whatever resources I had because to this day I hate to be wasteful. Today, I don't buy suits unless they are on sale, and I patronize a department store that offers the suits I like on sale twice every year. Ironically, in my early adult years false pride and the need to show my success outwardly made me waste a lot of money on automobiles (a very visible and American indicator of "having arrived"). Today, I buy preowned cars because I can still get the same warranty and I save thousands of dollars. I now have better places to use the money and know people who can use the money more wisely than for the luxury of a new automobile. I'm not about to spend all that extra money just for the new car smell because that is the major difference.

However, in spite of the fact that this sounds very contradictory to what I just said, I do believe that everybody, if humanly possible, should have the experience of owning a brand-new car at least once in his or her life, even though it isn't frugal. Though I'm too conservative to pay for it today, there is something about that new car smell, the perfect interior, and the pride of ownership that comes with the purchase of a new automobile. I imagine I feel this way because cars were the only things I wasn't frugal about in my younger years, and I've never forgotten the feeling I had when I drove off the car lot in my first brand-new car.

The frugality that I practiced in every other area of my life is probably the reason I felt like such a big winner when I got lucky with one of my purchases. When I was about fifteen years old I ordered a sport coat out of the Sears & Roebuck catalog. We were convinced that we got better value out of that catalog than in the local store. When the coat arrived, I was very pleased with it because it fit well and was warm and comfortable. A few weeks later I saw a pair of slacks advertised, and I ordered them, too. Much to my amazement and delight, the slacks were a perfect match with the coat. I was proud and grateful for that because then, for the first time, I had a full suit of clothes. In retrospect, I'm not certain that coat and pants were even of the same fabric, but the color matched perfectly, and I felt that I had gotten a double bargain.

After a few years of working with Mr. Anderson, Mama let me have a paper route for the *Yazoo City Herald*, which was published every Tuesday and Friday night. Actually, the job took three nights a week; on a third night I had to go door to door collecting the money my customers owed for their subscriptions. I received six cents commission each month from the already established customers, but if I acquired new customers, I made ten cents commission on those subscriptions. Every new customer meant an extra four cents. Not much, except that with four cents we could buy one pound of "fat back." Fat back was the part of the hog that was nothing but fat. But we used it to season beans, peas, turnip greens, collard greens, and cabbage, all of which were staples of the family diet. So at every opportunity I did what I could to acquire new customers for my paper route.

In those days even a small amount of money could tempt people to do the wrong thing, and I'm embarrassed to admit that I gave in to temptation myself. After I'd proven myself to be a good worker by putting dodgers in screen doors for several weeks, Mr. Anderson asked me to work all day Saturdays, from seven A.M. to eleven P.M., for seventy-five cents. I was thrilled. That first Saturday was a long, hard day, but the excitement I felt was intense. It was further enhanced when Mr. Anderson, apparently forgetting that he had already paid me forty cents for delivering dodgers earlier in the week, gave me a dollar and fifteen cents for my day's work. In retrospect, I know that I should have reminded him that he had already paid me for delivering the dodgers, but I suppose my elation and the thrill of knowing what the extra forty cents would buy was too much for this tired nine-year-old's scruples.

An extra forty cents represented a substantial amount of money. In those days you could buy a twenty-four-pound sack of flour, three pounds of sliced bacon, and sixteen small oranges for a dollar, so the dollar and fifteen cents, including the "tainted" forty cents, represented a significant amount of wealth to a nine-year-old. Needless to say, at that point in our lives every dime we children brought in we turned over to our mother, who carefully rationed every penny available to provide for the necessities of her family. Looking back, I'm amazed that in all of those difficult times we always had plenty to eat, a roof over our heads, and clothes to wear. I often say in my talks that I know we had plenty to eat because when I'd pass my plate for seconds, Mama would say, "No, you've had plenty!" All kidding aside, it was apparent to all of us children that in many ways our mother was a miracle worker.

By the time I was twelve, I was working all day on Saturday and five afternoons per week in the grocery store; I spent three evenings per week with my newspaper route; I helped with milking and other chores at the house; and I attended church on Wednesday evenings, Sunday mornings, and Sunday nights. I surely didn't feel like being at church every time the doors opened because I was about as busy as a boy can be! But Mama required us to go. I believe that in the long run her example of working hard, doing the right thing, attending church faithfully, and studying the Bible were the things that influenced her children most.

When I was offered an opportunity to make money without having to work, I jumped on it! This practically unthinkable business venture arose in the transportation sector of the Yazoo City economy. It was my first exposure to passive investments. I always rode my bicycle back and forth from home to work and parked it in front of the store, where it remained until I got ready to use it again. Rarely did I ever have to make a delivery on it, because Mr. Anderson had bought what he called a "truck" bicycle. It had a small wheel in front and a basket that carried about five times as many groceries as did a regular bicycle with a regular-size wheel.

One day my bicycle was sitting in front of the grocery store and the young brother of a man who had once worked as our butcher came in and said he would like to rent my bicycle. I asked, "How much?," and he said, "I will pay you ten cents an hour." I said, "Okay, how long do you want it?" He said, "Oh, three hours." So I said, "Okay, that'll be thirty cents." This became a fairly regular occurrence, particularly on Saturday. Before I knew it, I had myself a little side business. I'll have to confess that my self-image was a bit damaged, but not ruined, when I recognized I earned more in three hours from the bicycle rental than I did from my own labors. Besides, I already owned the bicycle, so I figured that was clear profit. Only later did I learn that the upstart capitalist was renting the bicycle to someone else for twenty cents an hour! But that was fine, too; had he not come along in the first place, I would not have been earning that thirty cents. The money always helped.

The grocery store was my primary job throughout my childhood, and over time, as I proved myself worthy of additional responsibilities, Mr. Anderson advanced my grocery-store career by moving me through a series of duties. I progressed from delivering circulars to sweeping floors, stocking shelves, waiting on customers, working the cash register, assisting Mr. Anderson in the inventory selection, and assisting Mr. Haining as a meat cutter. Each advancement was designed to teach me how to accept more responsibility, and was recognition and reward for the job I was already doing.

The entire time I worked for Mr. Anderson he was busy teaching me something new and important about life, people, or work. Mr. Anderson taught me that you couldn't make a good deal with a bad person. He also taught me to hustle, and if a customer was waiting and I wasn't hustling, he would often say, "Hurry up, boy! A dollar is waiting on a dime!" His point was that the customer was the foundation of our business. If I laid a grammatical egg any time during a conversation, regardless of who was around, Mr. Anderson, a former English teacher, was quick to correct me. With this training I learned to be very careful in the way I expressed myself. I started thinking through every statement I made before I said it, and there is little doubt in my mind that it had a positive impact on my use of the English language. I also credit Mrs. J. W. Parker with teaching me to love the English language and to use it properly. Between Mrs. Parker and Mr. Anderson I had nearly constant tutoring; for that I'm very grateful.

Role Models and Surrogate Fathers

I couldn't have asked for a more perfectly suited pair of male role models than Mr. John Anderson and Mr. Walton Haining. Though Mr. Anderson had no children of his own, he helped me grow into the kind of man my family would be pleased to claim.

Mr. Anderson was a powerful man in every sense of the word. His dark features often caused people to mistake him for my father. His compact physique (five feet, ten inches, and 205 pounds) commanded attention. While he didn't quite look like a door-to-door anvil salesman, he could have passed for a fullback or pulling guard on the Mississippi State football team.

Not only did Mr. Anderson have financial wealth, he had a wealth of humor. It showed when he called himself a devout Methodist, and then added, "But devout Methodist is somewhat of a contradiction in terms!" Today, the First Methodist Church of Yazoo City holds Bible study classes in the John R. Anderson Educational Building.

Walton Haining was a soft-spoken, gentle, Christian man—the perfect example of the biblical definition of meek. Someone mangled the third beatitude by saying, "The meek shall inherit the earth because they won't have the nerve to refuse it!" Wrong. Meek means power with restraint. Mr. Haining had power and showed it through his hard work and thrifty ways.

I do not ever recall hearing either Mr. Anderson or Mr. Haining use profanity or tell any kind of story that would have been inappropriate for a young boy to hear. They felt quite strongly that language was extremely important and should be used properly.

Mama recognized the importance of both of those men in my life.

During the time when Mr. Anderson was paying me seventy-five cents for working from seven A.M. to eleven P.M. on Saturdays, the man who owned the sandwich shop down the street offered me one dollar and fifteen cents to work for him from ten A.M. until ten P.M. Believe me, I wanted that extra forty cents and those four extra hours off.

Well, Mama had different ideas! She never even considered letting me make the change. And if you knew my mama, you'd understand why I never even considered going against her wishes. Mama had one of those serious front-porch/Red Wallace talks with me to set me straight.

"Hilary, in this day and time, forty cents is a lot of money to a small boy. I understand that. But the influence of Mr. Anderson and Mr. Haining can never be measured in money. The man who runs the sandwich shop may be a fine man, but I don't know him. However, I *do* know the two men you are working for now. I love you too much to let you work in a place of unknown quality."

I later learned that there were rumors of beer being sold at the sandwich shop. I'm sure Mama was aware of them when she decided to make that sandwich shop off limits for me. Mama had always been so consistent with her discipline and the respect she showed us that when she forbade us to do something, none of us ever looked back or questioned her decisions.

I Had to Pay for the Lesson on Responsibility

Talking about that forty cents reminds me of another lesson I learned that involved forty cents. We started our days early at my house because we had chores, including staking out the cows in lush, green grass after we milked them. We'd leave for school a few minutes before eight A.M., and we'd return home for lunch. If we were lucky, and we usually were, we got a ride back home with Mr. Phil Reeves, our debit insurance (insurance sold in low-income neighborhoods) man who lived a few blocks from us.

One day I was particularly eager to get back to school after lunch and get in a game or two of tennis. However, it was my job to move the cows, which at that time were grazing close to the railroad tracks. In my hurry, I did not properly stake the cows in the new location, and one of them got loose.

I know it got loose because I was confronted by an elderly black lady who pointed out that she had restaked the cow, but not until the cow had invaded her garden and eaten most of her turnip greens. I apologized profusely and took the cow home, thinking all was well.

About an hour later there was a knock on our door; there stood the black lady, telling my mother what had happened. My mother listened patiently, asked the lady how much of her turnip greens crop she thought our cow had eaten, and was told, "about eight bunches." Turnip greens sold for five cents a bunch. My mother proceeded to give the lady forty cents, and she, too, apologized for my carelessness.

Then my mother dealt with me. She pointed out that apologizing was the proper thing for me to do, but that it was not enough. It was also my responsibility, since I had been careless in staking the cow, to pay for the lady's turnip greens. Needless to say, I did not argue with my mother. Forty cents represented a full eight hours of work at Mr. Anderson's store. I learned very quickly that responsibility carries a price tag, and never again did I carelessly stake out one of our cows.

I believe that one of the great lessons my mother taught me that day and on numerous other occasions was that I had to accept responsibility for my own actions. Yes, my mother was very keen about the subject of responsibility, and she took every opportunity to impress on us its importance.

Even tougher was accepting responsibility when I had disobeyed orders and had been careless. A case in point: Every time I left the house to attend my Boy Scout meeting my mother's instructions were always the same: When the scout meeting was over, I was to come straight home. One night after my scout meeting at the Episcopal church, a few of my scout friends and I walked across to the school yard and played on the swings for a while, probably no more than thirty minutes, and then I headed home.

Some kids who weren't scouts were also playing on the swings when I left, and that night several of the swings were damaged. The principal of the school discovered the names of all the kids who were involved in playing on the swings after hours and required each of us to pay our equal share. Despite the fact that I was innocent and the damage occurred after I left, I still had to pay for my part, which came to one dollar and sixty-five cents. I thought it was grossly unfair, but again, my mother said, "When you're disobedient and the wrong crowd is involved, it will always cost you." How wise she was. Sometimes the lessons were painful, as they were in this case, but eventually, through lots of reinforcement, being responsible became a habit; that habit has been a standard I've worked to maintain.

This Time I Was Innocent

My younger brother, Horace, the one who as an adult came to be known as Judge after Papa, because that was his name—not because he was a judge—always accused our mother of letting me talk her out of things when I needed a whipping. On the other hand he complained he himself never was able to get by with anything. When he ran afoul of Mama's law, he always received a few strokes from the peach tree switch.

Consequently, one of the things Horace got the biggest charge out of was the time I returned home and my mother was waiting for me with a switch. As she prepared to deliver the first reminder that I had disobeyed her, I held up my hands in protest and said, "Now, Mama . . ." According to my younger brother, though I don't specifically remember these exact words, my mama said, "Now, Mama nothing!" and proceeded to give me a switching.

Well, the reason he got such a big charge out of it, he said, was that in this particular instance I was innocent! But he felt I deserved it anyway and felt vindicated himself because there had been so many times when I had been guilty as sin and somehow managed to talk Mama out of the switching. At any rate, he laughed about it on numerous occasions and delighted in retelling the story to our other brothers and sisters, his children, my children, and anyone else who would listen.

Whether he was dealing completely in facts I have no way of knowing, except that I do suspect there were those occasions when I did talk my mama out of a switching that I richly deserved. That incident provided my brother with lots of laughs, and he enjoyed laughing as much as anybody I know.

Two Cans of Tomatoes

In the Depression years, when I was a youngster working in the grocery store, the long, hot summer days were extraordinarily boring. We did something like 90 percent of our business between five o'clock on Friday afternoon and late Saturday night. Nearly everybody was paid by the week except state and government employees, and there weren't very many of them. When people got paid, they headed for the store, so we were unusually busy at those times. However, from Monday morning until Friday afternoon there was virtually nothing to do except be there for the rare customer who came in, restock the shelves, make certain everything was clean and orderly, and try to look busy.

One hot summer day, with absolutely nothing going on at the store, Mr. Anderson was a little frustrated that there was nothing for any of us to do. The electricity bills, salaries, etc., were continuing whether customers were coming in or not, so in one of his more frustrated moments he said to me, "Isn't there something you can do?" I responded that I didn't see anything that needed doing. He said, "Well, get the duster and dust off some of these shelves." He pointed at one mostly bare shelf that held only two cans of tomatoes.

I responded by stating the obvious, that there were "only two cans of tomatoes" on that shelf. But the way I said "only" really raised his dander that hot summer afternoon. His cheeks flushed, and his eyes got wide. He said, "Let me tell you something, boy. That case of tomatoes had twenty-four cans in it. We've sold twenty-two of them. That means I've got my money back and enough profit to pay the rent, utilities, and taxes. The profit I will make of those two cans of tomatoes is what we will use to pay your salary. Now, what do you think of those two cans of tomatoes?" I responded with enthusiasm, "They're absolutely beautiful, Mr. Anderson," and I proceeded to dust them off real good!

I learned that day that the success of the store determined whether or not I would get paid. It was a little incident but a big lesson, and I'm so glad I learned it early.

Not all the long, hot days resulted in boredom and frustration. Often during the slow times we entertained ourselves with various games. Besides being great teachers, role models, and surrogate fathers, John Anderson and Walton Haining each possessed a great sense of humor. By the time I was one of their "veteran" workers, I was included in their humorous pranks. Many of them took place Saturday night after nine o'clock, when most of the business had been conducted. One of our Saturday-night routines occurred after I had started spending most of my time working in the meat market. As I started to clean up, I would call out to Mr. Anderson (and, of course, all of this was prearranged), saying, "Mr. Anderson, the slicing machine is performing very poorly. It's hard to get it to do its job."

He would then ask what I thought could be done about it. I would respond that I felt that all it needed was some more "electric light juice." He would then say, "Well, give the boy (the latest hire) a bottle and tell him to go get some." I would do that and the part-time help we had brought in for Friday afternoon and Saturday would be the courier going after the "electric light juice." I would caution him that it would probably be reasonably hard to find this late at night, but then I would give him a list of three stores to go to, stores that were in on the game. Of course their stores were not busy either during this period of time.

So the youngster would dutifully take the one-quart milk bottle and head out to get the "electric light juice." Most of the time, by the time he entered the third store and heard the same story, that they were also out of "electric light juice," or an empathetic bystander would start laughing at the absurdity of the request and spill the beans, the youngster (who generally was about my age) knew what was going on. Invariably, our new kid on the block would return looking sheepish but, almost without exception, always took it good-naturedly. We all had a good laugh about the matter. It did give us something to smile about and made a boring period of time more enjoyable.

One of our favorites on Saturday nights developed out of cleaning out the storefront window, where the fresh vegetables had been on display. In those days we did not have a sprinkling and cooling system, and so after having displayed the fresh vegetables in the storefront window, each day we would gather up those that were left and take them back to the meat cooler to keep them refrigerated for the night.

Needless to say, displaying the fresh fruits and vegetables in the storefront window took a toll on the appearance of the display area; after a certain period of time, as the windows were being cleaned I would comment to Mr. Anderson that the display windows were looking very bad and that we needed to do something about them. He would say, "Well, what do you recommend," and I would suggest that freshening them up with paint was the only solution. Then he would ask what color I thought they should be "this time." I would always say, "Well, I think we need to add more color. Why don't we just get some striped paint and see if that doesn't dress it up?"

He'd say, "Well, send the boy out to get some." This one was also well set up. The first stop was always the Town and Country store where my younger brother worked. When approached, my brother would tell the youngster, "Well, we have some, but it hasn't been mixed yet and will probably be a couple of days before it's ready. Why don't you try the Nicholas store across the street?" They also were in on the act, and when our young man approached Grady Crawford, the son of the owner of the store, Grady would tell him, "Well, yes, we did have some, but the cat kicked it over, and so we won't have any more until next week. Why don't you try the Jitney Jungle?"

The people at the Jitney Jungle were in on the ruse, too, and we had carefully instructed the youngster that any color stripes would be acceptable, but since we had already used the patriotic colors of red, white, and blue so much, any color but those would be preferable. The young man at the Jitney Jungle would say, "Yes, we've got striped paint—red, white, and blue." Our youngster would say, "Well, that's the one color they told me not to get." Then, since we had assigned him no other stores, he would come back admitting failure. At that point, we could not contain ourselves, and we would all burst out laughing. It was fun, and it relieved a lot of the stress, strain, and boredom. And people were entertained as a result. No permanent damage was ever done, and invariably the "rookie" was glad to get out of the store for a bit, even if the joke was on him.

When we had an area that needed to be cleaned but was not responding to the normal process, Mr. Anderson and I would have a serious consultation, always making certain that the "new kid on the block" was within earshot. We would discuss the various cleaners we had used to try to remove the stain; finally, Mr. Anderson would say, "Well, we've tried everything else, why don't we give it the steam treatment?" I would say, "Well, where do we get steam?" He would then identify the hardware store about three blocks away from ours and say, "I think that's the closest place. Why don't you give [insert youngster's name] a bucket and tell him to go down and get a bucket of steam. That should do it."

Well, there was always a degree of skepticism in the facial expression of the youngster, but because any kind of job was difficult to come by in those days, he would dutifully take the bucket and head for the hardware store. Invariably he would bump into a friend (remember, Yazoo City was a small town and everybody knew everybody else) and reveal his mission in a brief conversation. The friend would laugh at him and our victim would turn around and come back, embarrassed, carrying the empty bucket with him. Again, we all got a good laugh.

Anytime a new employee came to work at the store, it didn't take long for him to notice the large crack in the glass counter near the cash register. Eventually the "rookie" would make the mistake of asking about when it might be fixed. That was our cue.

Mr. Anderson would announce ceremoniously and loudly enough to be heard by everyone in the store, "Well, Hilary, why don't you run down to the hardware store and borrow their glass stretcher?" "You bet, Mr. Anderson!" I'd reply.

"Oh, Hilary, on second thought, why don't you dust and rearrange those canned goods, and I'll send our new worker down there." I'd answer, "Don't you think that glass stretcher might be a little heavy for him, Mr. Anderson?"

"Nonsense, I have every confidence he can handle the job." And with that the new employee would set out for the nonexistent glass stretcher. When he closed the door behind him, everyone always burst into uproarious laughter.

Perhaps the most fun thing for me, as far as playing games in the grocery store was concerned, was thumping peas for a Coke. This was one we always used when a new salesman representing a wholesale grocery house came into the store and introduced himself. Let me repeat, nothing was going on in the store most of the time, and when the new salesman introduced himself, we always welcomed him warmly. The boss would generally ask what had happened to the other salesman and the new guy would give us some brief explanation. Mr. Anderson would say, "Well, it's nice to have you with us."

After they chatted for a moment and the salesman had taken his book out to show what was being offered that week, I would say, "Mr. Anderson, it sure is hot. It would really be nice if we had a Coke." He would respond, "Well, why don't you go get us one?" I would say, "Well, I was hoping maybe we could just thump peas for one." He'd say, "No, we're not going to do that anymore. You remember last time when I was the judge, as I always am, there was quite a discussion and a little arguing about it, and I just don't want any part of it." Then the new salesman would invariably ask, "Well, what do you mean, 'thump peas for a Coke'?" Mr. Anderson would explain,

"We just line up all three of you, and we put peas on the counter, and I count . . . 'One, two, three, go!' And the last one to thump has to buy the Cokes."

I would interject, "Mr. Anderson, if you'll judge one more time, I don't think anybody here is going to question your call." He'd always say, "No, that's what you said the last time." After further discussion Mr. Anderson would reluctantly agree to judge again who was the last one to thump. Then he explained the procedure, "All right, now, line up. This is not going to count. I'm just going to tell you what I'm going to do, exactly how I'm going to count it." Then he would say, "One, two, three, go. I'm not going to try to fool you, I'm just going to count it like that." Invariably the new sales-man, none the wiser, would comment, "Sounds simple to me."

Next we would line up, and the boss would say, "One, two, three, go!" and immediately the salesman would thump, look around, and enthusiasti-cally say, "I was first!" Then we would all laugh and say, "Well, actually, you were also last!" The salesman thought this wasn't quite fair, but since he wanted to make a sale to Mr. Anderson, he was stuck with buying the four Cokes. Now, although a Coke in those days was just a nickel, twenty cents for the four Cokes was a lot of money.

Incidentally, the RC Cola had just come out, and in those days Coke came only in six-ounce bottles. But the RC Cola was twelve ounces. I've al-ways been a bargain hunter, and the twelve ounces had considerably more appeal for me. The others would take the Cokes; I would take the RC.

Any and everyone was a potential target for a joke. The salesman for the Jackson Packing Company, the company from which we bought our whole-sale meats, would joke around with Mr. Haining, fill his order, and collect a check for the previous week's order. He often would jokingly say, "Well, I suppose I can dribble this on down to the bank," and Mr. Haining would always laugh and say, "Yeah, you sure can!"

One week when Mr. Haining signed his check he simply wrote "U. R. Stuck." The salesman, of course, never looked at the check because he had been dealing with Mr. Haining for years. The next week when he came in he was looking sheepish but was laughing out loud because the bank had returned the check and written on it, "You sure are!"

All of these pranks and jokes helped lighten what otherwise would have been gloomy times given the grim economic circumstances of America during the Depression years. When I first went to work in the grocery store, they tried to pull similar pranks on me, but my older brother had preceded me at the store and had forewarned me. When they sent me out to get the glass stretcher, I knew what the game was so I just stopped at Anderson's drugstore on the corner of the same block and sat down to read a couple of comics. They missed me at the store, and after about forty-five minutes they sent someone looking for me and found me there. The boss didn't fuss, but they didn't try to pull any more of those games on me. All in all, the cutting up made for an enjoyable experience and was part of my growing up.

The question is, What did I learn from all of this? I believe there were a couple of pretty good lessons. Number one, I learned that you can take even the most boring job and, provided it doesn't interfere with your responsibilities, create some enjoyment in the situation. But most of all, I learned that enjoying the company of other people and having a sense of humor were among the most effective ways to relieve boredom.

Humor at Home

Teasing wasn't confined to work. Under the tutelage of my employers I became quite a prankster on my own. When I was sixteen, I made a phone call to my older sister Turah and the conversation went like this:

"Turah, Turah Ziglar?" I asked in my highest-pitched voice.

"Yes."

"Turah, this is Mrs. Neismith," I said.

"Why, yes, Mrs. Neismith, how nice to hear from you."

"Turah, you know my daughter Nellwyn, don't you?"

"Yes, ma'am, I sure do. She's my best friend!"

"Well, I know she sure loves you. Turah, we are having a party in her honor tonight so I wanted to call to be sure you could be there."

"Oh, Mrs. Neismith, I am so honored that you would call and invite me, but my brother Huel is coming in tonight from the navy, and we haven't seen him in almost two years, and I just gotta be here!"

I paused for a long time, then I said, "Nellwyn is going to be so disappointed." I paused again and said, "I guess the best thing to do is just cancel the party—"

"Oh no!" Turah interrupted, "Please don't do that!"

"No, I think that since you are Nellwyn's best friend we just shouldn't even attempt to have the party if you can't be there."

As Turah's voice took on a tone of horror that she might be responsible for her girlfriend not having a party, I felt the slightest twinge of guilt and had trouble controlling my laughter. So in my deepest sixteen-year-old voice I said, "TURAH?" "TURAH?," and totally confused her. She was so upset about her options of missing our brother Huel or ruining her best friend's party that she didn't immediately recognize my voice. She asked if there were two people on the line, and then my uncontrollable laughter gave me away. Her aggravation with me was short-lived, quickly replaced with relief that her dilemma was resolved. She ended up laughing as hard and long as I did. To the end of her life, Turah Ziglar Allen had that wonderful sense of humor and the ability to laugh at herself. And I was still inclined to make similar phone calls even though my family long ago had figured out what I was apt to do.

Now I don't want you to think I was the one doing all the teasing! Not by any means. As a youngster I was extraordinarily naïve. I'll never forget when my older brother brought home some doughnuts from Webber's Bakery. Believe it or not, I had never seen anything quite like a doughnut. My bakery knowledge consisted of bread, biscuits, pies, and cakes. My older brother offered me one with the caution that I must not eat the hole in the doughnut or it would kill me. Such a warning was pretty frightening for a five- or six-year-old who had never laid eyes on a doughnut before. However, the lure of the doughnut was more than I could resist, so I started nibbling very, very carefully around the hole. Through great caution and restraint I did not break through to the hole. Needless to say, my older brothers and sisters got quite a charge out of that!

What would a childhood be without embarrassing moments? I had my share of them. In our family we bathed and washed our hair with ordinary bath soap because we seldom had any shampoo since it cost extra money. Never will I forget the day I got the rare bottle of shampoo confused with the hair tonic I used on my unruly hair. I had what in those days was known as a cowlick, on the left side of the back of my head. The disobedient hair would stick up in a thousand different directions, so I used quantities of the tonic to hold it down.

One day when I was ten years old I confused the rarely available shampoo with the tonic and doused it on my hair, carefully patting every stray strand into place. It was Saturday morning, so I headed off to work at the grocery store. Later in the day, I noticed that my hair was getting sticky, so I went to the sink in the back of the store and put some water on it. The inevitable suds formed and covered my head, so I had to stop and wash my hair right then and there. Since I had neither comb nor brush with me, all I could do was pull my hair back and arrange it with my hands. You might say my cowlick leapt at this opportunity to reassert itself. I was quite a sight, and I received many comments that were less than complimentary.

And what child hasn't caused his mother embarrassment on at least one occasion? I believe it was in late October or early November when I slipped out of the house to walk to school barefooted. The temperature was much colder than I had anticipated, and when I got about six blocks from school, a kindly lady picked me up, noticing that I was wearing no shoes, and took me to Ingram's shoe store. She bought me a pair of socks and shoes. To say I was proud of the new shoes, though I had shoes at home, would have been an understatement. When I got home and told my mother what had happened and of my good fortune, she was very embarrassed about it and told me that I must never do anything like that again.

The Community Helped

I have no way of knowing this for certain, but I believe that because of our plight and my mother's faith, independence and responsibility, a number of families in town found ways to extend to us helping hands so that it would not offend my mother's dignity.

I well remember Mrs. McKenzie, who lived several blocks away from us. She had several large fig trees that bore considerable fruit. She told my mother that if she wanted to, she could send us boys down to pick figs so that we could make preserves out of them. She pointed out that she could not gather all of them, and she was past the age of making preserves. Needless to say, my mother was grateful to preserve those figs, and they were a delicious addition to the hot biscuits that we enjoyed in the morning.

Mrs. John North, who lived next door to us, though she had a limited income, always encouraged us to show her our report cards at the end of each semester. Then she always gave each of us a highly treasured nickel, which delighted us. If the grades were not good, she would say, "I want to see these grades up next time."

When Mrs. J. C. Braddock came into the grocery store, I carried the basket (there were no carts in those years), following her through the aisles as she made her selections. When she was through shopping, I carried her bags to her car; she always gave me a nickel. She was very kind to me and I really looked forward to her coming to the store every Saturday.

Mrs. Mott, the editor and publisher of the *Yazoo City Herald,* always gave me credit for bringing in several more new accounts for the paper than I had actually earned. She never said anything about it; she just made certain that the extra money was always in my pay. That helped.

Even today, at age seventy-five, I remember quite vividly and am grateful for the care and concern I received from others when I was a child in Yazoo City.

Just a Little Bit Ugly

I have to confess that what I did in the following story was just a little bit ugly, but at least I've changed the lady's name. People were understandably a little tighter with their money in the years immediately following the Great Depression. One particular woman whom I'll call Mrs. T. W. (for Tight Wad) Blanks was so thrifty she was rumored to have invented copper wire when someone tried to take a penny away from her. Mrs. Blanks would handle every head of lettuce, every melon, and so forth to make sure she had the largest, freshest, and least-expensive produce there was to purchase.

One day I saw her studying the radishes and walked over to help. "Are these fresh?" she snapped at me. Someone of her stature who lived in a lavish home certainly couldn't be expected to make small talk with a lowly grocery clerk. I said, "Oh yes, ma'am! The freshest in town! Why, you shouldn't pick these up because we haven't even had time to wash the dirt off of them."

"Don't be impudent with me, young man!" she said, scowling at me. "How much are they?" Without missing a beat I told her they sold by the bunch at two for fifteen cents or three for a quarter. "Well, obviously I will take three bunches," she barked as she looked down her nose at me.

Mr. Anderson just about came unglued. He laughed so hard (after Mrs. T. W. Blanks left the store, of course), that he cried. Mr. Anderson was of the highest character, but he was bottom-line motivated, so he frequently marked up a new item that was selling too quickly—his own version of killing the goose that laid the golden egg. He truly enjoyed seeing this pretentious woman fooled into paying more than was necessary. He might not have been able to overcome all the social injustices enacted in our small town, but he could enjoy dishing out a tiny dose of revenge now and then.

While the Boss Is Away

During long, hot summer days, when there was nothing to do in the grocery store, time was heavy on our hands. Throughout the eventless mornings we waited with eager anticipation for the moment when Mr. Anderson headed home for lunch. He was in the habit of walking regardless of the weather, because he knew it was good for him. The minute he was out of sight, we would plan a visit to McLain's Ice Cream Parlor, which was just down the street. Since I was the gofer, I would get the ice cream for everyone. In those days it was two dips for a nickel, and I was entrusted to bring it back. Though it took only a few minutes to get the ice cream and for us to eat it, somehow it was the highlight of our day. I still have fond memories of that simple pleasure as a welcome interlude.

Small-Town Social Order

Yazoo City looked innocent enough with its pleasant, simple setting, clean streets, and beautiful trees, but our family had some struggles with the subtleties of the social structure that existed between "old" families and newcomers like us. Despite the sugar coating of cheer and friendliness that was customary in small towns, they still operated according to their own unspoken hierarchy. Respect and respectability was a function of a family's position on the social ladder in town. It was understood that one's rank was tied to one's income, education, industry, and apparent piety (pretty much in that order). When a widow with eight children living at home moved onto the same street with doctors and other prominent citizens, it could cause a stir. For that very reason, Mama laid down the law about the boundaries of our new yard and made it painfully clear to us that under no circumstances were we to stray outside those boundaries unless we were invited.

Because we were ushered into town under the protective umbrella of the highly regarded superintendent of education and the much-loved pastor of the First Baptist Church, our path of acceptance was easier and smoother than it could have been.

In Yazoo City the rich lived next door to the poor; only a small alley separated black from white; a raised eyebrow or a pointed frown effectively kept the "underprivileged" in their place. Mama sensed the class distinction more than it was shared with her verbally, so she taught her children about people's attitudes and ways in this regard, and helped us understand how good people might do bad things. She taught us how to respond appropriately when we found ourselves in difficult social circumstances. She would not tolerate our accepting the notion that we might be inferior to others, nor would she tolerate our acting superior to *any* other human being. You might say her own response to the situation was simple but profound: she was fair to everyone.

I firmly believe my mother's attitude of love and acceptance toward people of all races and socioeconomic backgrounds, at a time when racism and class distinction were the order of the day in the Deep South, had a profoundly positive influence on the man I would become. On this issue of race, my mama and papa were in total agreement. I vividly recall Mama telling us on many occasions that one of these days we would stand in front of a color-blind Lord and that we should treat our black brothers and sisters with kindness and respect. She always had a beautiful relationship with everyone, because underlying her treatment of people was the understanding that each one of us was special to God, and, therefore, we must be courteous to all of God's children.

Her habit of open-mindedness extended across genders, races, ethnic backgrounds, and social standings. The six people who had the most impact on my life were all women. Just think what I would have missed out on had I been sexist! Three Native Americans had a huge impact on me—one in my sales career, one in my speaking career, another in my spiritual walk. My closest friend for over thirty-six years is a Jew, and my favorite authors are Jews (Moses, David, Solomon, Paul, James, Matthew, Mark). My daughter-in-law is from Campeche, Mexico. Our head of product development and director of international operations is from India, and today I am affiliated with a large Japanese company with a Korean president. I shudder to think what would have happened to me had I been racist. I'm truly grateful that my mother would not tolerate prejudice in her home. I believe that when God used a black lady to show me that Jesus Christ is my Savior, He was honoring my mother because of the way she handled her relationships with all of His children.

Mama used day-to-day circumstances to teach us about people and life. In one instance a single woman with several small children ran up a bill of five dollars and forty cents with us. In days when "sweet milk" was ten cents a quart, buttermilk was five cents a quart, and vegetables could be bought in large quantities for less than a quarter, her bill was enormous. It represented over three weeks' salary for me at that time. Finally, her patience with the woman exhausted, Mama sent me to collect the debt. I struck out determined and resolute to recover the money that was rightfully ours. But I was too late. I found the house empty—the woman had moved in the dead of night! I was furious!

Mama in her infinite wisdom said, "Son, if she can live with it, we can certainly live without it." It was time to move on. She never mentioned the incident again.

I might point out that even in those times of hardship and hard work our mother never missed a real-life opportunity to teach us significant ethical lessons. Some people actually believe that "poverty is a cause of crime," but my mother always insisted that simply was not so, pointing out that honest people just do not take what is not theirs. They would ask for it, they would work for it; they would do anything but steal it. As it turns out, studies done later in Canada and the United States proved my mother right. In fact, according to these studies, during those Depression years, the rate of crime in both countries actually went down. I believe the reason is that Canadians and Americans were taught from their earliest years that stealing is both a sin *and* a crime.

Yes, the Golden Rule, "Do unto others as you would have others do unto you," was the philosophy that consistently guided Mama's everyday behavior. Had she known how some people in Yazoo City on occasion were treating her children she would have been heartbroken.

The Yazoo City Country Club Pool

The Yazoo City Country Club always fascinated me. It was a special place set apart for special people, and I knew I wasn't one of them. I was once invited to caddie for nine holes of golf, and I'll never forget the two and a half hours I spent on the course—or the two shiny quarters I was given as my pay! Later I sat in that clubhouse with the carpeted floors, looked out the picture window to see the glimmering swimming pool, looked past the pool to the beautiful golf course, and for the moment I felt like I was in a privileged make-believe world.

A few weeks after my first exposure to the luxurious watering hole of Yazoo City's elite, a friend whose family had a membership invited me to go swimming at "the club." Excited by the opportunity, I arrived well before the appointed time and stationed myself at the edge of the pool. I started getting worried that my friend might not show when he was fifteen minutes late. It was a beautiful summer day, and, as the minutes passed, I realized just how hot the sun was. By the time my friend was thirty minutes late I was sweltering and frustrated. I just couldn't resist the pull of the water any longer (I can handle anything but temptation). I jumped into the pool with a loud splash. As I was lost in the cool, refreshing joy of the moment, an angry voice called, "HILARY! Get out of that pool immediately . . . and stay out! And you can come to my office tomorrow afternoon after school!"

I knew and respected the man who ousted me from the pool. By Yazoo City standards, he was "rich and sophisticated," prominent in the community, and highly regarded. Definitely from one of the "top" families of Yazoo City, Mississippi. That night guilt and fear kept me wide awake. I felt guilty because Mama had taught me about boundaries, and I painfully knew I had crossed one that wasn't mine to cross. I was scared because I kept hearing that tone of voice that said, "You are in big trouble now!" I suppose I was a little humiliated, too.

When I arrived at Mr. DeCell's office the next day, I was reticent and repentant, but it didn't slow Mr. DeCell down for a second. He read me the riot act for several long and agonizing minutes. In the heat of the shame and humiliation that were heaped on my ten-year-old head that day I vowed that someday I would own a pool BIGGER than the Yazoo City Country Club's pool. That seemed like the perfect retaliation in my childish mind. I knew in my heart, according to Mama's philosophy, I was no better or worse than the next person. But if a swimming pool conferred status and recognition, I was going to have one, too. I'd show them I was just as good as they were.

I'm sorry to say there were more such incidents when adults I respected and looked up to instructed me in such a way that it undermined my self-esteem—or, as we'd say in those days, gave me an inferiority complex. I believe many adults think they are helping when they chastise a child, but often their criticism is done in the spirit of anger instead of love. And children instantly recognize it for what it is. This approach, in my case, just strengthened my inferiority complex in spite of all of the encouragement and reinforcement I got at home. However, there were far more people who, because of their respect for my mother and their admiration for the way she handled her difficult situation, were more than willing to cut us a little slack and extend a helping hand and a word of encouragement.

Trying to get over this hurtful sense of inferiority and prove to myself and everyone else that I was worthy of respect and admiration became a driving force in my early adult years.

Hurtful Moments in School

Some of my most painful memories have to do with feeling "less than" and humiliated in school. The day I was called to the front of my third-grade classroom to point out Arkansas on the geography map was especially humiliating. The night before I had fallen asleep on the floor next to the fireplace doing my homework and hadn't completed my work on the map. I was exhausted because I'd milked the cows earlier that morning and the newspapers that were supposed to be ready for me to deliver at three o'clock weren't ready until eight P.M. Normally my mother kept all of us around the dinner table after we'd eaten to do our schoolwork, but I'd had to go back to work that night. By the time I was able to start my homework I was just plain out of steam.

The next day I found myself standing at the blackboard, wondering if the teacher would accept my reasons for not knowing where Arkansas was located on the map, when she abruptly said, "Hilary, we are waiting for you to show us where the state of Arkansas can be found!" The situation was hopeless. I would only make a bigger fool of myself if I tried to guess. I felt the tears start to trickle down my cheeks, and I remembered a time in second grade when I'd found myself in the same embarrassing kind of situation.

The reason I hadn't gotten my homework done that time was very different, but the shame and humiliation that followed were exactly the same. The night before, Dr. Webb Brame from First Baptist Church had come by the house to tell my older brothers that the jobs he'd been trying to line up for them were officially theirs—Hubert would be working with the highway department at forty dollars a month (a significant sum in 1933), and Houston would work with the CCC (a government-sponsored organization that built bridges, dams, and parks—some of which still stand today) at twenty-two dollars per month.

My friend Red Wallace happened to be there at the time, and we got so caught up in the excitement over the good news and the celebration that ensued that all thoughts of doing homework flew right out the window! Mama pulled out some leftover jelly cake—a cake made from molasses and layered with jelly—and almost half of a sweet potato pie. That I can remember exactly what we had to eat is testimony to how special this particular occasion was for us. Sweets were in short supply in those days, but nothing was spared when Dr. Brame brought the good news.

Not doing homework had led to embarrassment and tears on that day, too! It almost seemed as if my teachers had a sixth sense and called me to work on the blackboard only when I hadn't completed my homework. The day I finally admitted that I couldn't find Arkansas on the map my teacher roundly humiliated me by saying, "No, you certainly can't! You probably can't even find the state of Mississippi! Take your seat!"

I can still hear the children's laughter. I tried to hide my stream of tears as I returned, hurt and dejected, to my seat. I was so humiliated and embarrassed. Some of the children even pointed at me saying, "Sissy—look at the sissy crying. He probably can't even find his way home!"

There was one sweet little girl with a tender spirit who cried with me, but that show of compassion wasn't enough to offset the rage I felt building inside at the injustice of it all. I couldn't wait to get out on the playground and take out all of my hurt on the boys who heckled me in class. Boy, I was gonna show 'em! I was gonna teach 'em a lesson they wouldn't forget!

I Became a Fighter

Incidents like the ones above, coupled with the fact that I was an unusually small child from an unusually large family, served to increase the painful inferiority complex I mentioned earlier. I was about as insecure as a child could be. My inferiority complex was aggravated by the embarrassment I sometimes felt about the clothing I had to wear, particularly in cold weather. Long trousers were scarce in our household. On occasion, I had to wear shorts with long stockings that Mother pinned to the shorts. While they were reasonably warm, they were an embarrassment to wear and caused unwanted attention and teasing.

One of the manifestations of a poor self-image is aggressiveness, and I overcompensated for my smallness in both stature and ego by physically challenging anybody who disagreed with me. Many people don't realize it, but a youngster who is small at ages eight, nine, and ten is more agile than a bigger child of the same age. As a result, even though I was small I could generally win a battle of fisticuffs with a youngster who probably outweighed me by fifteen or twenty pounds. If we got into an argument and could not settle it in a matter of moments, I would end up sucker punching the guy by hitting him first. The element of surprise gave me an unfair but decided advantage, which I'm ashamed to admit today. However, I never discriminated: large or small, black or white, rich or poor; if we disagreed, I generally struck the first blow.

My very first fistfight took place on the grounds of the elementary school, and it ended almost before it began. I just couldn't stand to see bigger, older kids picking on younger, smaller ones, and James Leverett was doing just that. I jumped into the middle of it and had gotten in a few good blows before a teacher pulled us apart and took us to the principal's office. James was crying pretty good. It was obvious he didn't know what had happened, because when he wiped the tears from his eyes and he saw me he said, "Are *you* the one?" I was so small for my age that James couldn't imagine that I had been able to pummel him like I did. Anger and resentment added considerably to my strength.

James Leverett and I managed to mix it up several times during our school years, and one of our fights stands out above the others in my mind. I was about fourteen at the time, and I'd long since earned a dubious reputation for being aggressive. I wasn't considered a bully, but the other kids knew that I wouldn't take any guff from anybody.

On this particular occasion James had been running his mouth about my mother being somewhat like the old lady who lived in the shoe . . . with all those children . . . and he topped off his taunt by stabbing me in the head with his Number 2 pencil. My first punch landed hard just above his left eye. Red Wallace told me later that the blood really started to flow from his forehead. My next punch landed dead center in the area directly under James's sternum and the "ooofff" sound of air rushing from his diaphragm told me I'd hit my mark. James crumpled into the fetal position, gasping for air, and Red started pulling me away saying, "That's enough. Enough is enough. Let it go." I yelled back over my shoulder that I didn't want to hear James say anything about my family or me ever again.

When school was out that afternoon my brother Huel and I headed home. As a show of his confidence and pride in my abilities, Huel was the brother who would volunteer me to fight the winner of any fight he happened upon. Usually I was happy to oblige. Anyway, James was waiting for me on Canal Street in front of Mitchell's Barber Shop. He said he wanted to take up what we hadn't finished at school. We were going at it pretty good when I got in a lucky blow and he started crying. When you're small and those things happen, the one who gets in the lucky blow is often the winner.

Just as I delivered the lucky blow, Mrs. J. K. Worley, the sixth-grade teacher who taught me to love reading and consequently made such a profound difference in my life and career, came along. She knew me and she knew my brother, so she asked him, "Huel, did you see these boys fighting?" He answered, "Yes, ma'am, I did." She said, "Well, why didn't you stop it?" He said, "It wasn't any use to, Mrs. Worley, my brother was winning!"

Well, while we can appreciate a touch of humor there and a sense of the fact that my brother was obviously on my side, one must understand that had I been losing, he would have stopped the fight. Today, of course, I know that whether I was winning or losing, since he was several years older than I, he *should* have stopped the fight. His only excuse was that he just felt James had it coming to him. We do rationalize things, don't we, when ourself or a loved one is involved?

One thing about fights in those days—to the best of my knowledge and experience, nobody ever thought about using a gun or knife. And, generally speaking, in 99 percent of the cases, when you knocked someone down or you had the other guy crying, the fight was over and there was no carryover.

I hate to admit it, but my scrapes were not limited to the likes of James Leverett, and they even included friends. Many of the scrapes we had were typical for our age group, but my insecurities and temper as well as my need to defend myself made me more confrontational than most children my age. Lintonia Park had a tennis court that was badly in need of repair, but that never dampened my love of playing the game. On late-summer Sunday afternoons, while there was still daylight for us to play by, we participated in hotly contested tennis matches. I don't know whether it was the result of overconfidence or insecurity, whether I so badly wanted to be accepted, or simply because I was overly competitive in whatever I did, but sometimes if a friend called my ball out of bounds and I didn't agree, I'd protest too long and too loud. I always wanted to win.

This spirit carried over into other areas of sporting competition. We played hockey using roller skates, broom handles, and tin cans crushed and shaped into a semiround puck. Our games frequently deteriorated into fights that we dubbed "hockey wars." As a rule, I was apt to fight over just about any kind of perceived slight or injustice, whatever position I played.

One of my playground encounters resulted in disaster. Once while arguing with Tom Ramsey, a Mexican classmate, I threw the first punch, but, as far as I can remember, that was the only one I got in. Tom Ramsey then proceeded to knock me down flat. I didn't have sense enough to stay there, so I got back up. This nasty routine, ending always with my face in the dust, went on for several minutes before the third-grade teacher, Miss Street, finally put an end to the massacre. I don't ever recall being so glad to see a schoolteacher in my life! However, in all fairness to myself, I will admit I scared Tom half to death. He thought he'd killed me.

Most of my fights were not of my own doing. My younger brother, Horace, could be quite antagonistic with schoolmates he didn't like—especially when he knew his "big brother" would take up for him if he got in trouble. He would always lose, and then I would enter the fight and take it from there. Long after Horace outgrew me in physical size during our teenage years (he got so tall he gave me the name "Short"), he'd still pick a fight and then solicit me to fight it for him. I often teased him in later years about developing the sales techniques that made him successful as an adult by honing his skills persuading me to fight his fights. I think the fights my brothers got me into were more a matter of family pride than anything else. It was their way of proving our worth and demanding respect. They felt it was my good fortune to play the role of hero in these childhood wars for honor.

I know this seems incredible, but my ever-ready adversary James Leverett, even after his last disastrous loss to me, felt compelled to come after me one more time to see if he couldn't redeem himself by somehow defeating me at least once. One day when I was riding my bicycle to work, I spotted James and two of his accomplices waiting for me across the street on the corner of the playground by my old elementary school. Scowling and raising his fist, he yelled out, "Me and these two boys are gonna whup you!"

I stopped my bike and sized up the situation—three against one were not good odds. Then I took action. I strode over there looking into the eyes of first one, and then the other, of James's friends, and I said, "If you two boys get involved, I'm gonna deal with you personally later." Then I paused for effect and added, glaring at them, "You can count on it!"

By the time Miss Bass, the elementary school principal, got to the fight, James was ardently wishing he had brought along more loyal—or tougher—friends. Neither one of the boys jumped in to help him at any point, with the result that I was cleaning his platter yet one more time. Miss Bass hurried over to us. She knew us both and said, "Hilary, you have somewhere you are supposed to be . . . [she knew I had multiple jobs] and you are in junior high now, so don't let me catch either of you fighting on these school grounds again!" With that, the fight broke up and everyone left; James Leverett and I never mixed it up again.

I'm not really sure if I was maturing or if I was just working so much that I didn't have time to get into trouble, but by the time I was in high school the petty fistfighting had pretty much stopped—with the exception of "the big one," which I'll get to later. It's possible that my time on the boxing team helped me satisfy my competitive nature through an acceptable outlet.

When I was in the seventh grade, I decided to go out for the boxing team. As a "street fighter," or, more appropriately, a "playground gladiator," I was pretty handy with my "dukes." However, when I got into the boxing ring, I very quickly learned there's a dramatic difference between a nonstop slugfest on the school grounds versus fighting in a ring under the watchful eye of a referee. Certain rules and procedures were under strict observance in the ring, and, more important, the fight moved from a freelance brawl to somewhat of a science.

I weighed in at eighty-two and a half pounds, and it's important that you give me full credit for that extra half pound. I was not the biggest guy on the boxing team; as a matter of fact, I was the second-smallest guy. The smallest was a classmate named Joe Stringer who weighed in at all of sixty-two pounds, so he and I were designated as sparring partners. Needless to say, I felt confident—and even a little guilty—being matched against such a little guy. However, he had been on the boxing team since the fifth grade and clearly understood the defensive aspects of boxing as well as the fact that a straight punch was the shortest distance to my nose.

I shall never forget the rude awakening I experienced about three and a half seconds after we started the first round and his left connected with the end of my nose. He apparently thought I had a short memory, because about two seconds later there it was again! I'm here to tell you that I never got so tired of stopping leather with the end of my nose in my life! Before the first round was over I was somewhat embarrassed, hurt (and hurting), and had about decided that I was really too busy to go out for the boxing team anyhow.

I was lucky in this instance because Coach Perminter, a man of real compassion, stopped the sparring (it was really more like pitch and catch, and I wasn't doing any pitching) after one round. He took me aside and started instructing me on how to protect my nose and throw a few jabs of my own. The next day Joe gave me another lesson—though it was not quite as painful. By the end of that week, because of my extra twenty pounds, I was able to defend myself a little more effectively. By the end of the second week, I was even able to get in a few licks of my own, and for the rest of the season we had some lively exchanges.

As a matter of fact, as my skill developed with practice and coaching, I acquired a winning record on the team. The worst I ever finished was second, and the only reason I stopped boxing was because of my hands—the referee kept stepping on them!

One of the chief pleasures in my life was occasionally getting to play tennis at the end of my work and school day. I bought a tennis racquet for fifty cents and managed to pick up used balls from older, better players who discarded them when they were about half used up. I was not fast, but I was quick. I could move in small areas as fast or faster than most of my peers. I became what others frown on and classify as a "junk player." I couldn't "put my opponent away," but somehow I managed to retrieve and hit balls back to opponents who had better technique than I had. As a result, I won matches against players who had better form and strokes than I did. What I did on the court wasn't pretty or conventional, but it worked for me.

In the ninth grade I tried out for the tennis team and made it. We had very few matches, but they were enjoyable. Then the state tournament rolled around. Everyone on the team was extremely excited. One of my biggest disappointments in high school occurred when the coach chose James Harry Graham, a classmate of mine, as the final member of the team. James was, by our standards, rich. He also was much taller than I was and had better, more classic strokes, even though I beat him on a regular basis. However, when the time came to leave for the tournament, the coach chose him instead of me, explaining that he felt a taller player had a better chance of winning and helping the team. Needless to say, I was very disappointed.

It wasn't until I was several years older, perhaps even after I became an adult, that I fully understood that the coach was probably embarrassed by my shoes, clothes, and fifty-cent racquet. One reason I believe the fifty-cent racquet was a factor was because one of the members of the country club, Charlie Graber, who was an excellent player (and an adult), noticed the special way I protected my racquet and let me practice with one of his—and it was really nice. He was amused that on those occasions when he was watching me and I fell in pursuit of a ball, I would always hold the racquet up so that I would not damage it. I did this out of habit because my own inexpensive racquet could not withstand the abuse a high-quality racquet could.

In addition to my formal studies in high school, I was getting a good education in the truth that life isn't always fair. There is a chance at that point I realized subconsciously the unfairness of discrimination for any reason whatsoever. However, it was not an issue I dwelt on because life was tough enough for us in those days, and to acknowledge and carry that additional burden for no good reason seemed like a waste of time and energy.

Outside of the boxing team, the tennis team, and a brief time on the track team, none of the other extracurricular activities interested me. The people in the high school fraternities seemed a little too fond of themselves—even my best friends acted differently when they were around frat friends. And, of course, I didn't have the extra money that fraternities cost. But the overriding reason I wasn't more involved in school functions was my work and church schedule. My family responsibilities saw to it that, whether I wanted to or not, I would remain an outsider.

One extra activity I did attempt for a time during my early teens was Boy Scouts. I'll never forget the wonderful scout camp I attended in Biloxi, Mississippi. We spent much of the day swimming in a crystal-clear little lake, and on warm nights we went into town where for ten cents we could swim in the Markham Hotel pool. We thought that was an unbelievable luxury.

Even though I look back on my time in scouts fondly, one of my biggest childhood regrets occurred while I was swimming in that lake at camp. I had carried two fifty-cent pieces with me to scout camp to take care of incidental expenses like the ten-cent fee to get into the Markham Hotel pool and to buy an occasional Coke or piece of candy. One day I made the mistake of putting the money in my swimsuit. The pocket was not very good, and while I was swimming I lost the two half-dollars. I was a beginner swimmer, but our compassionate scout counselor—an adult—spent some fruitless time diving to the bottom of the lake trying to retrieve my money. He didn't find it, and that really hurt because then I didn't have the funds to enjoy the treats the other kids were enjoying.

I loved the recognition we received at the Boy Scout Court of Honor when we were awarded the promotions and merit badges we had earned since the previous scout meeting. The recognition and values I was taught in scouting simply reinforced what my mother and the church had been teaching me. In the Boy Scouts I eventually achieved the rank of Star, but when I looked at the number of badges necessary to reach the next rank and the time and effort required, I was overwhelmed. My work schedule would not allow me to reach the next rank in a reasonable amount of time, so I dropped out. It was a fact of my life that Mama needed as much help as she could get from each of her children, and that included me. As a result, I actually became more comfortable with adults than I was with my peers.

I don't want it to sound as if we never had any time to relax or have fun because we were quite good at doing both. Many of today's readers will not be able to relate to things with which we entertained ourselves when I was a child, but, over all, I believe my generation of children was much happier than most youngsters are today. Here's a simple test. Can you supply the missing words in this oft-heard statement made by children today who have their own computers, televisions, CDs, Walkmans, and video games? Once a youngster is away from these electronic toys, parents are likely to hear this statement: "I'm ____! There's ____ ____ ____!" Chances are excellent that any parent is able to fill in the blanks: "bored! . . . nothing to do!"

When I was a child, nothing we had fun at depended on electricity or batteries. Hopscotch was a favorite with the girls, and occasionally we boys would join as well. We would take a Crayon and draw the form on the sidewalk, or, if there was open, grassless ground available, we drew the outline in the dirt.

My personal favorite was to shoot marbles for "keeps." We did this by placing the marbles in a circle about three feet in diameter. Each player put three or four marbles in the circle. Then we'd draw a line and "lag" up to that line. The one who could get closest to the line shot first, and we guys continued to shoot from the outer rim of the circle until we missed. (Girls seldom played marbles.) Then the next player had a chance to shoot. Any marbles you knocked out of the circle were yours to keep, so the name "shooting marbles for keeps" was born. I was one of the better players at this particular game. However, when I competed with Lawrence Moore, one of the boys who lived a couple blocks away, he generally cleaned me out, and I would have to seek less-talented opponents to renew my supply. Overall, however, my winnings were significant, and I usually had a pocketful of marbles.

As a matter of fact, those marbles served well for one of my other recreational activities, which, I am embarrassed to admit, I also enjoyed—though for many years I have been amazed that I even participated in this when I was a child. Phil Reeves, a neighbor who was a year older, and I were in contests against each other with our slingshots, which, of course, were handmade. We each took a branch out of a tree that had a "fork" in it and tied a strip of discarded inner tube to both sides of the branch, then sewed a piece of cloth or rubber to the inner tube section. From it we would shoot either a marble or a rock. Most of the time I had enough marbles to use. They were more effective and accurate, since they were consistently round. The part I'm not proud of is that unsuspecting birds were our targets. Phil and I kept score as to how many we shot and killed with our slingshots. In retrospect, I'm glad he always won, but in those days my competitive nature and lack of concern for the birds left me disappointed when he outscored me. I am glad to say that, by the time I reached age ten or eleven, I had abandoned this particular form of recreation.

Another favorite game when I was a youngster was to play "tops." In those days, a top was a little toy that had a large, round top and a steel ball at the bottom. We wound a hard string around the top and threw it to the ground. The top would spin for a number of seconds. We had drawn a circle on the ground and the contestant who was able to hit closest to the center of the circle was declared the winner. Unlike marbles, there was no such thing as playing for keeps; most tops cost a nickel, and a really good one cost a dime. The stakes would have been unreasonably high, and we would not have enjoyed the game. Some of us became quite proficient at hitting the center, or close to the center, of the circle. It always brought out our competitive instincts, and we would play that game vying with one another for sometimes as long as an hour. It was fun, kept us out of trouble, and increased our enjoyment of life.

Another exciting activity that we looked forward to was the annual soapbox derby race down Broadway, the steepest hill in Yazoo City. Soapbox derbies have been largely abandoned today in favor of other pastimes, but in those days, with very little else to do, they were extremely popular among children. The rules required that the driver had to be the builder of the racer, but the youngsters were permitted to receive guidance and instruction from their parents. On the big day of the race, it was obvious to virtually everyone there that most, if not all, of the entries were not built by twelve-year-olds but by fathers or much older brothers.

The races were run in heats, meaning that four racers were lined up together on a slanted launch, and at the word "Go!" they were all released at the same time. The first one across the finish line at the bottom of the hill was declared the winner. The winners then ran against other winners in their own heats. It generally took about two hours to complete the races, and from all up and down that hill hundreds of spectators watched and cheered for their favorites. It was quite a social event that generated excitement and enthusiasm.

Impromptu boxing matches, held at one of the feed stores around the corner from the grocery store where I worked, were another source of entertainment for us as children during that simpler time. There was a fairly large, open area in the feed store, and the contestants, recruited by the storeowners and others, would go at it with no referee. There were very few rules, but, in all fairness, the owner of the store watched over the matches and made certain no one got hurt. If there were mismatches, he would simply stop the fight, and that was that.

During those evenings of my youth we also played hide-and-seek. We'd take turns hiding in the backyard or next door, and we'd shout when we were well hidden, then the others would seek us. Needless to say, we were not hard to find because we didn't have far to go to hide, but we had a good time anyway.

I well remember hot summer nights when we would sit on the front steps of our porch at home and fight the Ford-Chevrolet war. Mr. Fred Shirley drove a Chevrolet coupe to deliver the mail; Dr. Tom Rainer, who lived down the street, drove a Ford. We boys and our buddies, primarily Louie Russell Williams and Red Wallace, would heatedly discuss the merits of the different automobiles. There never was a definitive conclusion as to which one was the best, but my sentiments were in favor of Chevys. My very first dream was to buy Mr. Shirley's used Chevrolet coupe when he bought a new one. I had plans for the sheer joy of driving it as far as it would go for three days of my one-week vacation, and then turning around and driving it back the other three days. The plan would provide for maximum driving time and would still get me back in time for church on Sunday.

Our imaginations were active, and, in the absence of an obvious occasion for fun, we were capable of concocting our own. In those days very few houses had garages, so the cars were parked on the street. In good weather the windows were rolled down so the car would be cool—or at least, perhaps, a little cooler in the morning. One of my buddies figured out how we could have a little fun by taking advantage of the situation. He took the slats from apple crates and slipped the slat under one side of the steering wheel, over the horn and under the other side of the steering wheel. The horn, which was always on a button in the center of the steering wheel, would start to blow loudly. Then we would dash to the next car and repeat the process. Our contest was to see who could get the most horns blowing at the same time. Generally speaking, the car owners had not gone to bed, or, if they had, they were not asleep, but it still would take them two or three minutes to get out of their houses to shut off the horns. We thought it was great fun and, as near as I can remember, always escaped punishment because no real damage was done and we were never caught in the act.

I remember another time I escaped punishment. Had I been caught, the greatest damage would have been done to myself. When I was a young teenager, I had already been working for several years, and a buddy of mine and I decided to hitchhike to the big city of Jackson, Mississippi, and spend the night in one of the hotels. While we were there we went to the zoo, walked up and down Capitol Street, staring at everything in sight, and over-all acted like a couple of country cousins come to town.

We checked into the Waltham Hotel, which was one of the best hotels in Jackson. I believe the room was four dollars, and each of us paid two dollars and an additional fifty cents deposit on the key. We were dazzled by the fancy surroundings and felt really special. Neither of us could sleep because of the thrill. After we settled in we each showered—that was certainly a privilege for both of us since our homes had only a bathtub. When we finished our showers, we got to talking about the beautiful towels the hotel provided us. Then we hatched a plan.

The more we eyeballed those towels, the more beautiful and desirable they became. We each decided we would take one, but how on earth would we get them out of the hotel? We had no change of clothing, no bag, no nothing—just us. We solved that problem by wrapping them around our bodies under our clothing. As stiff as two mummies, we caught the elevator to the lobby the next morning and walked up to the desk to turn in the key.

Just as we turned around and started walking away, the booming voice of the desk clerk called out, "Boys, just a minute!" Sheer terror gripped both of us. We froze. We knew in our hearts that we had just been caught stealing those two expensive towels from the hotel. Hesitantly and fearfully, we turned around. The desk clerk then said to us, "You forgot your key deposit," and handed us the fifty cents.

With a huge sigh of relief we walked out of the hotel and, I must also add, at the same time resigned from our lives of crime. As best I can recall, that towel was the only thing I ever stole in my life, with the exception of apples and peaches and pecans from neighbors' trees. I plead guilty to those thefts, and I remain grateful that the towel incident both began and ended my brief career in crime.

I knew that if my mama ever heard about what I had done I would be in trouble big time! And then I realized, somewhat belatedly, that if the hotel security had caught us and turned us in, that incident would have been on my record. I quickly decided that I was going to work for a living and not steal for one. I did not have the steely temperament necessary to be a good thief. Undoubtedly, the daily lessons my mama taught me (and had backed up with a peach-tree switch) had prepared me for that decision.

The pleasures of my youth were simple and few, but the good memories are many.

The War Years

A LIFE-CHANGING EVENT

On the first Sunday in December, shortly after I'd turned fifteen, Phil Reeves and I took to the woods. Since Sunday was the Lord's day, no work was allowed; Sunday afternoons were set aside for relaxing or having fun. Without a care in the world we climbed through the hills, forced our way through thick vines and underbrush, and explored the countryside. We weren't long into our expedition before we came upon some "wild" pecan trees that were growing in amazingly perfect symmetry. Not only that, they had produced an incredible crop of nuts! As luck would have it, Phil just happened to have with him a large flour sack! We then fell to discussing the attitude that Lawyer Henry, the man who owned the land we were playing on, might have about our gathering a few of his pecans. After a careful consideration of the facts as we knew them, we concluded that he had a lot of money, was a nice man, and wouldn't miss a "few" pecans. Also, we'd be careful to pick up only the ones he wouldn't mind our having.

It was one of those really beautiful days. The sun was shining through the trees, and the temperature, though it was December, was cool but not cold. Phil and I talked as we carefully gathered the "unwanted" pecans, and our conversation turned to the very important subject of what we'd do next. Phil suggested going to McLain's to get some ice cream and asked if I didn't work there sometimes. I explained that I didn't work *there* but that I did sell ice cream sandwiches for them at the local wrestling matches and that I'd even made a dollar a night on two different occasions.

Phil couldn't believe my good fortune and excitedly asked, "Did you get to see the matches, too?"

"You bet. You don't think people are buyin' ice cream when the action is going on, do ya? They buy between matches or when the matches are dull."

"Wrestling never gets dull for me!" Phil said. "I love to watch old Jack Curtis kick the stuffin' out of Sailor Watkins!"

"I used to feel that way, Phil, until my brothers Huel and Howard moved out to join the navy. When they left, we took in a boarder who was a former pro wrestler, and he told me the truth about all those guys."

"The truth? Hilary, what in the world are you talkin' about?"

"Fact of the matter is, Phil, those are exhibition matches and most of the time are not real contests. What really disappointed me was when I learned that our hero, Jack Curtis, switches roles and is the villain when they go to Mobile for a match!"

Phil looked so dejected at this news that I actually felt a little as if I'd just told him there was no Santa Claus. I tried to make him feel better by saying, "There's always a chance they will get mad at each other. Our boarder told us about one night in Montreal, Canada, when a guy got so mad he hit another wrestler over the head with a Coca-Cola case. Split his skull wide open and got blood on the people in the first three rows!"

Satisfied that wrestling was still worth seeing, Phil and I moved onto other important topics as we made our way back to town. We got about as far as Jackson and Seventh Street when we noticed the neighborhood seemed unusually quiet and deserted. Other than a radio playing somewhere in the background, there was not a sound to be heard. We were mystified and a little spooked. When we finally reached my house, my sister Evia Jane clued us in. The Japanese had attacked the U.S. Naval Base at Pearl Harbor, Hawaii. The United States was at war.

That day marked the end of my adolescence. The world took on a new weight. All frivolity seemed oddly a thing of the distant past. With a fearful heart I asked Mama if we'd heard from my brothers, Howard and Huel. She said we hadn't but that we must pray for them and keep our faith strong.

My Weekly Reader, a weekly newspaper about world events published for schoolchildren, had given us some indication of the tense situation in the world. And anyone who went to the movies saw newsreels from RKO News or Pathé News (depending on the distributor of the motion picture), featuring warlike rhetoric and battle scenes from halfway around the world. But nothing could have prepared us for the shock of the Pearl Harbor attack.

I resolved immediately to join Howard and Huel in the navy as soon as I was old enough. Patriotism ran deep in the Ziglar family, as it did in virtually every other American family at that time, and I decided right then and there that I could and would learn to be a naval aviator.

The Summer of Big Decisions

The war was in full swing by the summer of 1943, and I could actually visualize myself flying the Vought Sikorski Corsair or the famous navy Hellcat. We'd win the war, and I'd return to Yazoo City a hero. But the vision quickly faded when I considered the math and science course work I would need to complete before joining up. I also had a hernia that would have to be repaired before the navy would even consider taking me.

On top of all of that I was weighing what for me was the major decision about whether to continue to work for Mr. Anderson or go to work for Mr. Haining in the new meat market he had just bought in the A&P grocery store. All in all, they were pretty tough decisions for a sixteen-year-old boy.

Fixing the hernia was an absolute must if I was ever going to get in the navy, so I did that first. In those days having abdominal surgery meant that you stayed in bed for what seemed like forever. In my case it was for twenty days! The one good thing about being out of commission was that I had lots of uninterrupted time to consider my options. I had often seen my mama write in her journals when she was thinking deeply about things, and I decided that if it worked for her, it would work for me. I got out my pen and paper and wrote "U.S. Navy Fighter Pilot" at the top of the page. Then I listed the obstacles I had to overcome and the actions I needed to take to make my dream come true. First, I had to pass the physical, but I felt that would be a cinch since I'd had my hernia fixed. Second, I had to be seventeen years old, and, barring any unforeseen tragedy, that would occur November 6, 1943. Third, I needed to finish the proper course work, which meant that I'd have to register almost immediately for summer school at Hinds Junior College in Raymond, Mississippi, so I mailed off for the college application. Fourth, I'd need to make a formal application to the navy, but I couldn't do that until after my seventeenth birthday.

After seeing my plan written down on paper I felt comfortable that I knew what I needed to do to get started on my navy career. But I still had to decide what to do about work. So I took out a fresh sheet of paper and wrote across the top, "Work for Mr. Anderson or Mr. Haining?" I'd been agonizing over what to do and how to do it for quite some time before I decided to write down the pros and cons. Then I wrote "Mr. and Mrs. Anderson" on one side of the page, and I wrote "Mr. and Mrs. Haining" on the other.

I started my list on the Anderson side of the page. Mr. Anderson and his sweet, loving wife had always treated me like a son. Mr. Anderson showed his affection for me by teasing and joking, and Mrs. Anderson always had a hug and a kind word for me. When I'd started working for Mr. Anderson, Mrs. Anderson weighed me on the penny scales, she measured my height and wrote in my weight and height on the side of the scales and dated her entry. Every six months or so she'd repeat the process and brag on how I was growing so big and strong. Her interest and small kindnesses had a huge impact on me.

I thought long and hard about the relationship I had with Mr. Anderson. Was I really a surrogate son to him or just a boy who worked for Piggly Wiggly for several years? Consider the matter of the bicycle. I had paid off my first credit purchase—a twenty-six-dollar bicycle bought from Sears for three dollars down and four dollars a month for six months—on a Tuesday, and on Thursday the bike was stolen when I left it in a dark area outside during one of my Boy Scout meetings. Mr. Anderson *gave* me twenty dollars toward a twenty-two-dollar Western Flyer bike from the Western Auto store. Those twenty dollars represented more than seven weeks' pay for me. Mr. Anderson never asked or expected to be repaid.

I was also privileged to go to Mr. Anderson's farm on Wednesday afternoons to visit with the farmhands and to spend some one-on-one time with him. On one special occasion Mr. and Mrs. Anderson took me on a trip to New Orleans to attend a grocers' convention. It was the national convention, and World War II was under way. H. V. Kaltenborn, a well-known English radio commentator, was the speaker, and he announced that the largest convoy yet to reach England had just landed and that it brought much needed medical and food supplies to his war-torn country. The applause that followed his announcement was deafening.

Going to New Orleans with Mr. and Mrs. Anderson was an incredible treat for a small boy from a small town, and remembering that in the process of making my list I determined that I had been treated more like family than an employee.

In first light, Mr. and Mrs. Anderson's generosity toward me should have made the decision a simple one—and it would have had it not been for the man Mr. Anderson had hired to replace Walton Haining. I'm not sure if it was out of benevolence or in part because of poor judgment, but Mr. Anderson hired a man who had lost his own business because of "whiskey and women."

Unfortunately, the man brought his old habits to his new job. When Mr. Anderson left for lunch each day, the man would call his bootlegger (Yazoo was a "dry" county, meaning no whiskey allowed), who would quickly deliver his daily "half-pint of lunch." The man often wanted to play wrestle when business got slow in the afternoons, and his impaired condition meant that the playing sometimes got too rough to suit me.

Even the fun to be had with new young employees at the store took on a different feel. They were introduced to a new game in which they must place a nickel on their forehead, close their eyes, lean backward as far as possible, and then come forward and drop the nickel in the funnel that had been placed in the front of their trousers; if they succeeded, the nickel was theirs. The problem was that as soon as the new kid was "in position," Mr. Haining's replacement would bring out the previously hidden ice water, which he then would pour into the funnel at the front of the poor fellow's pants. The spirit of this game was mean and humiliating. In no way was it funny.

This man had made trouble in my life in the past, too. He was the same man who had caused Mama to get firm with me a few years earlier—though I must say it was as much my fault as his. When he had owned his own grocery store near our house on Grand Avenue, he hired me to help take inventory on a Sunday morning from eight A.M. to one P.M. He paid one dollar. Despite the generous compensation, Mama was against my working on Sunday instead of going to church, and she instructed me not to do it again.

Twelve weeks later inventory time came around again, and the man asked me to work once more. Since I was making seventy-five cents working from seven A.M. until eleven P.M. on Saturdays, you can see how inviting the Sunday work was to a boy my age. Well, without consulting Mama, I took the job.

Mama was . . . well, let's just say Mama wasn't pleased. But she sorted through the ethics of the situation carefully. She said, "Son, you gave that man your word that you would be there, and you will be there. But *this time* when you leave, give him your word that you will not be doing this again. Either you tell him, or I will!" That was the last time I worked on Sunday.

Anyway, thinking about working with Mr. Anderson's new man left me feeling cold. So I moved to the other side of the page to start my list under Mr. and Mrs. Hainings' names. Before I even wrote the first word I knew I'd be working for Mr. Haining—it just felt right. The memory of my second day at work as Mr. Haining's assistant at the Piggly Wiggly meat market came rushing back. Mrs. Haining had brought a batch of her world-famous (at least they should have been) pecan pralines to welcome me as her husband's new assistant. While she was there she found one of the old wooden Coca-Cola cases that held the bottled Cokes and placed it behind the meat counter explaining, "Son, this will help you watch what is going on in other areas of the store while you are waiting on customers." She didn't mention that without the case, the customers would not have known I was in the store. Those meat counters were high—and I was short! Mrs. Haining made me feel loved, respected, and appreciated.

Mr. Haining's gentle spirit allowed him to be more verbal in his appreciation of my work than Mr. Anderson, and I glowed under his praise. He'd say things like, "Thank you for your hard work today, Hilary," or "Hilary, you are one of the most dependable people I have ever worked with." Oftentimes he'd hand me a big package of turkey or another kind of meat, saying that it needed to be eaten right away or it would spoil; did I know someone in the neighborhood who might put it to use?

Mr. Haining had always taken the time to explain why he took certain steps and why he arranged the displays the way he did in the meat counter. He told me how he figured out how much to charge for the individual portions of meat since he had to "block the hindquarters and forequarters" into smaller cuts. He taught me how to wrap the packages and greet the customers. He also explained that if a customer wanted a four-pound roast a good butcher would cut a four-pound roast, but a good salesman would cut a five-pound roast and then sell the customer the other pound.

Mr. Haining didn't limit his teachings to facts about the grocery store. He often talked about family and would explain why certain people in town had bad reputations. He spent hours observing what went on in the store, and one day he told me to watch when a certain businessman came in. He explained that the man would cause a distraction when he got up to the counter, and when the cashier turned his head the man would slip a pack of cigarettes into his pocket. I was stunned when I observed the events unfolding just as Mr. Haining predicted, because I had thought the man was honest. Mr. Haining said, "We all just need to remember that we don't really get by with anything. There is always somebody watching, and if they're not, we still know it's wrong and that God is watching." I learned to be careful as I evaluated people. Often they were not as they seemed. I learned many things from Walton Haining that shaped my life for the better.

I thought through all I had written about Mr. Anderson and Mr. Haining, and I made my decision to work for Mr. Haining final. Telling Mr. Anderson of my decision to work for Mr. Haining was difficult, but he was most understanding. He said he hoped Mr. Haining would give me a raise (which he did) and that Mr. Haining needed a "dependable man" like me. Mr. Anderson thought the "experience at the new store" would be good for me, and when he shook my hand good-bye he held it for an extra long time. I'm almost positive I saw the glint of a tear in the corner of Mr. Anderson's eye.

Summer School

I doubt there has ever been a sixteen-year-old young man more motivated about summer school than I was in 1943. Attending it marked my second action step toward getting into the Naval V5 Program and the cockpit of an airplane. You can't imagine my shock and disbelief when Hinds Junior College required me to take a history course in order to graduate from high school! I could not imagine how history was going to help me fly that airplane any better. I needed math and science—not history! But I needed the graduation certificate to make application to the navy, so I decided to tough it out.

Coach Jobie Harris was my history teacher, and in many ways he changed and enriched my life. He taught me more than American history. He once said, "If you have an ability that goes beyond providing for your own needs, you have a responsibility to use that ability to reach down and help those up who do not have that capacity. As a matter of fact, if you don't reach down and help lift up those less fortunate, the day will come when due to sheer weight of numbers, they will reach up and pull you down."

That represented a new kind of thinking for me, and I loved it. Coach Harris did such a great job of selling his students on why history was important that I left his room determined to make history my major—and history was the only class I consistently made A's in during my college career. I'll always be grateful to Coach Jobie Harris for teaching me to love history and to reach down and lift up those who do not have the ability or wherewithal to lift themselves up.

Many of the most worthwhile things I have done the last thirty-plus years of my life—my work in the drug war, in the prison system, with churches, with schools and with the homeless—have been the direct result of what Coach Harris taught me in that brief period of time.

Coach Harris taught just one of the courses I took at Hinds Junior College that summer. For some reason, perhaps because the war was on and because skilled labor was needed in the shipyards, I decided also to take the welding course that was offered at the school. Despite the fact that my mechanical-dexterity skills were limited at best, I felt with diligence I could learn. The class was held early in the morning because of the intense heat that comes from the welding torch and the hot, muggy summer.

We got up at six A.M., went to the welding shop only about a half block from our dorm, and for the first hour we practiced welding. The instructor came in and taught us more technique and procedures for the next hour. At the end of the first hour there were a certain number of welding rods that had been used, only the stubs of which were left on the welding bench.

One morning a couple of the guys didn't show up until the seven o'clock hour. When the instructor came in, he asked the guys if they had had a productive morning, how hard had they been working, etc. Of course, all of us, including the two culprits, said we had been very busy and very productive. The problem was, the two guys who didn't show up until just a minute or two before the instructor had forgotten that the ends of the welding rods, which could not be used for further welding purposes, were conspicuously absent. When the instructor gave them a failing grade because they had not actually been there, had not been practicing, my eyes were really opened to one basic fact: You've got to play it straight; you can't cheat and gain any benefit except, perhaps, for a brief pat on the back from somebody you've tried to impress. However, the instructor was far from impressed. He was very upset with these two guys for trying to pull the wool over his eyes. As far as I know, that was the last time anybody tried to pull that particular stunt.

What did I learn as a welder? I learned, number one, that it was hot. I learned that it was something I was not especially good at. And I also learned that I was going to get enough education so that I would not have to do that particular job. I believe that was a good lesson. Over the years I've had people tell me that after a few days working on the highway out in the hot sun, or doing menial labor, they recognized they needed to go back to school and get an education.

I Learned Self-Control

At that time, the last two years of high school and the first two years of college were often taught at the junior college. In our freshman class we had some real athletes, guys who were big, strong and tough, and what's more, the freshman class outnumbered the sophomore class by nearly two to one. It was an old school custom that early in the term all freshmen were ordered out to take the traditional run. This really involved just about a mile run around the campus with the sophomores riding alongside on their bicycles taunting us or standing to jeer as we ran past. What prompted me to do it I do not know, but when the sophomores said to us (and remember, I was one of the little guys there!) it was time for the run, I blurted out, "We decided not to run." Shocked, the leader of the sophomores asked, "Who made that decision?" I said, "We all did," which was not quite true, but I figured the big guys would not stand for the run, and, sure enough, that's exactly what happened. We all stood around talking for a while, decided the run wasn't a good idea anyhow, and so we simply didn't do it. Maybe that's where some of my later difficulties at Hinds started, but at any rate, I was glad that victory took place when it did.

Luck was not with me in every social situation at Hinds. I was almost expelled when my competitive nature got me into some serious difficulties. I was attracted to a very pretty girl at the school, who I did not realize was dating an older and much bigger guy. That guy also had a reputation for being tough. I never actually dated the girl, but I did buy her a milk shake one day out of my limited funds.

I shall never forget that afternoon, though, when I was on my upper bunk in the dorm and four or five guys, including the boyfriend, invaded our room. I did not want to create problems with him, so I did not get off my bunk; I just sat on the side with my legs hanging over. He and his friends, including a guy named Duckworth—somewhat of a loudmouth—approached, and the boyfriend said to me, "I hear you've been trying to court my girlfriend." Well, I was willing to say almost anything at that moment, so I said, "Well, no, not really, though I did buy her a milk shake." Duckworth spoke up and said, "They tell me he's been doing a lot more than that!" Well, that made me furious and scared the daylights out of me at the same time. So I did something I don't remember doing either before or since. I screamed at him in a loud voice, called him a horrible name, and hopped down off the bed. He jumped me, and, as luck would have it, I got in that first lucky blow. By then I'd had the benefit of some boxing experience in high school, and, incredibly enough, my punch literally knocked him backward. He stumbled and fell into the closet.

The dorm manager, who was also an official at the school, heard the commotion. He got involved and chewed me out good, threatening to expel me from school. I pleaded with him, and after a couple of days he cooled down and said he'd put me on probation and let me stay. If he had made a different decision, I would have been kicked out of the program; I would never have met that beautiful Redhead who has been my wife for the last fifty-five years; I would have left college and probably never have had another opportunity to return—at least, not with the mind-set I had at that time.

The really scary thought is that I eventually realized the boyfriend was just teasing me and had no intention of jumping on me. As a matter of fact, he was so much bigger (I weighed 120 pounds fully dressed) and stronger than I was, he did not consider me a worthy opponent.

Out of all of this I did learn a significant lesson—namely, that I must learn to control my temper, especially if I were ever going to fly navy planes.

Back to High School for Senior Year

In spite of all the warning signs I'd received, there was yet one more big fight left in me when I returned for my senior year of high school. I was seventeen years old when I came across Grady Crawford pulverizing John Lyles, one of Horace's classmates. Lyles was gawky for his age and uncoordinated, and he wasn't faring well. I stepped up, got into Grady's face, and said, "Why don't you hit somebody your own size?" So he did! And the battle was on. It was fierce, and we managed to beat each other up pretty good.

That afternoon when I went to work, Mr. Haining saw that my right eye was swollen almost shut, my lip was split, and my two swollen and sprained thumbs stuck out of my hands at awkward angles. Our conversation went like this:

"What in the world? Have you been in an accident?"

"Sort of. Grady Crawford was giving 'what for' to John Lyles at school today, Mr. Haining, and he's too big and too tough to be jumpin' on Lyles! When I pointed that out to him he took offense!"

Mr. Haining was quick to note the irony involved. "He took offense, and you shoulda' used some defense!"

That made me laugh, and then I discovered that I had taken some really hard body punches. Everything on my body hurt and ached. I said, "Please don't make me laugh. I think I may have a cracked rib!"

"Did you crack it yourself, or did Grady do the dirty deed?"

"Please! Stop it! If you think I look bad, you should see Grady! We fought on the school grounds until there was such a crowd that to keep from getting in trouble, we went over behind the fire station. The police stopped us there, so we went back to a vacant lot across from the school. We must have fought there for about ten minutes before Mr. Frank Williams, the principal, came over and stopped the fight.

"Yes, sir. Once we got into his office I knew we were in big trouble . . .

and you're not going to believe this, Mr. Haining, but he looked me over real good, then he looked Grady over real good, and then he said, 'You boys have already given each other enough punishment. Now get out of my office and go wash your faces!' I couldn't believe it!"

"Hilary, you are very lucky that you weren't suspended—or worse!"

"Yes, sir, you're sure right about that! I think it was the five knots on Grady's forehead that got Mr. Williams's attention. I didn't realize it until we got to Mr. Williams's office, but I had my class ring on during the whole fight. You could almost read the words 'Yazoo High' on two of the knots!"

In an informal poll that Mr. Haining took of students who came to the store that afternoon, five thought I had won and four thought Grady had won. For months the topic of discussion at the school was who had won the big fight. Interestingly enough, once the fight was over, there was never talk of a rematch or even bitter words between Grady and me. When Grady eventually came into the store, we courteously gave each other credit for winning the fight, but when he left, he privately told his buddies he had actually won, and I assured Mr. Haining that I had actually won. I suppose that's as good a definition of a tie as any.

Mama and the Fight

My mama was alarmed when she saw me for the first time after my fight with Grady. I told her the story of what had happened, and she gave me a long, hard stare with her piercing blue eyes and said, "I'm inclined to agree with Mr. Williams that you have received enough punishment from this fight. Punishment is used to get your attention; discipline comes from a biblical word that means, 'to learn.' Son, I hope you learned something, too. There are better ways to settle disagreements. If you learned that lesson, the fight was worthwhile—if you didn't, you have a tough row to hoe."

I don't think Mama knew that side of me that made me strike out at others. I'd hidden it from her pretty well. I was obedient to her. I did as she asked and didn't give her a minute of trouble at home. I was dependable, responsible, and loving, and she would have been shocked had she known just how often I used my fists to settle problems.

Our one conversation did not overcome the years of insecurity and fear that drove me to fight, but Mama's words became psychological "anchors" that helped steady me in the years ahead and get control of my temper. When I again felt the urge to strike out, I could hear her saying, "Son, there are better ways to settle disagreements." That's a message I hope every young man can grasp early enough to save himself from real trouble. Keep your cool. Losing it might cost you more than just a whipping; it could negatively affect the rest of your life. Or, because of the violence in our society today, losing your cool could literally cost you your life.

My mother's training and influence on my life were things I appreciated deeply by the time I graduated from high school. To commemorate the occasion and express my gratitude to her, I wrote her a letter that I can still recall almost verbatim.

> *Dear Mother,*
>
> *The big day is finally here and I'm having trouble expressing my gratitude and feelings. I've watched the sacrifices, including all the hard work and faith you've used to make this event a reality. I know it means a lot to you, Mama, since I'm the first of your children to finish high school, but it means everything to me. It opens the door to college and a chance to serve in the Naval Air Corps, and then when the war is over who knows what will happen? This I do know, Mama, my gratitude extends into a promise that I will do everything I can to make you know that I am grateful for your love and sacrifices. I'm going to work hard, Mama, to make you proud of me.*
>
> *Your loving son,*
> *Hilary*

Extra Money

During World War II many things were rationed, including the rubber to manufacture tires for civilian use. All resources were going to the military as part of the war effort. My older brother had a dump truck, and he was hauling sand and gravel for the various military installations, like the shipyard at Pascagoula or army camps in Flora, Hattiesburg, and Columbus, Mississippi. Hauling such heavy loads required good tires, and because his work contributed to the war effort he could get new tires when others could not. I took advantage of this opportunity by selling his lightly used tires to local movers for anywhere from two dollars to as much as four dollars each. A load of furniture weighs only a fraction as much as a load of sand and gravel, so the tires were more than adequate for their purposes, and the money I earned (which also went to the family) was significant. To be able to increase the contribution I was already making was a thrill to me.

But sometimes it's just as much fun to *receive* as to give. And I got a lesson in just that at about the same time in my life. While a student at Hinds Junior College, when my funds were extraordinarily limited, I received a surprise money order for ten dollars from my brother Howard who was serving in the navy. You cannot imagine the delight, joy, and gratitude I felt for that ten-dollar gift. Every morning between classes a number of us would walk the two blocks to the corner drugstore and get a chocolate sundae or milk shake as a little break from our studies. They were fifteen cents each. The ten dollars financed quite a few chocolate sundaes and much unexpected pleasure for me during those thin times.

I mention the ten dollars and the circumstances surrounding it because many times, if we don't have much to give, we labor under the illusion that we may as well not give anything because our pittance wouldn't make a difference. Let me tell you—sometimes that little bit can make a huge difference. It certainly did for me.

PART TWO

Early Adult Years:
School, Navy
Aspirations,
Marriage, Work

The house I grew up in on Jackson Avenue
in Yazoo City

My father, John Silas Ziglar

Me in my high-school band uniform.
I'm about fourteen years old here

In my navy uniform, 1944

Me and the Redhead

The Ziglar family after Houston's funeral, 1964. From left to right, front row:
Evia Jane, Lola, our mother, Lila, Lera, Turah. Left to right,
back row: me, Howard, Horace, Hubert, Huie.

LEFT: Me with the pump!

BELOW: My beautiful family. From left to right: Jean, Cindy, Suzan, Julie, and Tom on Jean's lap.

BOTTOM: We're all a little bit older! This picture was taken at Suzan and Chad's wedding. From left to right: Tom, Julie, Suzan, me, Jean, and Cindy.

Cleaning my pool—the one
I always said I'd have!

ABOVE: With my son Tom,
our President and CEO, and
son-in-law Richard, our COO

RIGHT: With my editor
(and daughter) Julie

LEFT: With Lou Holtz in 1995

BELOW: The Redhead and me with Tamara and Peter Lowe

RIGHT: With Colin Powell

BELOW: With former
President George Bush and
First Lady Barbara Bush

LEFT: Our fiftieth
wedding anniversary

BELOW: The entire
family: children,
grandchildren, and
great-grandchildren

LEFT: Receiving the Cavett
Award from the National
Speakers Association

BELOW: My beautiful wife
and our dog, Taffy

The Dutch Uncle Talk

I mailed my application for the Naval Air Corps on November 8, 1943—
the Monday after my seventeenth birthday. In January 1944 I arrived in
New Orleans, Louisiana, to take my entrance and physical exams. When I
was given the word that I had done well enough on my entrance exam to
qualify for flight-training school, I experienced a huge boost in my self-
confidence. I had not been a very good student and was thrilled to know
that I had achieved what ninety-five out of a hundred applicants had not.
College would be the first phase of my Naval Air Corps training.

I was assigned to Millsaps College in Jackson, Mississippi, which was
only forty-three miles from home. This made it possible for me to travel
back home many weekends to be with my family.

The day before I left for Millsaps, Mr. Haining called me aside and gave
me a "dutch uncle" talk. The time had come to think about my future with
a capital F. He invited me to return to Yazoo City after my discharge from
the navy and work for him again. He said if I'd work for him for two years
to learn the business, he would help me get my own meat market. Then he
started sharing the really exciting news.

Mr. Haining pulled out his meticulous records and showed me that his
net earning for the previous year had been $5,117. In 1943, making over
$5,000 in a single year was some kind of exciting! I couldn't believe that any
one individual could earn all that money in just one year.

An incredible new horizon opened up before my eyes. I saw everything
so clearly. When the war was over, I would return to Yazoo City, earn $5,000
a year in my own meat market, and retire at age sixty-five. In those days
everybody retired at sixty-five. Then I would buy an acre of land because I
would need a big garden so I could sell vegetables to my neighbors to supplement my reduced retirement income. My vision of myself as a "little guy
from a little town" was slowly expanding.

Life at Millsaps

July 1, 1944, that long-awaited day, finally arrived. It was a Saturday morning, if memory serves me correctly, and I packed my bags with considerable excitement and delight at the prospects of my new venture. The days ahead looked bright, challenging, and full of opportunity for the taking. The mood at home surrounding my departure was more of a holiday feeling than anything else. As far as my mother was concerned, she was concentrating entirely on the fact that I was going off to college, that it would be many months before I would even get close to an airplane. She had plenty of time to worry about that when and if my flying days should come. Mama gave me no special advice or suggestions other than the standard, "Take care of yourself, son. I sure do love you. Be sure and write." The ordinary, affectionate, caring things any mother would say to a son going off to college— not to one going off to war. At that moment my siblings and mother were focused on the fact that I would be the first in the family to go to college, never mind my navy pilot plans. Making it to college was cause enough for rejoicing. I said the usual good-byes to my mother and my sisters and my younger brother, who were at home; after all of the hugging and kissing was done, I stuck out my thumb and headed for Millsaps College in Jackson, Mississippi.

My carefully structured and quite ambitious game plan when I qualified in January to join the V5 Program (which was the Naval Air Corps Training Program) was to become no less than a navy pilot! My trip to Jackson was uneventful. I arrived on campus in plenty of time and was immediately launched into the admission process, which included registering, having a brief physical (since I'd already had their more comprehensive one earlier), and getting all the required uniforms, equipment, paraphernalia, and books. I was about as excited as anybody can be. My dream had come true. I was headed for college and then into the navy.

For a little guy who had already beaten the 20-to-1 odds of qualifying, it was sheer delirium. Little did I realize the extent of the adventure that lay ahead of me. In retrospect, I've often made the statement that I believe every day during my two years in the military God looked down to make certain I was in position to accept all the good things and all the breaks He was sending me. It was almost uncanny the way He directed my steps and sent so many good things my way.

We were scheduled to enter classrooms on Monday morning. A loud bugle sounded reveille, and it came early. Necessity required us to rise early because after assembling for the orders of the day, we dressed, made up our bunks, and headed for the mess hall for breakfast. In my mind breakfast was always good, although some of the others did not think it was all that great.

We spent the rest of the day trying to keep up with the grueling training regimen. After breakfast we headed back to our rooms, then to our first hour-long class at eight o'clock, and then on to our next one-hour class. We then returned to the dorm, approximately a quarter mile from the classroom, changed into our running shoes and sweat clothes, and ran nearly a half mile back to the athletic field where we went through thirty minutes of calisthenics. Then it was back to the dorm for a quick shower and back to our desks (another quarter mile), all within one hour's time. I don't need to tell you that most of us sat at our desks pretty much out of breath. We were extraordinarily hot and pools of sweat collected around every desk. Yet early on the adventure was so great there was more excitement than complaints.

From eleven to twelve we were back in the classroom, and at noon we broke for lunch, which consumed another hour. Lunch was a particularly delightful experience for me, because, among other things, we were almost always served some kind of meat and a dessert. Meats and desserts were rarities back home. They were relatively expensive and not absolutely essential, so they didn't often make it to our table. Instead we ate lots of vegetables. My mother was a marvelous cook, and we always had plenty to eat, but for me the college/naval experience at that point was so exciting that everything about it seemed quite new and wonderful—even the meals.

The week itself was tough, but we had "liberty" on Friday night until eleven o'clock. On Saturday after reveille, breakfast, and assembly, we attended classes only in the morning. From Saturday afternoon until ten P.M. Sunday night we could check out for liberty.

The Friday-night liberty permitted me to practice using the self-control my mother so desperately hoped I'd learned. I recall one particular instance in which it was really put to the test. The scene was a Friday-night high school football game in Jackson, Mississippi. My home team, the Yazoo City Indians, was playing the Central High Tigers in Jackson. The stadium was just across the street from Millsaps College. Since I was from Yazoo

City, I was cheering for the Indians. I had just really gotten started rooting for the home team when a young man in front of me stood up, turned around, looked me in the eye, and said, "That's the last I want to hear about you cheering for Yazoo City. If you do it again, I'm going to bust you one!"

I've got to tell you that every ounce of my nature up until then would have invited the young man to go down under the bleachers and we would settle it there. But the rules were very clear that if I were involved in any altercations, whether on or off campus, I would automatically be discharged from the program. Since the war was beginning to wind down, the need for more pilots was becoming very limited and the navy was looking for reasons to kick men out of the program. I sat there for a moment, my mother's words, "Son, there are better ways to settle disagreements," ringing in my ears; I bit my lip, got up, and walked away. I learned that if something were truly important to you, you could hold your temper and restrain yourself from foolish action. That was the first time I'd ever avoided a confrontation, and I'm glad I did because my whole life would have been different had I lost my cool and gotten into that fight. I would have been shipped immediately to the Great Lakes naval training base, and my college days would have ended. In short, every facet of my life would have changed, and I believe it would have been for the worse.

Back to the discussion of weekend liberty. Each weekend I had the privilege of going home, but I often opted to stay at the dormitory because I had discovered a niche market that needed to be filled—and money that I wanted to earn. We had navy uniforms, which we were required to keep clean and pressed. I learned that one of the janitors at the school had a washing machine and was willing to wash our uniforms for fifteen cents each. That included the jumper and the bell-bottom trousers. The laundry charged seventy-five cents to wash and press our uniforms, so I bought an ironing board and an iron, gave the janitor fifteen cents for washing the uniforms, and then I pressed them and delivered them to my buddies for fifty cents. I consequently made thirty-five cents on each uniform. I generally did this on Saturday afternoons. I could press somewhere between ten and twenty uniforms in an afternoon. In those days, if buses did not run close to where I was going, a taxi, which cost more, was my only other option for transportation, so picking up a few extra dollars each week was very significant for me. Especially since my navy check was only thirty-one dollars per month. The extra three-fifty to seven dollars per week was important for social events, which escalated dramatically after the following incident.

The One

On September 15, 1944, at 9:08 P.M., I met the belle who would eventually become my bride. God certainly blessed me when He sent her my way. I met her in Jackson, Mississippi, at the YWCA, which was hosting a party for the sailor boys from Mississippi College and Millsaps College and the personnel from the Mississippi Ordnance Plant in Flora, Mississippi. When I walked in and saw her, I was immediately smitten. I know that God arranged our meeting because she had never been to the YWCA before, and neither had I. She never went back; neither did I. As I've told people for years, there was no point in going back when I had found exactly what I was looking for on the first trip!

The night we met, the Redhead was staying with a girlfriend who just happened to live across the creek from my dormitory at Millsaps College. I walked them home from the bus stop and had to climb through an unlocked window to gain entrance into the house because the parents had not left a key with their daughter. The Redhead gave me her phone number that night, and because nickels were scarce, we made arrangements that whenever I called her (I knew what time she got home from school), I would let the phone ring once and hang up. Then she would pick up the phone and call me back, and we would engage in an extended conversation.

We did much of our courting over the phone. In addition to the regular phone conversations we had nearly every day, incredibly enough, we decided to write each other letters every day, too, and for many months this was the rather intensive courtship process we followed. I'm convinced that through those phone calls and letters, as we shared our thoughts and feelings and revealed ourselves to each other, we were able to get better acquainted than 99 percent of the people who marry.

Early in our courtship when I first introduced the Redhead to my family, my older brother heard her tell my mother that, since she was the baby in the family, she was occasionally called Baby Jean. My brother latched onto that and to a degree I did, too, at least temporarily. A few weeks after we met, the Redhead told me that when I dropped into the antique shop where her mother worked to chat with her a moment or two, the manager and owner of the store told Mrs. Abernathy (whom I always called Miz Ab, as did most other people), "Miz Ab, that boy's gonna marry your daughter." According to the Redhead, her mother got tears in her eyes when she heard that because at that time the Redhead was the ripe old age of sixteen and we had been courting for only a few weeks. Nevertheless, the manager's instincts were 100 percent right. I had marriage on my mind a short time after I started courting her.

Along the way, however, it was not always "peaches and cream" or "smooth sailing." I've even forgotten the occasion, but something happened that upset me, and I revealed my immaturity by simply walking out on the Redhead. When I went home that weekend, my mother wanted to know what had happened, and when I told her it was all over, she very sadly shook her head and said, "Well, son, she really is a nice girl and I like her very much."

You see, I'd already taken the Redhead home to meet my family, and she had captured the heart not only of my mother, but of my older sister as well. She and I had gone out a time or two with my sister and her boyfriend, who later became my sister's husband. If ever a disagreement came up between the two of us, I now had three women on one side, while I was on the other. The Redhead, my mother, and my older sister were always in agreement. I never had a chance. After all, it was my word against thousands of theirs.

So when I told my mother that it was all over, she was very sad, and without being too forceful she encouraged me to do what I could to mend that fence. She always loved the Redhead, and the Redhead always loved my mother. They were certainly on the same page when it came to right and wrong, and doing the things that should be done. It was no coincidence that I fell in love with her.

Learn by Watching Others

My mother's opinion of whom we dated had acquired great weight with my brothers, sisters, and me over the years. As a child I witnessed the disastrous results when someone in our family didn't listen to my parents' opinion about the person they were dating. One of my sisters married a man several years older than she who had raised some red flags, I am told, in my father's mind. Papa pointed out that any man who could come visiting and courting on any day of the week had a serious work ethic problem. My sister was young, and she was persuaded that he would be fine. Disaster was the result. He turned out to be abusive to her and, as my dad would say, was just "a sorry man." Ultimately, one of our older brothers literally kidnapped her, with her permission, and brought her home for good.

A number of years later one of my older brothers became involved with a much younger girl from a family that had an incredibly bad reputation, and the girl herself lived up to the bad reputation. The brother made a bad choice, and the choice was his. The inevitable results were a divorce and a split family.

Yet another brother made a poor choice, and he, too, ended up getting a divorce. The advice my mother gave me, and from my own observations in two of the marriages that had been made at that point, led me to believe that I needed to choose a bride very carefully. She told me that I should never date more than once or twice a girl whom I would be unwilling to marry and have as the mother of my children. Since Mama seemed to know what she was talking about, I took her words to heart and did what I could to mend that fence with the Redhead.

Miz Ab Liked Me, Too

One of the more delightful experiences the Redhead and I had when we were dating was the time Miz Ab gave me five dollars to take her daughter out to dinner. There was a nice restaurant called the Rotisserie, where we could get a shrimp salad and what they called a bell steak—a small filet— as well as coffee or a soft drink. For the two of us the bill came to five dollars. At that stage of my life I did not quite understand the tipping process, and so I think I dug into my own pocket and left maybe fifty cents. The cab fare to the restaurant was twenty-five cents, and the cab fare home was another twenty-five cents. Needless to say, when I got her back to her place, I rode the bus back to the dorm for only a nickel. Yes, you could court for a whole lot less money then than you can today—but then, there was a lot less money around.

The Hedge Jumper

While I was at Millsaps College for the training program during World War II, our liberty was on Tuesday and Friday nights, starting after dinner, which took place at five-thirty P.M. We had the usual assembly with the bugle blowing and being at parade and the other great things the military does, and then off to see the Redhead I would go.

I would catch a bus from the campus to one block from her house, and when I disembarked I walked very quickly. Since it was warm weather most of the time, she, her mother, and her sister would be sitting on the porch enjoying the early evening. They had a hedge about two feet tall that I had to pass before I could turn right and then right again a few feet to get to the front porch. Many times, in my enthusiasm to see her again, instead of walking the thirty feet down the sidewalk to the entrance to the yard, I would cut the route short and simply jump over the hedge. Occasionally their minds were somewhere besides on my imminent arrival; they would be talking and having fun and not really watching for me to come flying over the hedge. Then suddenly they would see me up, flying through the air, and sailing over the greenery. Invariably my appearance elicited one, two, or three shouts—not of fear, but certainly of surprise. That was one of the little rituals we went through courting, and it always produced in the ladies the same reaction followed by laughter.

After exchanging a few pleasantries and courting the rest of the family, as quickly as it was practical to do so, the Redhead and I would head up to the bus stop. We invested ten cents for both our fares and made the trip to a downtown movie and bought the tickets which I believe were, at that time, twenty-five cents. We splurged on a bag of popcorn apiece, and to this day the Redhead says I would always eat all of my own and two-thirds of hers. And that was our financial investment for the pleasurable evening together.

As a general rule we would then walk home because it was only a little more than a mile, or we would ride about half the distance and then get out at Poindexter Park, which was only a few blocks from her home. It often took us longer to get through the park than it did for us to make the rest of the walk. However, we spent many pleasant hours together, and in retrospect I believe this is what built the relationship that has endured now for fifty-five-plus years of wedded bliss.

The Plans Kept Changing

Just six weeks after I'd started on my grand adventure, the navy discontinued the flight-training program because it was evident the war was winding down and they already had more pilots than they felt they would need. Then they put us into the V12 Program, which had the objective of keeping us in college an additional twelve months, then sending us to Midshipman's School prior to commissioning us in the regular navy. However, that program, too, was discontinued, and I was sent to the University of South Carolina as a member of the Naval Reserve Officer Training Corps.

What's truly amazing is that I was able to stay at Millsaps College for all of sixteen months. Had any one little thing worked out differently, and had I been shipped out shortly after meeting that Redhead, I'm not at all certain we would have survived the separation. Yet there's no doubt in her mind that we would have seen it through, because she felt God had put us together from the very beginning, that our relationship was preordained.

I sometimes ponder the complicity of all the coincidences it took to get us together, and one overwhelms me in particular. I spoke earlier of my history teacher, Coach Jobie Harris. As a youngster he was active in the Boy Scouts of America. His scoutmaster, unbelievably, was the Redhead's father, Thomas B. Abernathy, who was not only the first scoutmaster in Mississippi, but also the first scout official in the state. Mr. Abernathy influenced little Jobie Harris by teaching him the many character-building principles included in the Scout Oath, the Scout Law, and the Scout Motto. He also took an additional interest in him and served as a role model and mentor. As a result Mr. Abernathy was a huge force in Coach Harris's life.

Obviously, there is no way that Mr. Abernathy could have known that when he was investing extra time with little Jobie Harris, he was preparing the boy who would become the man who would have such a huge impact on his future son-in-law, making him a better man, a better husband, and a better father to his future grandchildren.

Fascinating, isn't it? How a sincere interest in a young boy could affect not only the boy but also the man, husband, father, and even his grandchildren many years after his own death. And the story isn't even close to being over.

In November 1945 the navy shipped us out to attend the University of

South Carolina for the first four months of our NROTC training. I left with considerable reluctance because I had been dating the Redhead for over a year, and the thought of being without her was really tough to bear. I have to tell you that I could not wait for Christmas break to come so I could get back home and renew our courtship. Those holidays were a delightful time for us, and during my Christmas visit home she unofficially agreed to become my wife when I was discharged. Once that was settled, everything was right in my world.

My trip to the University of Columbia, South Carolina, was uneventful. We went through the normal procedures of checking in, being assigned our quarters, and being issued the new uniforms (which were very similar to the uniforms being worn by the chief petty officers in the navy). Regardless of our new improved status, however, they did not give us a raise in pay. I was somewhat overwhelmed by the size of the university. Millsaps College consisted of five hundred students, a small campus compared to USC's student body of twenty-five hundred.

My buddies and I were very busy keeping up with the routine of going to class and performing a host of other duties similar to those we had at Millsaps. The studies were no more intense, and the continuation of a structured routine was very good for me.

I had dodged a bullet at Millsaps College, and I did not want to put myself in jeopardy again. When I had taken the navy entrance exams, the math questions were primarily common sense, everyday math equations involving arithmetic—addition, subtraction, multiplication, and division. Apparently, I scored very high on the test because they put me in an advanced math course at Millsaps—and I was lost from day one until the end of the semester. I got a big, fat F, and it was a five-hour course.

At that point, with the war winding down, the brass weren't inclined to be lenient in regards to any shortcoming a recruit displayed, and we really had to be on our toes just to stay in the program. However, the navy recognized they had made a mistake in assigning me to that advanced math course, so they gave me a reprieve. They put me in a simpler course the following semester, which I managed to pass, and thus I was able to make the trip to South Carolina.

I was fortunate to be assigned three roommates with whom I got along quite well. While we were living together in the dorm, I got an enterprising idea. We students were restricted to the dorms at night, so every evening guys would come to the windows on the ground floor selling ice cream to us as a captive market. They seemed to be doing quite well, so I figured that when I was discharged from the navy, I could come back to South Carolina, get permission to sell sandwiches, milk, and coffee cake around the dorms at night, and make a pretty good living.

At the end of the first semester at USC, the navy again had a change of plans. The war had ended, so they offered us choices. One was that we could go to Great Lakes Training School in Great Lakes, Illinois, for six weeks, go through boot camp, and then be shipped to an outgoing unit where we would probably be for another three or four months before discharge. Since the war was over, the navy did not feel it was necessary to be training even more deck officers (our new status after the pilot program had been shut down). Because I had maintained a steady correspondence with the object of my affection, and was eager to be back by her side as soon as I could, I opted to go to Great Lakes for the six weeks, knowing that I could head back home after being discharged in only about four more months.

At Great Lakes my good fortune continued. They had what they called Battalion Watch and Battalion Work Week, Regimental Watch and Regimental Work. Each of us was required to participate in those assignments. However, an amazing thing happened to me. I developed a severe yet fortuitous case of tonsillitis; for a little over two and a half weeks I was in sick bay and out of commission. When I finally recovered, they sent me off on a work detail to the Officers Quarters. I walked in through the back door and found in the kitchen a young man who was doing a miserable job of cutting some meat. Since I had actually managed a meat market during my grocery-store years, I asked the young man to let me have his knife for a moment. He handed it to me, and I picked up the long, straight, round rod on which those knives were sharpened and gave him a lesson. Then I started to cut the meat as it should have been cut. At that precise moment the lady in charge walked through, watched me for a moment, and asked my name. I told her, and she said, "You're now permanently assigned to the Officers Mess until you're shipped out."

The result was I got to eat in the kitchen the same food the officers ate in the dining room. There was an abundance of milk, which was rare and very much in demand at the time. I felt very privileged and honored that my meat-cutting skills had earned me this position.

One experience (which I'm not proud of) was funny, and yet, though it was wrong, it provided me a little extra adventure. A lady from Denmark with only about two teeth in her mouth was baking some beautiful apple pies for the officers. They smelled devastatingly good! I laughingly said to her, "I think I'm going to snitch one of those pies and take it back to the barracks for my buddies and me." To my surprise, in her broken English she encouraged my rascally plot. She said, "That would be good. I like to see good boy get pie."

The next day, when I returned the empty pie plate, she asked, "How you do that?" I said smilingly as I walked out, "I slipped it under my jacket when nobody was looking, and my friends and I thoroughly enjoyed it!" She laughed and said, "That good! I knew you boys would."

As it developed, in addition to getting to work in the Officers Quarters in the morning, I was assigned to do some typing since I also knew how to type. The last two weeks of the program I spent all of that time typing the pay chits (vouchers) for the 144 people in our company. Later, when I was assigned to Washington as a recruit typist, my buddies couldn't believe it! How could a guy who spent two weeks typing 144 names, serial numbers, etc., then be recommended for an assignment in Washington (actually, Bethesda, Maryland)? But that's where I landed!

When I got there, after working less than a week as a recruit typist, I applied to go to the hospital to have my still problematic tonsils removed. Since I'd had a long record of tonsillitis, the order was accepted, and I was sent to the hospital. While there, a second doctor was called in to perform a minor procedure, and his involvement created an interesting situation. Each of the two doctors thought the other was going to discharge me, so for thirty days, with liberty every night, I stayed in the hospital eating good food, lying around, goofing off, and having a good time. I actually worked only one week during the five weeks I was there, and then I was eligible for discharge. They gave me a choice of being discharged either in Baltimore (which is just a few miles from Washington and Bethesda), or New Orleans. Always the man with an eye for opportunity, I opted for discharge from Baltimore. It was roughly fifteen hundred miles home, and they paid seven cents a mile for travel. I knew I was going to hitchhike, so I accepted the hundred and five dollars in travel reimbursement, which went quite well with my two hundred dollars in discharge money, stuck out my thumb, and headed home. I actually spent only about twelve dollars for food on that trip.

Yes, it was a marvelous experience. I was discharged on June 30, 1946, and they required us to sign up for four years in the reserves. Another one of those "interesting little things" happened at that point. On June 30, 1950, exactly four years later, they froze the reserves for the Korean War. I possibly missed going to Korea by just one day. I say possibly because by then I was married and we had a daughter, so I was never called back into service. Needless to say, there were some in the same situation who were in the reserves who were called to duty in the Korean War. Again, I believe God was looking after me.

Back to Yazoo for the Summer

Upon my discharge from the navy I returned to my roots and to my job with Mr. Haining at the meat market. After the war ended, many of the things that had been rationed or unavailable began to be available again. One such product was sausage packed in oil, which was much more flavorful than sausage packed in water, as it had been during the war years. Mr. Haining paid me a five-cent commission on each can of water-packed sausage I sold. He wanted to move it out of his inventory before the better sausage became readily available. I'll never forget the first day he made the deal with me; I made more in commission on that sausage than I made for working the whole day. Right then and there I knew I *liked* working on commission. This would prove to be an important discovery for me in coming years.

Another thing I knew I liked that summer was Jean Abernathy! By the time I was discharged from the navy, I knew that the Redhead was the one with whom I wanted to spend the rest of my life. Actually, I knew before then and had asked her to marry me on several different occasions. But I never had purchased a ring to make it an official request for her hand—and she had never officially answered me either. Since our family was pretty much an open book, everyone knew I had bought the ring and was going to pop the question that weekend, including my chatty little nephew. Five-year-old Silas Ziglar, who was living at our house at that time along with his parents—my older brother and his wife—let the cat out of the bag concerning the proposal and the ring.

A couple of hours before the opportunity for me to ask the Redhead the big question presented itself, Silas asked her himself (when I was not around) if I had given her the ring yet. Obviously, I did not learn about this until long after I had proposed. So to say that the Redhead was not surprised would be a gross understatement. Despite being tipped off ahead of time, she acted as if she didn't know or suspect a thing when I presented the ring to her and asked her to marry me. And she officially said yes. The plans for us were sealed. Our marriage was definitely a thing that was going to happen.

Overcoming Temptations

I returned to the University of South Carolina in the fall of 1946 and was able to secure permission to sell sandwiches, milk, and coffee cakes around the dormitories at night. After a reasonably good start, with money coming in to pay living expenses, a couple of the guys in one of the rooms in which I stopped to sell, said, "Zig, we'll roll dice with you. Double or nothing." Well, unfortunately, I'd had some craps-shooting experience while I was in the navy, and I thought I was pretty good. But when I was in the navy there was very little money available, so all losses were limited to two or three dollars. Even then those two or three dollars had a way of slowly escalating to five dollars and then as much as ten dollars. Anyway, I readily agreed to the offer, figuring I would lose about as often as I won, but I would pick up some extra sales because everybody's always looking for something for nothing.

Soon the guys down the hall were making the same offer, and I was always happy to accept. As a result, night after night, many guys who were not hungry but sought the "something for nothing" routine challenged me to roll the dice. Which I agreeably did, rationalizing that at worst it would be a wash and at best it might be good for my sandwich business. I'd been doing this a few weeks when one night one of the guys said, "When you finish your route, why don't you stop by and we'll have a little game?" I did stop by and we had quite a game.

By the end of the evening I had lost every dime I had, a full thirty-nine dollars. This was before I had my car, and I had to borrow cab fare to get home. That night I made a far-reaching decision. First, I realized that I simply could not afford that kind of loss. I was doing okay, but in those days thirty-nine dollars was a substantial amount of money. Second, I realized I thoroughly enjoyed gambling to the point that the thrill of the game overrode my good judgment. This was a tendency I had to nip in the bud. I decided that it was simply not wise for me to continue in a habit that could become addictive and be very destructive. I believe I do have an addictive personality, and I realized at that point in my life that it would lead me nowhere but into trouble if I did not change my ways. That was the last time I indulged in a dice game or any other form of gambling.

My decision not to gamble anymore was fueled also by the fact that in the past I had occasionally gotten involved in a game of blackjack, which I found exciting and very enjoyable. I enjoyed it far too much and couldn't afford the losses. These experiences taught me that my ego and overconfidence were potential sources of trouble. For that reason, I intentionally never learned to play poker. Knowing myself as I did, I realized that after about the second or third game I would figure I was pretty good and that, of course, would be when the good players would clean me out big time!

Today I won't even place a friendly two-dollar bet on the golf course. I will gamble for bragging rights only, and we have lots of fun doing that, but no money changes hands. I realized that had money been involved on the golf course, my highly competitive nature would have driven me to hope that my fellow players would hit their shots out of bounds, in the woods, or into the water. As a matter of fact, I'm so competitive, I've struggled with that very attitude even when there wasn't money involved.

Ron Ezinga, the president of our company for a number of years and a good friend of mine (who is fully as competitive as I am), and I took our competitiveness to the golf course when Ron was working with me. After about a year, we totaled the results. Each of us had won exactly the same number of matches, and we had also tied a number of times. In short, we were even.

But my feelings and behavior on the links were very revealing to me when I had a chance to stand back and consider them. I realized there were many times that I hoped Ron would miss the putt, knock the ball in the water, or hit it out of bounds so I could win the match. That is not golf, nor is it my general nature. All of my life, but particularly since I became a speaker/trainer/writer, I have looked for, pulled for, and encouraged people to do their best. So, for me to be pulling for Ron to miss a putt, etc., was frightening to me and left me disappointed in myself. With this in mind, one Monday morning, after we realized we were exactly even, I announced at our company devotions that, effective immediately, I would no longer compete with Ron. We would play on the same team so that I could honestly pull for him with both my head and my heart. That's what happened, and it's been much better since. Though he long ago moved back to Grand Rapids, Michigan, I believe it was one of the best decisions I've made. Even now when we occasionally play golf, even though I still want to win as badly as he does, I can honestly say that I pull for him on each shot, despite the fact that the last time we played he clobbered me.

Because of my addictive, overconfident personality, there was another gamble I was unwilling to take. I refused to learn to ride a motorcycle even though they were very appealing to me and looked like lots of fun. By the time a motorcycle was within my reach, I knew myself well enough to know that once I had learned how to turn it on and off and stay upright, I'd figure I was pretty good with one and start hotdogging—and that's when I would be in danger of getting seriously hurt or even killed.

In retrospect, the insight I gained into the dangers of my habit of overconfidence is the reason that, after the navy pilot plans fell through, I did not pursue my dream of flying airplanes. I am an impatient person and want to see the big picture quickly. Deep inside I knew that I was not emotionally geared to follow the rules, regulations, safety procedures, and all that goes with taking an airplane off the ground and returning it in one piece. I knew if I followed my urge to fly, it wouldn't be long before I had brought disaster on my head through my impatience. Besides, I caught on pretty quickly to the idea that I loved selling, commissions, training, and helping people. After I was discharged from the navy I never looked back.

But no matter where I was or what I was doing, I learned I had to be on guard against certain weaknesses inherent in my makeup as a person. Something would always come along with a siren's song and tug my heart in the wrong direction. Self-discipline and self-control would always be extremely important in my battle against situations that appealed to my thrill-seeking, sensation-loving personality. I had to be vigilant about things that felt too good because sooner or later they wouldn't be good for me at all.

It wasn't long before I encountered another such potential trap. Selling on commission made it necessary for me to do a lot of traveling in my car. When driving late at night, I would get sleepy. I had developed the peculiar idea that a fire in my hand would help keep me awake, so I started smoking cigars. This was long before the general public understood the scientific

evidence of the dangers of tobacco. I continued to smoke cigars with abandon until I had a physical demonstration of tobacco's harmful effects. I was
in the cookware business at the time and won a trip to London and Paris
with the Redhead. While there I developed a sore throat; when I would
take a drag from the cigar, even though I did not inhale, it was extremely
painful. I realized at that point that if smoking caused pain in my throat
when it was sore, then it could not be good for me when I was not suffering from a sore throat either. So I decided to quit.

It's interesting—at least to me—to note that even though I had never
inhaled, the nicotine that entered my body through my mouth had become
to a very small degree addictive to me. Without my knowledge or understanding, my body had decided that it was a nice, pleasurable feeling, and
it missed smoking. On countless occasions during the following weeks I
was tempted to pick up another cigar but declined to do so and, as a result,
avoided an addiction to tobacco. For this I am grateful. It's a very difficult
habit to break.

I truly believe God gave me the insight I needed to avoid becoming ad-
dicted to gambling, smoking, and alcohol so that I could live the life I've
lived, being a positive influence on others instead of a negative one. All the
temptations were there, and by nature I was perfectly willing to indulge.
But God had other plans and graced me at critical points with the insight
and self-knowledge that allowed me to resist them. I go into more detail
about my brush with alcohol later in the book.

Married Life

I continued my correspondence with the Redhead when I returned to the
University of South Carolina. I missed her more than ever since I'd just
spent a whole summer of seeing her whenever I had a free moment. I
missed her so much I kept trying to sell her on the idea of getting married
earlier than we'd originally planned, which was at the end of the school
year. But we were so miserable apart, and I was so persistent, that we decided a wedding over the Christmas holidays would be ideal—but even
that wasn't fast enough to suit us, so we got married two days before
Thanksgiving.

November 26, 1946, was our wedding day. Since the Redhead lived in

Jackson, Mississippi, and we had decided to get married in South Carolina, I was responsible for making all the wedding plans. I had arranged for the church, the minister, the maid of honor, the bridegroom (that part was easy), the flowers, the honeymoon hotel, and everything else. The wedding was scheduled for four-thirty P.M. so we could catch the bus to Charlotte, North Carolina, where we had reservations at the old Barringer Hotel.

In those propeller-driven airplane days, there were considerably fewer communication facilities available to keep everyone informed of schedule changes, and the Redhead's transfer in Atlanta was delayed because of the weather. She had no way to get in touch with me, and I, in turn, was anxious about notifying everyone involved in the wedding about the delay. I called the Barringer Hotel twice to assure them that we were coming and begged them to please hold our room even though it would probably be very late when we got there. They agreed to do just that.

The Redhead arrived almost four hours late for her wedding, but I didn't mind one bit when I saw her in her soft blue wedding suit with a pink blouse and pretty pink hat. We were married that evening at eight-thirty P.M. When we finally checked into the Barringer Hotel after midnight, we began a fifty-five-year honeymoon that's still going strong.

Like most brides and grooms, we were enthralled with each other, but because we had been courting for two years, two months, and eleven days, we were pretty well acquainted. Incredibly enough, being very young and inexperienced in the art of pleasing a wife, I had arranged this honeymoon to include a football game between the University of South Carolina and Wake Forest University. But the Redhead's nature is such, and we were so much in love that she happily went to the game and cheered for the home team.

On Sunday morning, December 1, we returned to Columbia and found a minisuite at one of the lower-priced hotels where we planned to stay until we could find a place to live. That Sunday night right after our honeymoon trip I faithfully got my grocery cart and sandwiches, coffee cakes and milk, and made my run through the dormitories, selling my wares in order to meet the needs of our new home.

We spent about five days in the minisuite before we saw an ad in the paper and rented a room from a lady we affectionately started calling Ma Bruce. We had a bedroom and kitchen privileges, and we survived there for about four months before we found an apartment with Mrs. Norabelle Hall, a lady probably old enough to be our mother. We had two rooms there, as well as kitchen privileges, and the accommodations were much more convenient for us.

Big Mistake

As a young married man I made some incredible misjudgments that were basically self-centered and derived from erroneous ideas common among males in those years. Never will I forget a simple little incident a few weeks after we were married. It's a perfect example of what clods men can be when laboring under mistaken notions about women. The Redhead was all of eighteen, and for the first time in her life she was separated from her mother, who was widowed when the Redhead was just ten years old. Growing up, the Redhead had done a little cooking at home, but very little. Now, all of a sudden, she was a housewife, married to (as the English would say) a young bloke who harbored the illusion that his wife was supposed to cook three meals a day for him, regardless of how she might feel.

One evening she was just tired of cooking and wanted to go out and enjoy at least a sandwich that she did not have to prepare. I was very unhappy about this. I expected her to cook; she was supposed to cook. She was my wife, and that was her job. My job was to provide the money that bought the food that she was to prepare for me. I had done my part; now she had to do hers. We had quite a little to-do before I finally gave in and proceeded to pout like a spoiled brat for the rest of the evening. To say it was not a pleasant experience would be the understatement of the day. My selfishness and immaturity along with a complete lack of empathy made for a miserable evening for both of us. Wonderful lady that she is, she forgave me, and I recognized how wrong I was and resolved to do better.

The Beginning of My Car Habit

Soon after the Redhead and I married we recognized our need for a car, so we managed to buy a 1940 Studebaker Commander, well used, for $645. It was a good car, but it had never been driven the way I drove it, day and night with frequent stops, and it was only a few months before we had some serious problems, necessitating an overhaul of the engine. This really set us back financially and added to our already difficult situation.

While we were living with Mrs. Hall, the Redhead, after about eight months of tolerating me, grew terribly homesick. She was just barely nineteen years old, and she wanted desperately to go home to see her mother. I agreed and bought the bus ticket for her trip. She was scheduled to return on a certain day at a certain time, but just a few hours before her bus was due in she called to let me know that she would be in the next day at that time. A day late! I found this completely unacceptable. *My* wife was supposed to come home to *me* on the agreed date so she could be with *me* and cater to *my* self-indulgent whims.

Now even though I was actually twenty years old when this happened, I pretty well reacted with the attitude typical of a ten-year-old child. I was really upset with her outrageous unilateral change of plans, and like a general dressing down a private, I said, "I want you to be on the bus tomorrow without fail." It wasn't a suggestion—it was a demand. Regardless of my offensive behavior, the Redhead showed more restraint in the situation. If she was upset by my belligerent attitude, she didn't tell me, but I later regretted my childish outburst and apologized to her. This was not my proudest moment.

During the first two years of our marriage we argued more and disagreed more about little things than we have over the last fifty-three years. We simply were getting adjusted to each other and were displaying considerable immaturity. This despite the fact that I had worked all of my life and had assumed responsibility for providing for all of my own needs by the time I was twelve, and had contributed to the family from that point on as well. Yet, I was thinking primarily of myself and did not empathize with her and her needs.

What is particularly regrettable about my behavior is that my wife has a much better handle on finances and manages money better than I do. Many of my decisions, especially in regard to trading cars, moving, and changing jobs, were the personification of financial foolishness. But the Redhead also came from a background where the husband was considered the last word on financial decisions, so she did not complain.

Over a period of time I slowly but surely learned about sharing decision making with the Redhead. Yet it wasn't until I became a Christian that I fully understood that my wife and I were equal partners, that while I was the head of the house, she was certainly entitled to have all the information available so she could have input in the decision-making process. My basic problem was that I did not clearly understand the word *equal*. At least, it had not been clearly explained to me. When we became closer and more conversant about sensitive matters, my love and appreciation for her grew and as a result our decision-making process has been much better than my decision-making process.

The good news is that, whatever our disagreements and disputes, we never once considered separation or divorce. We had both learned growing up that marriage is a commitment involving a lifetime. So gradually through the months and years we adjusted to each other. When our daughter Suzan was born, and became a common bond between us, we got over much of our childish behavior (especially on my part). I can joyfully say that these days we seldom disagree. I emphasize seldom because we're still human, and, as I often tell people in marriage seminars, neither one of us is perfect. But I'm quite grateful that she is not perfect. If she had been, she certainly would not have married me.

We stayed with Mrs. Hall for many months, and in the summer of 1947, after less than a year of marriage, the sandwich business started to fall off. The hot summer months came, enrollment dropped dramatically, classes were cut to only four days a week, and the dormitories were not air-conditioned. Our income dropped to almost nothing.

One day the Redhead saw an ad in the paper for a "$10,000-a-year sales person." I applied. The interview went well. They said they would be in touch, and I took them at their word. They didn't get in touch with me, however, and a month later I wrote them a letter saying I was very much interested and would like to work with them. Bill Cranford, the field manager, called me, and I went out with him on two presentations. He sold them both so easily I was completely confident I could do the same thing. He agreed to put me through training but because of his past experiences with college students he made it clear that he was not guaranteeing me the position. At the end of the training, if he felt I could succeed, I would then be given the opportunity.

Apparently my performance was satisfactory, and Bill gave me the job, but I had to buy my sales samples in order to start work. In addition, I had to get a suit of clothes and a hat. Yes, in those days, since we were selling heavy-duty waterless cookware for the WearEver Aluminum Company, I had to wear a suit and hat. Besides the suit and hat, I also bought a briefcase, all for a little less than fifty dollars—which I had to borrow.

When the school year started again I enrolled, but at that point my heart and interest lay in selling and not in finishing my education. I found I gave up important study time to concentrate on what truly interested me, and a couple of months into the new school year, recognizing that I was not going to be able to both sell and study well, I officially withdrew from college. Soon after withdrawing from school, Bill Cranford, the field manager who brought me into the business, opened Lancaster, South Carolina, to me as a territory, and with considerable excitement we moved there.

However, when we made the move to Lancaster, South Carolina, we needed more dependable transportation, so I swapped in our Studebaker Commander for a little Crosley automobile that was light and uncomfortable. Nevertheless, as long as I drove it under fifty miles an hour, it was dependable. Making that swap, as sensible and prudent as it was at the time, marked the beginning of my almost nonstop habit of car trading and new-car buying. The process became like a drug to me, and I always wanted a different (read that new) car. And the funny thing is, just as with any addiction, there is always some kind of rationalization handy to justify getting a new or different car.

In my work for the cookware company I drove to Columbia every Monday morning for a sales meeting and then back to Lancaster that afternoon. I was also driving a great deal during the week to see customers in the small towns and communities outside of Lancaster. With all that driving I had plenty of time to think about *what* I was driving. I was not very happy with that little Crosley automobile. So after a fairly good week of sales, in a burst of ill-founded, well-intentioned optimism and enthusiasm, I managed to scrape together a few extra dollars and with it traded the Crosley in on a brand-new Hudson automobile, which sold for $2,403. This was reasonably soon after World War II, and Fords, Chevrolets, and Plymouths were oversold and much in demand, whereas the Hudson was a relatively unknown car, though an excellent automobile.

I drove the Hudson around pleasantly enough for a few months, and then for some weird reason felt that I must have a sedan, since what I was driving was a coupe. So I foolishly traded—and business promptly dropped. I hasten to add that it wasn't completely the fault of my purchasing the automobile, but I could not meet the payments for it and had to turn the car in and settle for a Pontiac that was several years old. It was dependable transportation, though, and served me well.

When we first arrived in Lancaster, South Carolina, all we could find in housing was a bedroom with kitchen privileges with James and Doris Ballard. We became close friends with the entire Ballard family and with Bill and Iris Hunter, the daughter and son-in-law of the Ballards. To this day Iris is still a good friend. Bill died of cancer in 1999, and we really miss him.

After a couple of months living with the Ballards, we saw an ad for a situation in which a widower had accommodations that seemed to be a little better and involved free rent. All we ("we" meaning the Redhead) had to do was cook one meal a day for Mr. Holland, the landlord. That made the arrangement financially feasible. However, it wasn't long before we realized that though the rent was cheap, the price of living in Mr. Holland's place was high. Mr. Holland was demanding and complained a great deal, but mostly he was lonely, in want of company and conversation. We really did feel sorry for him, but we were also newlyweds, and the prospect of spending night after night visiting with him when we were really eager to be alone was more than we could take. After a short time we sought other housing.

We saw an ad run by Mr. Estridge in the Lancaster paper offering an apartment above a store. The condition was we had to agree to buy the furniture that was already there and the price was five hundred dollars. That, for us, was a substantial amount, but we agreed to pay for it on a monthly basis. The furniture included a reasonable number of pieces for both the bedroom and living room. It also included a stove, which gave every indication of being from pre–Civil War days, and a refrigerator that appeared to be a relic from World War I, but both did work. We gladly made the deal, though, because we wanted to be by ourselves. We had had enough of this sharing space with other people.

At that point my sales were spotty and my career was in trouble. I was not making a living, but the grocery store trusted us for our groceries and the service station trusted us for gasoline. We struggled along and then got the marvelous news that we were going to have a baby. I was so excited I did not really think about the cost, and on May 10, 1949, our daughter, Jean Suzanne Ziglar, made her appearance.

In those days things were done differently, and the Redhead suffered through a twenty-seven-hour labor. Thank God, she was none the worse for the wear, and our beautiful baby was a delight to see and hold. However, the hospital bill was sixty-four dollars, and I did not have the money to pay the bill. I had to make two cookware sales to get my own baby out of the hospital. You've heard about "captive audiences." I found a potential customer who literally could not escape my sales presentations. One of the desperate sales I made to spring mother and child from the hospital was to the lady who was the joint occupant of my wife's hospital room! When the Redhead had Suzan, doctors kept new mothers in the hospital for several days. The Redhead's hospital roommate was Christine Davis, and she and her husband, Harry, became good friends of ours. I've long ago forgotten who the other sale was, but I managed to raise the sixty-four dollars, make our exit from the hospital, and go on to the joyous experience of loving, admiring, and raising our beautiful little girl.

The Redhead has told me on numerous occasions that one of the reasons she was initially attracted to me was my obvious love for children. She was right on that score. We've been fortunate to have always had, with one brief exception, a close relationship with all four of our children. I'll discuss the exception later.

In Lancaster, I had some ups and downs—but mostly downs. The first two and a half years were extremely hard. Sales were difficult. Money was always in short supply. We basically lived from hand to mouth: bought groceries on a very limited budget, frequently purchased fifty cents' worth of gasoline at a time. It was not a good experience. But those meager times created one of my most vivid memories. One week I had done incredibly well and decided to "bank" fifty dollars, which meant that I put it in my underwear drawer under some T-shirts to save for a rainy day. After that I completely forgot about the money, and I happened to run across it at a time when our need for cash was almost desperate. I've never seen two twentys and a ten look so good. Fifty dollars was a lot of money—only fourteen dollars less than it cost to get Suzan out of the hospital when she was born.

We lived like that, holding our breath in anticipation of my selling that next set of cookware and collecting the commission, for most of the time we were in Lancaster. Then one day I went to a meeting where Mr. P. C. Merrell, the divisional supervisor from Tennessee, took an interest in me and persuaded me that I could be the national sales champion. He convinced me I had the ability to succeed and that I simply needed to believe in myself and work on an organized schedule. His encouragement ultimately catapulted my sales and management career into high gear.

He said, "You have the ability to be a great one." To be honest, I'd never heard words like that. As a child raised during the Depression, I had concentrated on "survival" and not on being "great." Now here was a man for whom I had the utmost respect, a man who was my hero, a man of integrity, and he was emphatic that I could be the best cookware salesman in the country. His belief in me caused me to believe in myself. For the first time in my life I had hope that maybe I did have more to offer than I'd ever realized. I turned his words over and over in my mind and got more excited by the minute.

By the time I got back to Lancaster and was packing up for my demonstration that night, I was really fired up! During the cookware demonstration I realized for the first time that my prospects were not dealing with "a little guy from a little town who would struggle all his life." Now with the picture I had of myself, because of Mr. Merrell's integrity and his strong endorsement of me, they were dealing with the national champion. That night for those three couples my enthusiasm was measurably higher, my confidence was strong, I was relaxed and having fun, and the three couples all bought without a question. It's important to understand that in the two and a half years I struggled so hard to learn how to sell cookware, I *had* learned how to get prospects, make appointments, conduct demonstrations, answer objections, and close the sale. The salesperson was trained and ready. The man, however, was not.

Dr. Joyce Brothers said that you can't consistently perform in a manner that is inconsistent with the way you see yourself. Mr. Merrell changed the way I saw myself—a little guy with an inferiority complex from a small Mississippi town could never be the national champion, but a great salesman, which is the way Mr. Merrell identified me, could be. The change was dramatic. Mr. Merrell got the man ready.

He got me ready by giving me instruction as well as encouragement. He told me that if I believed in myself and went to work on a regular schedule

I could do some truly great things. Immediately, I began leaving the house every morning at exactly the same time so that I would be knocking on a prospect's door at exactly nine A.M. I followed the same schedule rain or shine, whether I wanted to and felt like it or not, and I don't ever remember looking forward to knocking on that first door—or the second or third! By the fourth or fifth door, however, I was feeling comfortable, and from that point on I truly enjoyed making my sales calls.

I could hardly sleep when I went to bed that night. I woke up a new man. My confidence did a 180-degree turn, and results were immediate and substantial.

I started selling like a house afire, and in a matter of two or three months I was given the opportunity to move up to a bigger territory, Florence, South Carolina. Since I knew of the pending move well in advance, I started asking the people to whom I was selling in Lancaster if they knew anyone in the Florence area. As a result, when I arrived in Florence in the spring of 1950, I had several people lined up to call on for booking dinner parties. By then I was selling exclusively at dinner parties. The hostess actually had the most important job in the sales process. She invited couples to attend the cookware demonstration and received a really nice gift based entirely on having the party at her home with anywhere from four to eight couples present. In those days, people were far more inclined to go out at night, and in rural areas they especially enjoyed getting together to visit. The cookware demonstration was merely an excuse for them to socialize over a good meal and have some fun.

This is where an outgoing personality and a sense of humor were very helpful to me. I instructed each hostess on how to invite their guests and explained that the guests' only obligation was to bring a big appetite with them and be prepared to have an enjoyable evening. I always emphasized that at the last minute things would inevitably happen to change the plans of some of the couples, and so the hostess should invite at least two more couples than she could accommodate. I also told the hostess that she would probably have at least one decline for every acceptance, and for her to be neither surprised nor disappointed. Those things just happen.

I would arrive for the demonstration two hours before the guests so I could prepare the meal and have everything ready. I always saved one fast cooking food to prepare after the guests had arrived so that I could demonstrate how to use the cookware. The hostess kept the guests in the living room, and when everyone had arrived, I was invited into the living room and introduced. Then I made my "living room talk," impressing them with the way I remembered their names, which, incidentally, I had committed to memory before they arrived. I welcomed them, assured them they would love the food, that there was plenty to eat. But I also cautioned them that since I was a salesman I would probably try to sell them something.

Nobody was surprised at this, and everybody generally laughed. Then I would say, "I don't know what experience you've had with salespeople, but I have been told that some of them will actually stretch the truth just a little. How many of you have heard that?" Everybody would laugh and hold up their hands, indicating that yes, they had heard that. I would say, "So with this in mind, I'm going to ask you not to believe anything that I have to say, because you've been forewarned. However, let me ask you to do two things. First of all, how many of you believe your hostess is an honest lady?" Needless to say, all would agree. Then I would say, "If she says something, I'm going to ask you to believe her. Would you be willing to do that?" Again a little laughter and they'd say, "Of course." I'd then say, "Second, I will also ask you to believe what you see with your own two eyes. Will you do that?" They'd laugh again and say, "Yup." I would smile and say, "Well, now, if you'll do those two things, I warn you—you're going to end up cooking in this beautiful set of cookware in your own home, because seeing is believing." Then I would invite all of them back into the kitchen where I quickly cooked the cabbage and explained how we had cooked everything else, getting the hostess to validate what I was saying, including the fact that I had used no water and that the roast did not shrink.

During the meal we did not bother them. We simply saw to it that they had what they needed to enjoy the food.

When the meal was over I made a short health presentation, reconfirmed what they had already agreed to, and made the appointments to see them the next day in their own homes. Next I would say, "As most of you can see, I have fun doing this. And as most of you know, many of your neighbors are cooking this way." Then I mentioned the names of a number of local people who had purchased the cookware, just to let them know they were not the "Lone Rangers" when they decided to cook this healthy, money-saving way.

That's how I sold my cookware and how I got most of my recruits through the dinner parties. Just a few months after arriving in Florence I qualified for the field dealer's position, and the next year I was the highest-paid field manager in the United States.

Yes, my career was picking up nicely, but I still had some work to do on my addictive personality. It was destined to trip me up and undermine my best efforts at every opportunity. When we moved to Florence, I had once again decided I had to have a new car and was able to buy a new Dodge, which was quite dependable but also very slow. After just a few months with it, my business was exploding, and I was able to realize, or, you might say, rationalize, a long-held dream: namely, to own a new Cadillac automobile. At that time the car sold for only a little over thirty-seven hundred dollars, and I was so proud of that car! I used it and loved it, and it possibly helped in my recruiting and building. Then, when I was promoted to divisional supervisor I rationalized that the Cadillac was nearly a year old, and I thought I had to have a new car at least every ten or twelve months, so I swapped the Cadillac in on a new Lincoln and drove Lincolns for several years.

One of the most serious mistakes I made as a young man was a result of the ridiculous idea I had that if anybody else had a new car, I needed to get a new one also. This kept us in financial hot water for a large portion of those early years. I always had to hustle to pay my growing bills, keep the electricity on, and put food on the table. I was always overextended financially because I was positive every week would be a great one. Sometimes I miscalculated.

My newfound success encouraged me to indulge in other forms of what I'll call "amateur high-rolling." The first extravagant time the Redhead and I ever had on vacation was the result of the fulfillment of one of my dreams—to spend at least one night in the Waldorf Astoria in New York City. The movies of the day made the Waldorf look like one of the most sumptuous, luxurious places on earth. So the summer following my appointment as field dealer, when business was exceptionally good, the Redhead and I decided to go to New York for a week's vacation and spend at least one night in the Waldorf Astoria.

I called the Waldorf from Florence, South Carolina, and was told that the room rate was twenty-four dollars per night. Feeling the exhilaration of the newly rich, we reserved the hotel room for two nights, left our daughter with the lady who was working with me at the time, and off we went. On the outskirts of New York, fearing this all might just be a dream (how could we suddenly afford to do this?), I called the Waldorf again, confirmed the reservation, and verified the twenty-four-dollar room rate. Satisfied by the reality check, we continued on. When we arrived at the Waldorf I was wearing a red-and-blue sport shirt that I thought was quite debonair. To put it plainly, I still remember the color because it was just a little "loud."

We walked in and everybody else—and I do mean *everybody else* (all of the men, that is)—had on very conservative dark suits. I walked to the desk to register and said to the clerk, "Now the rate is twenty-four dollars a night, isn't it?" He smiled and said, "Yes." Then he leaned over and whispered discretely to me, "Can you handle it?" I grinned and said, "Well, yeah, I think so for a couple of nights, anyhow!" And so there we were, in a nice, big gorgeous room in the Waldorf Astoria.

That evening we walked out on the streets surrounding the Waldorf for about two hours, just walking and looking, taking in the sights. There's an old adage that says you can take the boy out of the country but you can't take the country out of the boy. When we at last walked back to the hotel and into our room, I was shocked at what we found. The first thing I said was, "Sweetheart, somebody's been in our room!" The bedcovers had been turned back. We had never heard of anything like that! When we finally realized everything was in place, that this was a service the hotel offered its guests, we laughed about it and had a good night's sleep.

They really were two outstanding days. We did the usual tourist thing—we went to see the Statue of Liberty and the Empire State Building; we took a tour of the harbor and went to Staten Island, etc. We didn't want to miss a thing about what made New York, well, New York in the popular mind. On the third day, as we'd planned, we headed out for New Kensington, Pennsylvania, which is just outside of Pittsburgh. We went to the home office of my company, WearEver Aluminum, to meet with the vice president of sales. His name was Mr. A. P. Miller, and though he was fairly short in stature, he was ruggedly built and very impressive. We had a marvelous visit. During the hour we spent with him, he gave me some wonderful suggestions about recruiting new salesmen, and I was really pumped up about my future in selling cookware when the Redhead and I left there.

Here's where the fun starts again. We had just spent the night before in one of the premier hotels in the world, but the only room we could get in New Kensington was, to be kind, not quite in the same category. We did not even have a bathroom in the room—it was down the hall. We also were in an internal room, looking out on an alley, and there was a huge pipe just outside our window. Since the hotel was not air-conditioned, not only was it extremely hot in our room but also the pipe blocked a major portion of the view to the alley. It was really quite a transition—we had gone from the sublime to the ridiculous in just one day!

The next day we left and took a route that would allow us to see some of the Blue Ridge Mountains on the way back to Florence. On our return trip we spent one night at a beautiful resort hotel, but the price wasn't nearly the exorbitant twenty-four dollars we had paid to stay at the Waldorf. Just a few years earlier a trip like this one would have been beyond my capacity even to dream. I have fond memories of it to this day.

PART THREE

*Three Steps
Forward, Two
Steps Back*

Not too long after we moved to Florence and the year before our New York vacation, WearEver, our company, had its annual National Booster Week. All of the field sales force was encouraged to do nothing but sell for a full week—no recruiting, no training, no service calls, no collection calls—just sales. In preparation for concentrated selling, I sent my wife and daughter to Jackson, Mississippi, to visit with her mother. Our convention, the climax of the special sales week, was going to take place in Biloxi, Mississippi. I was going to finish working the big week, drive to Jackson, pick up my family, and head for the convention.

I also planned to stop in Atlanta on the way to Jackson and spend at least a portion of the night with my friend Bill Cranford, the man who first hired me and gave me the break I'd really needed. During the National Booster Week, I had the biggest week of my career—up until then—by far, selling over two and a half times as much as I had ever sold in a single week. I arrived in Atlanta at about two-thirty in the morning, since the drive from Florence took roughly five hours. Supercharged by the drive and my excitement over my recent successes, I awakened Bill. He put the coffeepot on and for the next two to three hours I gave him every minute detail of the entire sales week, explaining how "I said this and the prospect said that; I said this, they said that; and I said this and they bought." I gave him a blow-by-blow description of every single sale I made that week.

It was well over two hours later when I finally finished recounting my triumphs and suddenly it hit me—I said, "Oh, my goodness, Bill! I've done nothing but talk, talk, talk, beating my gums. I'm suffering from an advanced case of 'I' trouble, and I'm terribly embarrassed. Please forgive me, Bill. So how are *you* doing?"

As only the diplomatic and compassionate Bill Cranford could do, he smiled his most pleasant smile and said, "Zig, don't give it a thought! You have every reason to be proud. You've done a tremendous job and made a fabulous effort, and I commend you for that. But let me remind you that I was the one who recruited you, brought you into the business, and trained you. As you recall, for over two years I conducted the sales meetings for you every Monday morning, called you on the phone when you were discouraged, went up and worked with you when you were threatening to quit the business. And Zig, as proud and grateful as you are for what you've been able to accomplish this week, you will never know real joy until you have experienced what I have just experienced. You see, Zig, I'm even prouder of you than you are of yourself. I get more delight from what you've accomplished than you get, and as I say, you will never know real joy until you've experienced helping someone else achieve success."

Bill Cranford taught me a very important lesson that night: that real joy comes when you make a positive difference in other people's lives, helping them achieve their goals and dreams. I've even built my philosophy—*You can have everything in life you want if you will just help enough other people get what they want*—around the principle that Bill taught me in the wee hours of that morning. I emphasize that this is a philosophy, not a tactic. This is not manipulation, which you do for your benefit. You don't do something for somebody else and then sit back expecting him or her to do something for you. That's back scratching at best and manipulation at its worst, and it has no long-term benefits. True joy comes when you inspire, encourage, and guide someone else on a path that benefits him or her. That's what Bill Cranford and the twenty-five other people on my Wall of Gratitude did for me.

One of the most amazing facts of life, and in reality the reason it works so well, is it's just a different way of putting the Golden Rule into practice. When you treat other people as you wish to be treated yourself, you will invariably put them first. I can validate in a hundred different ways in every profession and in every phase of life that this philosophy really does work. And by work I mean produce genuine happiness and satisfaction in the hearts and minds of everyone involved. It is through losing yourself in helping others find what they want and need that you yourself find real joy.

Because of the confidence-building (encouragement) of Mr. P. C. Merrell and the constant support of Bill Cranford, in 1951 I finished number two in the nation out of seven thousand salespeople, and the following year was the highest-paid field manager in the United States.

When we first arrived in Florence to assume responsibility for my new territory, we found a small apartment in a private home and stayed there roughly three months. When the Gregg Apartments opened, a new and spacious apartment complex, we moved in and had real breathing room for the first time in our marriage. We made friends with many of the residents and even recruited two of them as part of our sales organization.

About a year later we moved into our first house. It was on Indian Drive in Florence, and stood about 150 yards from an extremely busy through street. Since we couldn't hear the traffic noise inside the house, we never gave it much thought. That is, until one day, somehow, some way, we lost sight of our daughter, Suzan, who was slightly less than two years old at the time. I went outside, looked around, walked into the street in front of our house, and was horrified to see our Suzan in the middle of the busy through street.

I had my car keys in my pocket, so I dashed over to the car, backed it out, accelerated as fast as I could for the 150 yards, and stopped just before I got to the through street. Traffic was almost nonexistent during those several seconds, and I have to tell you that when I jumped out of that car and grabbed my Suzan in my arms, I wept as I had not wept up until that time—tears of relief, gratitude, and joy. It was inconceivable to me that we might have lost her by letting her out of our sight for a few seconds. I had just had the fright of my life and had discovered the aching vulnerability of being a parent, always subject to the incomparable pain of losing a child. We learned a big lesson that day about locking doors. The shock of that event undoubtedly lifted both the Redhead and me to a greater degree of responsibility and maturity than we had achieved before.

Florence, South Carolina, is where I really hit my stride in the cookware business. We had lived in Florence a little over two years when I was promoted once again, this time to supervisor for North and South Carolina. A few weeks later we moved to Charlotte, North Carolina, because it was in the center of the territory, and it cut my driving time considerably. We were there only three months when management divided the territory between the former supervisor and me, and moved us to Knoxville, Tennessee.

While in Knoxville our daughter Cindy was born, and I experienced a rather strange feeling when we found out we were going to have her. I seriously doubted that I was capable of loving another child as much as I loved our first one. Although I did not express it to anyone, I was genuinely concerned. How was I going to be a good father to both girls and treat each of them fairly? I wasn't sure I had the emotional resources to love two children as much as I already loved Suzan. That concern lasted about three and a half seconds after I held that beautiful new little girl in my arms and realized how precious she was—and is—to this day.

My career successes, however, would not keep pace with the joy that the Redhead and I were experiencing in our growing family. Almost immediately after I agreed to split the territory with the previous divisional supervisor, disaster struck and our business dropped dramatically. In direct sales, where the salesperson goes to the customer at his or her home or place of business, the field manager is the key position. I had four field dealers in my division under my supervision, and almost immediately one of them had a heart attack; one of them almost cut off his big toe and spent three weeks in the hospital; and a third one had an integrity problem. The fourth had been promoted when I was and did not have the experience necessary to handle the much bigger assignment. Almost immediately, rumors started circulating in the company that I was unable to do my job, that I had been promoted beyond my level of competence, and that the company was thinking about replacing me.

Casting about for solutions, I picked up a copy of Dr. Norman Vincent Peale's book *The Power of Positive Thinking*. I had been moping and groaning and crying because I had nothing to do with the difficulties in my division and yet my fate was tightly tied to its performance. I was suffering for things beyond my control. Dr. Peale's book was just what I needed. His book taught me that though I am not always responsible for what happens to me, I am responsible for how I *handle* what happens to me. Immediately my attitude changed for the better. I realized I did have a large degree of control over my own behavior in the face of the difficulties, even if I had nothing to do with producing them myself. My new confidence and enthusiasm proved contagious to my coworkers, and my division had a dramatic turnaround. We actually finished fifth out of sixty-six WearEver divisions in the nation that year, and my promotion had not even taken place until that April. What a difference attitude makes!

Things were much better, and I felt like I was back on top—but the feeling didn't last as long as I'd hoped. It soon became clear that something was seriously amiss with the compensation from the company for the work that I was doing. My checks didn't reflect my production as far as I was concerned. I'm certain the new pay scale was explained to me when I accepted the divisional supervisor position, but in my excitement and enthusiasm I naturally assumed the promotion also meant more money. I had been excited all month—until payday. When I received the first check after having assumed my new responsibilities, I was shocked to discover that my income was now dramatically *less* than it had been when I was a field manager. I was, to say the least, stunned and disappointed. Had our division been failing, I could have understood it, but we were successful. With that national standing—finishing fifth the first year and third the next, being beaten only by Kansas and New York (which had considerably larger populations than South Carolina)—I felt I was doing a good job, and certainly my income should not have been less. In all fairness to the company, they explained to me many times why I should work harder, be gone from home several nights a week, and use my car when I worked in the field with the field managers. They also explained why they expected me to pick up the tab when we ate in restaurants. I followed them up to a point, but then in my view their reasoning broke down. I never did understand why I should earn nearly ten thousand dollars less than I had as a field manager, considering the extra work and responsibility I had taken on in my new position. After explaining it to me many times, they finally threw up their hands and said I wasn't trying to understand—and they were right.

After the second year I felt I simply could not continue enthusiastically in this position with the company with an eye to the future. Eventually I was called into the home office for a meeting because my concern finally got their attention. To this day I will never forget the interview. It was with Mr. A. P. Miller, our national sales manager, who was highly respected—and feared—throughout the company. When he learned of my discomfort and my plans to leave, he looked at me very directly, and in his deep voice said he was surprised and disappointed, because he felt that someday I would become a district manager. My response was one I doubt he had ever heard from any of his underlings in his many years with the company. I said to him, "Mr. Miller, I appreciate that vote of confidence, but the reality is if my next promotion costs me as much money as the last one did, there is no way I could even afford it." Needless to say, the rest of the conversation was noticeably cooler.

Another significant event in my career followed. It was clear to me that

I wanted to leave WearEver, but I had not made any definite arrangements to seek employment elsewhere. However, two and a half years earlier I had met Mr. Bob Bales in Florence, South Carolina, when he was conducting a motivational seminar. I had never seen anybody have so much fun, do so much good, and, I thought, make so much money. That evening, when he finished the seminar, he went out with the Redhead and me for dinner and conversation. Captivated by what seemed to be a wonderful way to make a living, I eagerly expressed to him my interest in becoming a speaker myself. I sought his counsel and direction. He encouraged me to have a few birthdays, set some sales records, hone my skills, and see if I could affiliate with the Dale Carnegie Institute, a privately held training company that teaches public speaking, communication, leadership, and sales-training skills. To my delight, he suggested that, yes, there might be a future for me as a speaker. I had the natural talents and determination. I showed promise. By then P. C. Merrell had already taught me that what one person said to another could have a huge impact on his or her performance and, in fact, life and career. That night I made the decision that I did indeed want to be a motivational business and career speaker.

I followed his good advice. After two and a half years of setting sales records and having birthdays, I remembered what Bob Bales had said, and I wrote a letter to the Dale Carnegie Institute in New York City. Several years later I learned that they had saved my letter as the classic example of how not to write a letter. It was a glaring display of "I" trouble. I described in glowing terms all of the remarkable things I had done: how successful I had been; how "I did this" and "I did that." Fortunately for me, as they later explained, I also included the records to support my self-congratulatory statements. Based on the hard evidence I'd supplied to back up my claims, they flew me to New York City for the interview. I liked what I heard, and the Dale Carnegie people liked what they heard, so our growing little family, the Redhead, Suzan, Cindy, and I up and moved to New York City in the summer of 1955 to go to work with Long Island Dale Carnegie Institute franchise owners Mr. and Mrs. John Mason. The Masons hired me to sell the newly developed Dale Carnegie sales course, and I developed the talk they used to sell it during the introductory phase.

One thing that made an indelible impression on me was that John Mason was also a newspaper executive in addition to being the sponsor for the Long Island Dale Carnegie Institute. One day I stopped by his newspaper office to have lunch, and as we were leaving he said, "I need to stop right here." Outside of his office was a pay telephone. In those days a call cost a dime. He made a brief call and then we were on our way again. During lunch he explained to me that he felt it was wrong to use the newspaper telephone or newspaper time to conduct business that had nothing to do with the newspaper but rather concerned his Dale Carnegie operation. I respected more than I can explain in a few words the deep integrity of a man who was that committed to a principle. He made a big impression on me and set an example I wanted to follow.

I was excited about being part of the team that would introduce the sales course to the New York area. They had just brought John Cooper aboard to head the operation, and he was going to be working directly with Mr. Percy H. Whiting, author of *The Five Great Rules of Selling,* a dynamic fellow who was the man responsible for making the Dale Carnegie Institute a nationwide enterprise. I loved what I was doing. I enjoyed the challenge of introducing the sales course, learning to teach the public-speaking course at the same time, and going through the instructor's training course.

However, one major problem was created by the new situation. I was not seeing enough of my family. Leaving my girls asleep when I left home early in the morning and finding them asleep when I got back that night was not my idea of how to father children. In addition, I don't need to explain to you that the culture shock I felt coming from Yazoo City, Mississippi, where I was raised, to New York City was substantial. I was a fish out of water and had to learn to thrive in an entirely new environment. The customs, attitudes, and even the language of New York were as foreign to me as I was to them. One of my first New York moments came when I stepped on an elevator going to the tenth floor of a building in order to talk to a prospect about enrolling his people in the Dale Carnegie sales course. When I entered the elevator, I said to the operator, "Ten." The gentleman looked at me, smiled, and said, "And what part of the South are you from?" Well, at that time, I did have quite an accent—and it was funny, particularly to New Yorkers. Naturally I knew in my heart that I talked normally, but those New Yorkers sure did talk funny.

My attention was further distracted, and my curiosity piqued, by a new start-up operation that seemed to offer even greater opportunities than the

Carnegie Institute. A friend of mine named Bernard Haygood, with whom I had worked in the cookware business, had become affiliated with his brother-in-law, Jimmy Glenn, in an organization called Nutrilite Food Supplements, which I believe was the first company to use the system of multilevel marketing to distribute products. Lee Mitinger and William L. Castleberry had created the concept, and persuaded Carl Rhenborg, the founder of Nutrilite, that he could market his products more effectively through this system. The prospects for success seemed excellent, and everyone involved was really excited about it. Actually, Jay Van Andel and Rich De Vos, who would later become legendary in the world of sales and marketing, had joined the company and were setting the woods on fire in building the organization. They are the entrepreneurs with the Midas touch who later started Amway and, in turn, bought the Nutrilite Food Supplement Company. To this day Nutrilite is still a part of the Amway organizational structure.

While we were in New York working with Carnegie, Bernard would call me pretty regularly and tell me about all the wonderful things that were happening with Nutrilite and the multilevel marketing organization they were developing. I enjoyed the New York experience, but I realized the living arrangements it required were not fair to my family. Finally, the lure of the homeland and a more normal home life was too strong. After three short months I reluctantly resigned from my Carnegie affiliation and headed back home to South Carolina where our third daughter, Julie, was born shortly after we returned. What a delightful addition to our family she made. We felt we pretty well had our family completed by then, though, candidly speaking, I had wanted a son. But with three beautiful little girls in the family at this point, a son didn't appear to be in the cards.

We had been back in Columbia for some time when little Cindy gave us quite a scare in the way only a child can frighten her parents. One beautiful summer day we all had gone swimming at Sesquicentennial State Park with our friends Earl and Sybil Small and their children. The park was full of people intent on enjoying themselves, seriously going about their business of having fun. The scene was one of activity and distractions and potentially very confusing. People were everywhere, going in and out of the thirty-acre lake swimming. Suddenly one of us realized that Cindy was missing. We anxiously looked all around our little area on the shore of the lake but could not spot her anywhere. We all became extremely concerned, and I approached the lifeguards, asking them to clear out the lake and announce on the loudspeaker that our daughter was missing. The lifeguards, however, had better things to do than bother about a missing child. Quite callously, I thought, they shrugged off our worried request and went about their other activities. Even as our panic mounted by the second, they refused to make an announcement, and did not tell people to stop going into the lake. By their general lack of interest in helping us, they essentially said that we should find our little girl ourselves.

Well, after a few wild and frantic minutes of searching everywhere for her, Earl Small found her playing with a group of children some distance from our area and brought her back to us. Our rejoicing was great, as you can imagine if you are a parent. Everyone cried and hugged and cried some more, and, as best I can remember, we were so exhausted emotionally by the search-and-recovery mission for Cindy that we just packed up, left the lake, and returned home immediately. There is nothing quite as soul chilling as fearing that your child has disappeared and that you might not find her.

A "Wandering Generality"

To know where I was mentally at this time, you need to understand that when I returned to South Carolina from New York City, the prior four years of my life had been unusually successful and productive ones. I had set records in the cookware business with the number of people I had trained who then in turn went on to become very productive in the business themselves. In New York, though I stayed only a few months, I accomplished some significant objectives both for the people I was working with and for myself.

All the early encouragement and confidence Bill Cranford and Mr. Merrell had given me, I was now convinced, were only recognition of my real capabilities. I had proven them right. Yes, I had worked hard and paid my dues. Nothing had been handed to me. I played by the rules and for four great years took home the winnings. When you start thinking like that, friends, you better watch out. You can start believing you're capable of anything. The bottom line was, after achieving some significant personal goals during those four years, I then stopped growing—and started swelling. There's quite a difference.

Riding high on my recent accomplishments and my streak of good fortune, when I returned to Columbia, South Carolina, I became a "wandering generality," unwilling to waste my precious time and energy on efforts unworthy of my abilities.

I got into the Nutrilite business with my old colleagues, but it didn't take long for me to discover that it was difficult in 1955, when nutritional supplements were not well known or accepted, to make a good living distributing them. I gave it my best shot, but I realized within five months that I simply could not survive in that business, so I went back into direct sales with Arcadian China. After a brief but moderately successful run with them I decided to try my hand in the insurance business. The first company sold a compensation plan (health and accident insurance), and when a better plan was made available by yet another company I went for it. Next I tried a life insurance company that sold an "investment" policy only to find that it wasn't all they had promised it would be.

It wasn't too long after that a product called NutriBio caught my attention. NutriBio was a new concept in nutrition with very exciting marketing plans, and I just knew that it was going to be wildly successful, so, casting off china sales with no remorse, I jumped into it with both feet. This impulsive move, the first of many, launched our long and winding downward financial slide.

During that period, when I was trying just about everything that came along, I did make one notable exception and exercised, for me, uncharacteristically good judgment after a fling with an idea. I had discovered yet another new company that designed and built an exciting new product that I felt would have a huge market, this one primarily for people who had some type of physical handicap or who suffered from mild dementia. I could see a market for it in retirement homes, nursing homes, hospitals, and any home where there were senior citizens or those with physical disabilities. The device, I felt, was unique. Not only would it be a major improvement in sanitation but it would also be a wonderful convenience for people who had physical difficulties.

To show how far over the edge I was at the time in my quest for opportunities worthy of my attention, this particular product was perfectly suited for a *Saturday Night Live* skit, had the show been in existence at the time. Considering myself a comedian on the matter, I laughingly referred to the product as ideal for overweight people with short arms. On a more serious note, however, truly disabled people who had either no arms, deformed arms, or arms that simply would not function would really benefit enormously from this new appliance. I forget the official marketing name given the device, but I referred to it in my own shorthand as an "automatic bottom washer." When a person went to the bathroom for "number two," as we referred to it then, once he or she had finished, a gentle stream of warm water conveniently and effectively bathed that part of the body. Since the water was warm and soothing, it would also be ideal for people suffering from hemorrhoids. The fly in the ointment of my grand plan, however, was brought to light by my daughter Suzan's earnest question when she found out I was contemplating marketing such a product: "Dad, what will I tell my friends you do?" Even though it still had hints of humor, her inquiry was absolutely serious. I immediately realized, on hearing her question, that I could not put my family through that kind of embarrassment and ridicule. No child of mine was going to have to say her daddy sold bottom washers for a living.

Frankly, in retrospect, I'm amazed that people would give me so many different business opportunities at that time in my life because I had become pretty arrogant, and my inflated ego made me a poor listener. My ego was such that if I did not have my way with whichever company I joined, I would very quickly let them know that I did not have to tolerate their ignorance and ineptitude. I always knew a better way and was always frustrated that they did not understand the terrific contribution I could make to the company if they would just do it my way.

On top of my high and mighty attitude about work, I displayed incredible clumsiness and ineptness in my relationship with the Redhead. I was operating under the unenlightened belief that the man of the house was supposed to be in control of everything and make all decisions himself without benefit of wifely counsel. It was simply my right as head of the household. What the Redhead had to say or think about issues was beside the question. I would buy and sell cars without conferring with her, and I'd quit and start new jobs without discussing it with her first. I would make the deals, then tell my wife what I had done. Not good. Not bright, either.

But the Redhead didn't fuss too much. Not even when I was in seventeen different deals over a five-year period—and really, that's all they were—just deals. All my wheeling and dealing involved moves to Nashville, Tennessee; Greenville, South Carolina; Atlanta, Georgia; and back to Columbia, South Carolina. I left several of those companies honestly thinking that though they had been in business fifty years they were doomed for failure because they wouldn't take my advice and do things my way. The bottom line is there *was* failure involved. But it was mine—not theirs. Even though it was my dire prediction that they were going under, they somehow managed to survive. I almost didn't.

During this most difficult period of my life, and actually during our entire marriage, we've had any number of setbacks and some very dark days. But the stabilizing factor, what kept me going, was the love, support, and encouragement of that beautiful Redhead of mine.

Mixed in with a number of these side trips and detours was one of the more pleasant and meaningful experiences of my life. My old cookware manager, Bill Cranford, introduced me to Dr. Emol Fails. Dr. Fails was a professor at North Carolina State University and also had his own consulting business, Fails and Shepherd, out of Raleigh, North Carolina. Dr. Fails became a mentor and a friend to me and taught me the importance of self-worth, which incidentally has nothing to do with arrogance and an overbearing sense of self-importance. He was an encourager, a man who believed in me and helped develop my quest for knowledge, personal growth, and improvement. He had the capacity to make me feel important, while at the same time he carefully mentored me on the importance of being humble as I continued to grow and develop my ability. I had not up until that time considered humility a critical factor in the mix of essential virtues necessary for success in life.

Dr. Fails invited me to participate in some of the Chamber of Commerce seminars he was conducting in North Carolina. We had an amiable and effective division of labors in our presentations. He covered the nuts and bolts of business practice just as he did in his seminars for the general public and the specialized seminars he did for the heating and air-conditioning industry. I, on the other hand, provided the encouragement, motivation, and inspiration that had to go with the "perspiration" in order to succeed at any endeavor. I told them they *could* do it and Dr. Fails told them *how* to do it, so, as a team, we covered all of the bases. The partnership proved to be a good arrangement, and I gained valuable experience and quite a few dollars in the process.

One memory of my time with Dr. Fails that stands out in my mind was an engagement for heating and air-conditioning businesses in Cleveland, Ohio. Dr. Fails and I were there in the dead of winter. I arrived the night before the seminar. Though snow was falling and it was bitterly cold, I was ignorant of how quickly a winter storm can change a landscape, and I walked a full two blocks to a theater. By the time the show was over and I got out of the building, so much snow had fallen that it was well over my shoes. I got awfully cold and damp that night on the way back to the hotel, and I was truly grateful that we didn't have that kind of snow in Columbia, South Carolina. But I had acquired a new respect for the importance of checking out local weather conditions.

The most memorable part of that trip, however, was my surprise at the size of the compensation Dr. Fails offered me for my work. I was stunned when Dr. Fails gave me a very generous three-hundred-dollar speaking fee for the engagement. That was very early in my speaking career, and in my own heart and mind I did not feel that I deserved that kind of fee. However, Dr. Fails was adamant and said I sold myself short, that I had made a bigger contribution than I realized, and that I needed to recognize the contribution. At that stage of my career and financial life, I was more than thrilled to cash that check.

In the midst of all of this, between engagements and conversations and just getting to know each other quite well, Dr. Fails told me something that for the one and only time caused me to regret that I had not gotten my degree from the University of South Carolina before I left school and jumped into the sales profession. He told me that if I had a degree, he could use me as an associate professor in his department because in my field I was certainly qualified to do an effective job of teaching. He pointed out that the association with the university would give me additional credibility in many areas of business. However, I did not dwell on the missed opportunity for a university connection very long because I don't believe in sawing sawdust. But I did determine to continue my education through the seminars that I was able to attend, as well as through the many books I've read over the years.

One of the most distinct honors I've ever received came to me when Dr. Fails's widow invited me to give the eulogy at his funeral. She said that before his death Dr. Fails had himself requested that I deliver his eulogy and that he said he had always felt as if I were his son.

My Most Miserable Year

In 1959, after spending a frustrating year in Nashville, Tennessee, where my brother Judge and I worked as the home office general agents for a new life insurance company, my judgment only got worse as my aptitude for creating catastrophes improved. In the next twelve months I managed to move my family's misery index to an all-time high. The Nashville insurance company, we discovered painfully, had taken its product to market before it was ready to sell. It didn't take long for us to figure out what the problems were and to determine we had boarded a ship that wasn't going to sail very fast or very far. Ever on the lookout for the next big thing, I resigned my position with the insurance company and joined what I thought was a new enterprise with great potential, a small company called Vigor-Wealth. Associating with Vigor-Wealth required that we move our family to Greenville, South Carolina. And the whole situation proved disastrous in no time.

Vigor-Wealth was a line of nutritional products that was scientifically sound, but, sadly enough, the company lacked the financial resources to really capitalize on the market. I made the move for at least one reason that was wrong: I was getting out of something that I knew was destined to be a long and difficult struggle and was using Vigor-Wealth as an escape hatch. While the product was good, the lack of available capital was almost immediately obvious. A deciding factor for me was the fact that a well-known speaker and author of national reputation had publicly stated that with his reputation at stake, while serving on the board and as an adviser, he could not afford to let the company fail. This was one of the lures that attracted me to the company. Yet what he said and what he did were two different things. In a matter of weeks we realized that we had made yet another bad move, one that would not have that pot of gold at the end of the rainbow but that rather promised only more frustration. So after just three months in Greenville, disgusted with the way things turned out with Vigor-Wealth, we moved to Atlanta, Georgia. Surely, I thought, we would get a break soon; the streak of bad luck couldn't continue forever.

Along with the frustrations that generally go with bad choices, I was disturbed to notice that my tendency to blame circumstances seemed to be growing. And yet, I still felt I had the ability to make the right connection and get my career back on track and achieve success. The long series of blind alleys couldn't continue indefinitely. In retrospect, I realize that I was fast running out of legitimate reasons for feeling so optimistic, but with a family I had no choice. I kept looking for the right opportunity. My willingness to work was never in question, and so we made the next move.

When we arrived in Atlanta we moved into a thousand-square-foot house, and with a wife, three children, and enough furniture for a two-thousand-square-foot house, we were overcrowded to the extreme. Yes, we were an extremely close family, too close in those days. It was an unproductive way to live, and all of us needed more space. The move to Atlanta marked the beginning of my most confusing and frustrating year ever. The more I tried to gain control of my career and the fortunes of our family, the more the situation spun out of control. In a weird kind of inside-out version of the way things should go, the harder I worked, the worse everything became. In Atlanta I first went to work for Arcadian Fine China, a reputable, old-line direct sales company, selling fine china, crystal, and table appointments. I got off to a reasonably good start, but along came another new product, and after only a couple of months I moved to the "greener grass." Actually, I was very happy and enjoyed my relationship with Arcadian, but the new Japanese company had what I considered to be a much better product with a better guarantee and benefit for the customer, so I made the switch for positive reasons and not negative ones. I saw it as a product that was easy to sell with more income possibilities for the future.

A few weeks after making the move to the Japanese company, I discovered that I had yet again fallen into another trap of my own devising. By then you would have thought that I would have taken a break from my snap decisions to jump from one thing to another at the drop of a hat. But, no, I still had the confidence that generally goes with ignorance. I believed that I would eventually hit my stride again and build a sales career like the one I had enjoyed so much for several years before I got on the binge of trying everything new that came along. The Redhead, as always, was very supportive of what I was doing, though she was concerned and nervous about the ongoing moves. One day she remarked that she wished my mind was not always so open to every opportunity that presented itself. However, she still had faith in me and that was especially important because during those years her loyalty and confidence in me were put to a severe test. At that time I needed somebody to believe in me. She did, without knowing from one day to the next what we would be doing for a living or where we were going to get the money we needed to survive.

When the latest china-sales position did not work out, I got a call from my brother Judge about a sleep-teaching course built around the delivery system of small records to be played on what was called a Dormaphone. The product used a series of inspirational recordings by Dr. Ben Sweetland and worked by programming the listener as he or she slept. A listening device that was placed under the pillow aided this. During the night at three preset times the machine would come on and tell you that you were capable of doing some wonderful things. This was supposed to carry through to the waking day and create a new you filled with self-confidence and creative energy. I didn't buy into the concept lock, stock, and barrel without checking it out fully myself. But amazingly enough, when I tested the Dormaphone in our own home, I found the system had a very positive impact on the mental attitudes of both the Redhead and me. I really got excited about selling it. I became convinced that the sleep-teaching system using the Dormaphone was a terrific product to represent. Finally! I thought, after a long dry spell, I'd found something that I could believe in because of the results. I was absolutely thrilled to have the opportunity to really get behind it and market it wholeheartedly. Sure enough, my customers immediately started getting results, and I was soon enjoying the same type of success I had enjoyed during those good years I had spent in the waterless cookware business.

My brother had the Dormaphone franchise for seven states, and I myself was assigned Georgia, Alabama, and Florida. Fairly quickly I trained a man and woman from Mobile and another in Pensacola, each of whom opened offices and were doing quite well. Then Dr. Sweetland paid a visit to Atlanta with a stopover in Mobile, and we had a nice visit. He and my brother were in conflict about a certain matter, and, following my instincts for self-preservation, I asked Dr. Sweetland to give me the assurance that if

he severed the Dormaphone relationship with my brother, I would still re-
tain the three states I was working. He indeed made that promise, to my
great relief, but at that precise moment a regional transportation strike took
place. Truckers refused to drive, and I was unable to get the product to sell.
This was truly a devastating blow.

The strike lasted roughly six weeks, but when it ended our business
took off again, and the nicer office I had opened just before the strike
looked as if it had been a wise move. Yes, we were ready for business to
boom, and it did. Things were finally cookin'. My optimism recovered; we
were on a roll. This was going to work. All I had to do was stick with it.
Eventually we would dig ourselves out of the financial hole we were in. And
then one day, without warning, I returned to the office from lunch to find
a telegram under my door from Dr. Sweetland, congratulating me on being
permanently assigned the entire state of Georgia and Florida east of the
Apalachicola River. I doubted congratulations were really in order. Trans-
lated accurately, Dr. Sweetland's message actually was, "We have now taken
away from you the offices in Pensacola and Mobile, and all of the salespeople associated with those offices. Good luck, fella." No explanation, no
advance notice. It knocked the wind right out of my sails. Over night our
income potential with Dormaphone had dropped through the floor.

I was absolutely crushed. After all the hustling, scrambling, fear, and insecurities of the previous few years, just when my career and our home life
were beginning to thrive once again and we were achieving some stability,
Dr. Sweetland had pulled the rug right out from under my feet. For the first
time in my life, that I can remember, I was completely devastated and discouraged. Our franchise offices were still struggling desperately to play
catch-up as a result of the transportation strike when the blow from Dr.
Sweetland came. I couldn't believe it. My trust in him was destroyed. Hurt
and angry, I immediately resigned my position and started looking for something else.

For the first and only time in my life, my spirit was broken. I was so far
down I didn't know which way was up. I could not even bring myself to get
out and seek gainful employment. To this day I wonder what I would have
done had I not been taught responsibility as a child, that when I had made
my commitment to my family, I was responsible for them. So at last I responded to an ad in the paper about selling cancer insurance. It was liter-

ally a door-to-door proposition. I was given absolutely no training. In my despairing frame of mind, I forced myself to make two calls and then realized that I could not bring myself to pursue that particular career either. Needless to say, during this period of time with my confidence down, my career in turmoil, the way I felt about myself was not good.

But, as always, it was onward and, I hoped, upward. What could I do but blindly go on? I had a wife and three little girls depending on me. I had suffered many defeats, but I could not let myself be defeated.

Casting around for a life rope, next I saw an ad in the newspaper for Southern Land Timber and Pulp Company. They were a direct sales company selling stock to build a paper mill in Blakely, Georgia. It was an excellent sales opportunity with very good commissions; the company was well financed and organized, and eventually raised more money than any other company in history with that type of funding arrangement. If memory serves me correctly, their initial goal was to raise $45 million through the sale of stock.

I started selling for Southern Land Timber and Pulp Company like a house afire and was doing well when the stock's issue was fully subscribed and we came to a halt. That put us on hold for the time being until another stock issue was authorized. Management told us there would be a three-week delay in our selling in order to get approval for the new issue from the Securities and Exchange Commission. The three-week delay turned into six and the six into nine. There was a delay and then a delay and then a delay. Finally, the issue was granted, we went back to work big-time with renewed enthusiasm, and again business was booming.

This second issue lasted approximately five months before it, too, was completely subscribed. The company gave the sales force the same song and dance as before—it would take three weeks to get the new issue approved, and then at the end of the three weeks they told us in three more weeks they were going to have a big meeting to plot the strategy and do the training for selling the next issue. The bottom line is they kept us waiting another three months. Of course, in the meantime, our finances were completely depleted. The little headway we had made as a family toward solvency and security vanished. Regardless of how lucrative selling the securities could be, I finally realized that I simply could not continue to live and operate on that kind of unpredictable basis. The emotional costs were too great to bear.

While I was working for Southern Land Timber and Pulp Company, we were living in Stone Mountain, Georgia, and we attended the Indian Creek Baptist Church on a fairly regular basis. We loved the people and the church, and the pastor was outstanding. On several occasions I came close to committing my life to Christ, and incredibly enough, I was almost voted onto the deacon board, which would truly have been a travesty and certainly not in the best interests of the church, Christ, or myself. Ultimately, I was not elected to the board, but I enjoyed my worship experiences. Unfortunately the benefits I derived from them were limited because I did not have that personal relationship with Christ necessary to have faith that God was going to help me with our problems. That was something I thought I would have to deal with on my own. In retrospect, I now know that had I committed my life to Him, then I would have taken an entirely different approach, would have prayerfully sought direction, and I believe things would have been better at that moment. Yet I am convinced that one of the reasons God let me struggle so long was so that when good things did start happening, there would never be any doubt in my mind about Who was in control—and there never has been any doubt. During all those years, as a general rule I was optimistic, upbeat, and confident; I just knew that tomorrow would be better. In short, I had everything except the power, and it was not until I met Christ that His power and His love made the difference in my life.

During the months I spent in the Atlanta/Stone Mountain area, I was about as miserable as I've ever been in my life. Nothing was going right. Everything I touched turned to ashes. This despite the fact that I loved the city (still do!) and loved the people, and the Redhead had more friends there than she had ever had anywhere until that time. The source of the problem, of course, was in me and not in the city. But when you start with a house that's far too small, make a series of devastating mistakes in judgment, get involved in jumping around from job to job, and at last face disappointment because someone you trusted let you down, it all adds up to considerable frustration. I was confused, bewildered about what was happening in my life, and unsure of how to proceed. I felt like a blind man groping around in a dark room. And the more I struggled, the more our situation deteriorated.

To this day, with the benefit of all of these years of perspective, one of the most amazing things to me about that chapter in my life is that during all these difficult times the Redhead and the children were in full support of me, and were loving and loyal in every way. Had I not had that blessing, I would have been truly lost.

As if I didn't already have too many balls in the air, it was also during these crazy mixed-up months that I was still trying to develop a speaking career. Against all odds, I did manage to get a few engagements, one of which was with the U.S. Navy for a week in Pensacola, Florida. But the fee was so minimal that it scarcely paid expenses.

When the Redhead picked me up from the airport on my return from Pensacola and the navy speaking assignment, she had brought Suzan and one of Suzan's little friends with her. Needless to say, full of myself, I was talking a mile a minute, giving them all of the exciting details about the trip, when I overheard Suzan's friend ask, "What does your daddy do?" Suzan responded, "Oh, he sells that positive-thinking stuff." Her friend said, "Positive thinking? What's that?" My daughter answered, "That's what makes you feel real good even when you feel real bad." Interesting from a small child, isn't it? She was at least partially right. She understood the irony of our circumstances even at her tender age. Here I was peddling optimism, personal improvement, yes, even success, when in fact I myself, or at least the way I was living at the time, was a notably poor representative of such things. And yet, as even little Suzan seemed to grasp, and since I was not yet a Christian, it was only going to be through consistent belief in the value of positive thinking that I would be able to persist and eventually overcome our problems. From the mouth of babes such great wisdom . . .

It's a mystery to me, and a source of relief as well, that despite my own personal discouragement, the children did not have a clue that I was struggling to the degree that I was. Even the Redhead did not know the full extent of my unhappiness. I don't know how I was able to hide this from them, but mercifully they did not have the additional burden of carrying my personal pain along with their own discomfort at our living circumstances. I look back on those years of dread and anxiety now as years that gave me a chance to sink to the bottom on that one occasion and get fairly close to it on several others, as far as my spirit was concerned, and still manage to survive.

After a five-year hiatus from the cookware business, I did something I said I would never do, under any circumstance. I got back into the cookware business. We were in a terrible mess financially. If memory serves me correctly, I needed seventeen hundred dollars a month—and please understand this was in 1960—just to pay my debts. This was *before* I paid for the necessities to live: our rent, car expenses, or groceries. I had dug quite a deep and dark hole during my "wandering generality" days. When I got back into the cookware business I was in Atlanta, Georgia. I returned to the business with Vita Craft, a fine china and waterless cookware company, and quickly realized that I needed to get back to Columbia, South Carolina, where I knew so many people and had enjoyed so much success in the business. My many contacts there would give me the best opportunities for selling the products successfully.

We moved back to Columbia, bright-eyed and optimistic with the full intent of making a big smash selling Vita Craft's cookware. I was setting up shop so I could get down to business when a friend of mine, Jerry Walters, a fine man who had worked with me in the WearEver business, came by to show me the cookware he was selling for a different company. He challenged me to a side-by-side comparison of the two brands. So we did, and the reality was, there was no comparison. His Saladmaster cookware was clearly and definitely the superior product. Jerry said to me, knowing exactly which hot buttons to push, "Zig, you have always believed in quality products. How could you, in good conscience, not sell the superior product?" Of course he had me there. In addition, if I joined Saladmaster, I would be an independent franchise owner and so the profit from each sale would be larger. It was yet another "better deal." Should I take it?

The good news is, I had conducted one cookware demonstration in Atlanta, and, after a five-year absence from the business, on that very first demonstration I felt right at home. I knew in my own heart and mind that I had made the right decision to get back into cookware. Therefore, when Jerry Walters approached me with the Saladmaster line, proving to me it was clearly a superior product, I had no hesitation about making the change. This time I was getting back big-time into the business where I had enjoyed such success earlier in my career. I can truly say I was a happy camper, though I still had a long way to go to get out of debt. Now I had legitimate confidence that I could make the climb out of the hole we were in and obtain the success I had enjoyed earlier in the business.

Saladmaster

When I was in the process of deciding if I wanted to sell Saladmaster cookware instead of Vita Craft, I flew to Dallas to meet with Mr. Harry Lemmons, the founder and president of the Saladmaster Corporation. While there I met another young man, Hal Krause, from Kansas City, Missouri, who was part of an organization called Future Homes, which sold heavy-duty, waterless cookware, china, crystal, and other hope chest items primarily to single working women. Hal was also looking at the Saladmaster opportunity. We hit it off immediately and sat up almost all night discussing our plans and our futures. After hours of sorting things out and comparing what the two companies had to offer, Hal decided to stay with his company, and I decided to join Saladmaster.

There was even another reason that I made the change, and that was, namely, because the financial hole I had dug for myself was so big. I needed a big leg up if I was ever going to come out of it. I found it in Saladmaster's CEO. Mr. Harry Lemmons loaned me the money to pay some pressing bills that could not wait for monthly payments and got me out of a very tight spot. I've always been grateful to Mr. Lemmons for that. His confidence and trust in me renewed my career in a significant way. It was just the kind of personal endorsement and encouragement I needed to get my life back on track.

Two things about selling the cookware vividly stand out in my memory. First, I had to airmail, special delivery, all of the credit contracts to Dallas, where the Saladmaster Corporation was located. I always requested, of necessity, that they send me my money via Western Union so I could continue to operate and retrieve the sets of cookware from the warehouse in which they were stored. Western Union was located on Main Street in Columbia, South Carolina. I became quite well known to all the clerks there, because I would frequently double park and run into the office; if the cashier shook her head no, I knew the money had not arrived, and I would scoot back out. If she grinned and nodded her head yes, I would quickly pick up the check, sign it, get the cash, and race out the door.

Never will I forget my "jackpot night." I had a demonstration with my barber and he had gotten together a marvelous group. That night I sold $1,995 worth of heavy-duty waterless cookware—stainless steel—and all of it, except a $195 credit account, was in cash. When I got home late that night, the Redhead was awake and waiting for me. Like two kids we sat on the bed and counted it. We stacked it every different way that $1,800 in cash could be stacked. There were several hundred-dollar bills, several fifty-dollar bills, many twenties, a few tens and fives, and a lot of ones. We counted, recounted, and wept with joy, because this bonanza meant that at least for the next couple of weeks we could live in a more organized manner. I would not have to have money wired to me. I could pick up several sets of cookware from the warehouse to deliver and would not have to go back and forth, getting the money then getting the cookware. It was sheer ecstasy. I'll never forget that experience. I know what it is when you've been struggling for so long a time that you're almost convinced that's the way your life was meant to be, and then all of a sudden you hit that home run. The astonishment at the breakthrough leaves you almost without words. The difference in your life is wonderful. Finally I was reestablishing myself as a stable producer and not a wandering generality. I had been through a nightmare of spinning my wheels and doubting myself and everyone I worked with. I wasn't sure how or why, but my long-sought-after productivity and self-respect were returning. I was overjoyed.

Columbia, South Carolina

So many things seemed to go better when we moved back to Columbia. Our daughters settled easily into their new schools and neighborhood and made lots of new friends in record time. The Redhead was reunited with girlfriends she'd made in years past, and I was back on track with my selling.

We bought a house that was much larger than the two previous homes we'd lived in in Atlanta and felt as if we had breathing room for the first time since we started our family. Our house was on Timberlane Drive and had been built on land reclaimed from a swamp that had been pushed back with fill dirt. There was virtually always water across the street, as well as wildflowers, fly-catcher plants, a few snakes, turtles, and tiny fish along the way. Julie even saw an otter there once. The environment was familiar and evoked fond memories. In some ways it reminded me of the home my family lived in before my father died. The children in the scene now were my own, though.

One day Cindy and her cousin Sarah Kathleen decided to explore the swamp, got off the beaten path, and lost their way. As darkness approached, the Redhead, my brother Judge, sister-in-law Sarah, and I walked up and down the street yelling our lungs out for them. They finally heard us, called back to us, and we were able to go in and retrieve them safely. Yes, that was not quite as frightening as the other previous lost-child incidents, for us anyway, but Cindy still reports being scared when she thinks back on all the snakes and creepy crawlies in the swamp.

Another memory that involves that swamp is when Cindy gave Julie a small, blue, plastic boat for her birthday, about a foot longer than she was tall. Every now and then heavy rains in our part of town would cause the swamp to overflow and flood up to the front steps of our house. One of the neatest photographs I have from that time is of Julie riding in her little birthday boat and rowing all over our front yard.

Angel Driving

Good things kept happening even when I wasn't in control. One night as I drove home to Columbia, South Carolina, from a cookware demonstration fifty-five miles away in Lancaster, South Carolina, I fell asleep at the wheel. Apparently I drove over seven miles in that condition, and made a left-hand turn and drove approximately two more miles before I awoke to the flashing lights of Military Police in Fort Jackson, South Carolina. They had followed me onto the base and told me I had gone through the entry gate at approximately sixty miles an hour. I had driven so deep inside the fort that MPs had to lead me out. When I arrived home, I was still stunned and told the Redhead what had happened. She was both shocked and relieved, and she told me she had been praying especially hard for me that night. I believe an angel was sitting by my side and driving the car. Some skeptics would say I was not really asleep. My friends, I was *sound asleep.* Someone far greater than any of us was looking over me. I'm convinced of it.

It's obvious to me today that God had plans for my life even that long ago. When I think back on that night, I still feel the wonderment of the moment. It's an unforgettable feeling to pass through a dangerous situation unscathed, knowing full well that if the Lord hadn't been with you disaster would have struck.

Another reason I believe that God has sent His angels to take care of me is because when we attended the WearEver Aluminum Convention at the Edgewater Gulf Hotel back in 1951, something happened that indicated I was being prepared for a long life, even at that moment.

The hotel was very old but absolutely beautiful and a choice place to spend time. The convention was well attended, and everyone was feeling busy and productive. On one occasion I needed to run back up to the room for a moment. As I was approaching the elevator, something occurred in the lobby that distracted me for merely a second or two. I continued on my way toward the elevator and a young man in front of me stepped in. At that instant the elevator suddenly bolted upward at an incredible rate of speed. The young man ahead of me, who was quite agile, was able at the last instant to pull his leg inside the elevator or it would have been severed. Had I not been distracted and not slowed down, I also would have been in the process of boarding the elevator. Had I stepped on the elevator at that time, there is no way I could have escaped instant death, because more than just a leg would have been involved in my case. I probably would have been crushed and killed. Even though I wasn't especially devout at that time, I sensed that God was involved in preserving my life. Yes, I believe in angels, and yes, I do believe God has sent them to protect me, specifically on the occasions I've related. Only He knows how many other times coincidences (God's way of staying anonymous) have occurred when my angels were on guard.

Good Advice from the Boss

One of the reasons my career with Saladmaster was successful, and the reason I stopped wasting my life as a "wandering generality," is because Divisional Supervisor Frank Grubbs, a former minister, came by when I joined the team to give me some sound advice. What he said completely turned my career around. He pointed out that free advice is generally worth about what it costs, and I could either accept or reject what he was going to say, but he felt an obligation to tell me a few things.

Frank pointed out that over the preceding five years I had tried virtually every new deal that came along—and the bottom line was I was broke and in debt. He said, "Zig, everybody knows you're a great salesperson. You've proved that beyond any doubt. You don't need to prove it anymore. What you do need to do is look at your future. You need to reestablish your financial base and establish your reputation in this business. So I'm going to encourage you, when people come along with a big deal—and you can count on it, they will be coming along with those big deals for you—simply say to them you've made a commitment and for the next year you're not going to listen to any offer from anyone. You reestablish yourself and rebuild your reputation for productivity. If the good deals are still good deals a year from now, then go with them. If they're not good deals a year from now, they're not good deals now."

To be completely candid, it was difficult for me to listen to what Frank Grubbs had to say at the time. My ego was so inflated that I felt I was much better qualified for his job than he was. Who was he, I asked myself, to be giving advice to me? Even so, I heard the truth in what he was saying and recognized that Frank Grubbs was doing me a good turn, even a favor. And though I did not like him as a person then, long ago we did, in fact, become friends. We still enjoy periodic phone visits and correspond with each other after all these years. Because of Frank Grubbs's sense of responsibility to me and his wish for a better future for my family and me, I did indeed reestablish myself as a reliable and productive employee, and, eventually, I dug myself out of debt. For that I will be forever grateful to Frank.

When I returned to the cookware business in March 1961, I finished as the number five Saladmaster dealer in the nation for the rest of that year. The following year, the first full calendar year I worked for Saladmaster, I was number one out of more than three thousand dealers. I also won my first international trip selling Saladmaster, a trip to London and Paris. I have fond memories of our many surprises and good times while we were there. Some parts of the visit, however, were a little less than comfortable because the Redhead and I weren't familiar with the customs and accommodations, and I also developed the sore throat I mentioned earlier. During our trip we stayed in some of the older English hotels, and the plumbing left something to be desired. On the other hand, since it was the coldest winter in fifty years in Europe, the steam heat, as old as some of the buildings themselves, did an adequate job of keeping us warm.

Never will I forget one dining experience while we were in London at one of those old hotels. The gulf that can separate cultures, even two that share the same language, can produce some silly situations and misunderstandings. We entered the dining room and sat down for lunch and ordered. I told the waitperson that we would like to have our coffee to start the meal, an ordinary and easily satisfied request stateside. The waiter's response was, "Yes, sir! Right away, sir," and he returned with the salad. A little later, when he brought the entrée, I said, "You know, it would really be neat to be able to eat our lunch and drink our coffee at the same time." He said, "Yes, sir! Right away!" When we finished our entrée he brought dessert and I said to him, "The thought just occurred to me that it would be really nice to have coffee to go along with our dessert." He said, "Of course, sir. Right away." When we finished our dessert, he said, "Coffee will now be served in the foyer." He had never said no, but their tradition was such that he wasn't about to bring that coffee until the proper time and place all coincided. It really drove home to me how different and varied people are the world over, and how the benefits of travel broaden and enrich your education.

After London we flew to Paris and thoroughly enjoyed doing the touristy things. We saw the Cathedral of Notre Dame; we went up into the Eiffel Tower. But easily the most beautiful place we saw was the Palace of Versailles, along with its gardens. They were absolutely remarkable, beautiful almost beyond description. We thoroughly enjoyed our time there. However, I will never forget how difficult it was to order meals because, at that time in our history, the French were not exactly enamored of Americans, and I suspect that in many instances they really could speak English but did not wish to do so. The food was delicious, but it was frustrating not to know what we would get when we ordered from the menu. The language barrier was significant. The French love their language as much as we Americans love English.

One night we became so frustrated with our inability to communicate in the restaurant that we decided we would not go to one; instead, I was elected to walk down the street to a café, a store that is similar to an American deli. I had to point out what I wanted, so I decided to do so with enthusiasm. After all, it was their country, their language; neither one of us was at fault. I walked into the café and they greeted me in French; I responded, "Viva la France," with considerable enthusiasm. On hearing me, the guy lit up like a lightbulb and repeated back to me, "Viva la France!"

Then two or three of the patrons there joined in, crying, "Viva la France!" When I pointed to a specific item in the store that I wanted, I would say, "Viva la France!" By the time I left there, every time I would say it, everybody in the café would join in by replying, "Viva la France!" That experience remains a funny and pleasant memory.

The other little thing that wasn't exactly enjoyable but, I'll have to confess, was exciting, was our ride in one of the Paris taxis. I thought New York had some cabdrivers who were reasonably wild, but oh, I was sadly mistaken. We didn't know what wild was until we got to Paris. On two different occasions our cabdriver and another cabdriver exchanged verbal barbs as they leaned out windows. Though I speak no French, I do know a little Greek—his name is Nick. Anyhow, I have no idea what they were saying but I have an idea they were not wishing each other well. As a matter of fact, their faces got red, they shook their fists, and I thought I was about to witness physical violence at that very moment. However, I was assured later by some of my English speaking friends we met in Paris that it was just standard fare; neither of the drivers had any intentions of engaging the other in fisticuffs. As a matter of fact, I was told that one of them was probably scared and the other one was glad of it! But still it was one of those little moments that rates a footnote in the passing parade of life.

My First Big Break as a Speaker

Shortly after I'd gotten involved with Saladmaster, Hal Krause, the young man I'd met when I went to interview for the Saladmaster job, and with whom I sat up all night talking about the opportunity, persuaded the management of his company, Future Homes, to invite me to address the organization. You need to understand what an incredible opportunity this was for me. At that time, about the only organizations inviting speakers to come in and make presentations were the Chambers of Commerce, the Sales and Marketing Executives, and the General Motors Speakers Bureau. The pickings were pretty slim in those days. My presentation to the Future Homes group went exceptionally well. I formed some friendships with the management as well as some of the distributors and salespeople in the organization. At that point, Hal Krause decided to go to law school in Washington, D.C., but the entrepreneurial bug was simply too strong for him to get away from business. He conceived the idea of American Salesmasters, an entity that would be primarily organized to give recognition to professional salespeople in America. He invited the management of Future Homes, Cal Misemer and Doyle Hargedyne, along with a young man named Dick Gardner, who was part of the cookware organization, and myself to join. We each were stockholders in the company.

The first session of American Salesmasters was held in Kansas City. Hal and I sold all of the tickets; however, we were very naive and believed the businesspeople when they told us that they were coming, but they would buy their twenty-five-dollar seminar tickets at the door. We reasoned that they were stable, responsible businesspeople. Therefore, we could depend on them to keep their promises and commitments. To our great surprise, a very high percentage of them simply did not follow through on their promises. In our advance marketing of the seminar, I had made most of the presentations to every organization, it seems, within fifty miles of downtown Kansas City. I used all of my best motivational, inspirational material to convince them they needed to hear our program. We expected about two thousand people to be there for the sales training, and to hear the personal growth and motivational topics presented from the stage. Only six hundred showed up for the big day. We had a lot of empty seats as well as an empty bank account.

I so well remember: I served as both master of ceremonies and as one of the speakers. At that time I was always introduced as H. H. Ziglar; "Zig" didn't attach itself to me until shortly after I started speaking full-time in 1970. (I'm not sure who started calling me Zig, but I do know that I never asked anyone to call me Zig or purposely changed my name.) The other speakers were Dr. Kenneth McFarland, who was recognized several times by the Chamber of Commerce as the "number one speaker in America"; also, Elmer Wheeler of "Don't sell the steak, sell the sizzle" fame; Joe Batten, who had written *Tough-Minded Management*; and Senator Milward L. Simpson from Wyoming.

It was quite a heady experience for me, but to be perfectly honest, I was in over my head. I was on the program because Hal Krause was my friend, and we had started the company together, so it was really one of those grandfather deals, almost nepotism. I only had one talk, and I'd given it to virtually every person there. I was not the best speaker on the program. As a matter of fact, I was the one speaker who should not have been there. But it was a launch date, and the talks I made selling those tickets, as many as eight talks a day, served as an important step toward launching my speaking career. I will always be grateful to Hal Krause because he believed in me as a speaker and communicator and, through many other Salesmasters events, helped give me national exposure, which enhanced my career substantially. As a matter of fact, the support of Hal Krause had the greatest positive impact on my speaking career. Without him and others I name later, I seriously doubt my career would have gotten off the ground.

Another reason the very first American Salesmasters convention in Kansas City stands out so vividly in my mind is I met my best friend, Bernie Lofchick (Brother Bern) there. The convention was over and I was headed to the old Muehlbach Hotel where I was staying. As I walked toward the elevator his booming voice interrupted my thoughts, and I turned when he called, "Zig! Where you goin'?" I explained that I was on my way to dinner, and he said, "Well, if you'll go with me, I'll buy!" That was an offer that enticed me enormously—especially since Bernie was so friendly and outgoing.

You must remember, my performance at this first Salesmasters conference was not up to my standards or, I felt, to the standards of the people with whom I shared the podium. Bernie's friendliness and support were balm to my embarrassment and hurt feelings.

Dinner with Bernie was an incredible experience. In my lifetime I have instantly bonded with only three men—and Bernie Lofchick was the first. Our backgrounds and interests were so similar that it was a natural. We understood each other from the very beginning. Both of us had lost our fathers when we were very young; both of us had worked in butcher shops when we were young; both of us had gotten into direct sales early in our careers. Each of us had such great love and respect for our mothers that it was almost eerie. Almost from the start we referred to each other as Brother Bern and Brother Zig. He was the first person outside my immediate family who believed that I had something to say and would have a real future as a speaker. If Bernie hadn't walked into my life at that moment, I don't know what would have happened. His optimism, enthusiasm, encouragement, and belief in me over all these years has not wavered one iota. To this day, he still listens to my recordings every day and gives me credit (though he was already enormously successful before he met me) for much of his progress. His family and mine are exceptionally close.

Since we've become friends, Bernie and I have shared virtually every experience that men who are brothers can have. I've shared in his grief in the loss of his mother, brother, and sister. We have shared worries about our children and a host of other things. He was the first person outside of my immediate family I called when our daughter Suzan died, and he was there for the funeral to give his words of love and encouragement. The story he told me of his son, David, who was born with cerebral palsy, and how they battled it with the help of doctors, nurses, a personal trainer, and the undying conviction of Bernie and his wife, Elaine, that David was going to have a bright future, is one of the most inspirational stories I've ever heard. It has been a life-changing story to me and to countless other people to whom I have passed it along. I document it carefully in *See You at the Top* and reference it in several other books and on my tape programs. Bernie and I talk on the phone regularly and have occasional visits together; not only is he my dearest friend, but he also serves as an adviser to help us steer our business in the proper direction.

But of all the things Bernie Lofchick has contributed to me and our relationship, the unflagging belief he has in me and the encouragement he has given me to continue my speaking and writing has been of utmost value. Bernie Lofchick believed in my ability as a speaker long before I believed in myself. Everyone needs a Bernie in his or her life. Without one I suspect it is impossible to realize your full potential and to have the heart and stamina to stick with the ambitions of a lifetime.

Here are some excerpts from a letter he wrote to me in 1994. When you read what he's written, you'll know why I love him so.

Dear Brother Zig:
You are a Brother in the truest sense.

I do not always show my appreciation or gratitude for your never-ending support, advice, counsel and the appreciation, encouragement, confidence and love you share with me.

This is my small attempt to do a little catch-up before this year is over.

. . . You have consistently supported Israel throughout the years, and

the Jewish people, and I truly appreciate this. If this is Christianity, and it is, how can we not love and respect Christ, and what he stands for? Why wouldn't one love how you always say grace, so positive, and you know how much we admire and subscribe to the positive aspect of every event.

May your world always be as beautiful as you make it for others.

Thank you for choosing me to be your Brother.

Brother Bern

I really do love that Brother Bern!

After I'd had about three years of selling Saladmaster cookware successfully, the public speaking and training bug bit me pretty seriously. I increased my efforts to promote myself as a speaker, giving freebie presentations at Lions Clubs, Rotaries, and Jaycees—speaking whenever I could. During the time I was promoting myself as a speaker, I continued selling the heavy-duty stainless-steel cookware. Whenever I had an audience at hand, I spoke about how to have a better attitude and how to see things differently. If I were speaking to a sales group, I'd talk about making the appointment, closing the sale, and asking for the referral. My topics changed as the times and audiences changed as the need arose.

Once I again had a little wanderlust and listened to the siren calls of several companies that were trying the new multilevel marketing system. The term *multilevel marketing* comes from the fact that a person can bring a friend, relative, neighbor, or stranger into the business and draw an override, or commission, on what that recruit (known as the "first level") produces. They also will draw an override or commission on the people their first-level recruit brings into the business, and then, in most cases, a smaller commission on the third level, often extending all the way down to seven levels.

In addition, there are no territorial restrictions, as long as the company is registered in other states. This means you can sponsor people miles away from where you live and still draw a commission on what they produce. The products, goods, or services are shipped from one or more sources directly to the consumers. This alone gives considerable benefits to the concept of

Wall of Gratitude

THE PEOPLE WHO HAVE SHAPED MY LIFE

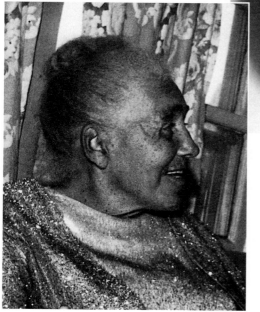

ABOVE LEFT: Lila Wescott Ziglar

ABOVE: Jean Abernathy Ziglar

BELOW LEFT: Sister Jessie

ABOVE RIGHT: Suzan Ziglar Witmeyer

ABOVE: Mrs. Dement Warren

BELOW RIGHT: John R. Anderson

ABOVE LEFT: Walton Haining

ABOVE: Mrs. J. K. Worley

BELOW LEFT: Mrs. J. W. Parker

ABOVE LEFT: Coach Jobie Harris

ABOVE: W. P. (Bill) Cranford

BELOW LEFT: P. C. Merrell

ABOVE RIGHT: Bob Bales

ABOVE: Dr. Norman Vincent Peale

BELOW RIGHT: Dr. Emol Fails

Hal Krause

Harry Lemmons

Frank Grubbs

Bernie Lofchick

ABOVE LEFT: Mary Kay Ash

ABOVE: Mary Crowley

BELOW LEFT: Cavett Robert

Dr. and Mrs. W. A. Criswell

Dr. Kenneth H. Cooper

Fred Smith

multilevel marketing because the territory is unlimited. There is a distinct possibility that those you bring into the business will bring others into the business who will be even more productive, and, hence, make the business more financially rewarding.

The neat thing about the network marketing concept is that you truly hope each person you bring into the business will be more productive and more successful than you. Here's why. The more successful they are, the greater income you will realize from that individual and his/her organization. This is a built-in encouragement to a training system that will make the recruit more productive. My philosophy—*You can have everything in life you want if you will just help enough other people get what they want*—is certainly applicable in multilevel marketing.

One major disadvantage to the program is the fact that there are some who are superb at selling an idea but in many cases they do not follow through with proper training. Today, most multilevel companies, especially those who successfully retail their product and are over five years old, recognize the benefits of follow-through and training, and are doing a considerably better job than when multilevel marketing was a new concept.

At this time I met a gentleman named Charlie Madden, who introduced me to his sixty-five-year-old mother who was doing extremely well as an Amway distributor. I was intrigued by the opportunity she set before me. The Amway Corporation, as I mentioned earlier, was started by two World War II veterans, Jay Van Andel and Rich De Vos. They had been by far the most successful distributors functioning in the Nutrilite System and were familiar with the concept and very excited about it. Amway is short for American Way, and the products they sold were products necessary in every household—shaving cream, toothpaste, cleansing products, dishwashing powders, soaps, and an unlimited number of other items. This made the products quite salable because everybody used them. When a person was brought into the business, he or she automatically became a consumer, and as part of the sponsor's organization, profits were realized almost immediately.

The thing that intrigued me about what was happening to Charlie Madden's mother was the fact that she was a grandmother and at age sixty-five had managed to build an organization of several hundred people in a reasonably short period of time. I joined the team and immediately got busy. I became the first direct distributor in South Carolina, a significant achievement because in a multilevel organization, if you can establish a reputation for success in the beginning, it gives you a better chance for explosive growth, and that's exactly what happened in my case.

Then I spoke at an American Salesmasters convention in San Francisco, where I was introduced to a man named Mark Evans who was in the Holiday Magic organization, another multilevel marketing program. At that time I was primarily money motivated, because money had been in such short supply in my unbelievably up-and-down, roller-coaster career. When Mark reached into his pocket and pulled out a huge roll of hundred-dollar bills, I'll have to acknowledge that I was impressed. I was so impressed, after I got the rest of the story, that I decided to give up my Amway business and go full speed ahead with Holiday Magic. I formed a partnership with a gentleman named Mel Lanius, and we were off to the races! Holiday Magic was a cosmetics organization started by William Penn Patrick, who was an entrepreneur with a touch for organization and inspiration. He persuaded a recognized Hollywood makeup expert to become part of the team, and they created a skin-care product and cosmetics line that was different and good. They also developed an offshoot of the multilevel system that involved a process which enabled those who joined to buy an inventory and participate in a promotional structure that gave an individual considerable opportunity to satisfy not only his need but also his greed.

Initially I did not recognize that the Holiday Magic system was a smooth talker's dream and was wide open to abuse. Strangely enough, it took me nearly two years before I saw this facet of the business through a long series of events.

Most of the recruiting was done through opportunity meetings where a speaker would make the presentation, and those in the business would bring their friends, relatives, and guests to hear the presentation. It was an exciting, very persuasive presentation. As a result, those who made good presentations from the beginning had an excellent opportunity to build an organization quickly, and since motivational speaking was the field I had started participating in, it certainly gave me a great opportunity.

Mel Lanius was a successful insurance general agent and was quite good at persuading people to take the final step. Together we made quite a team!

It was in Holiday Magic that I really hit my stride by virtue of the fact that we were building a very successful organization. After a reasonably short period of time, Holiday Magic, recognizing the need for more training all over the country, initiated a position called instructor general. Both Mel Lanius and I qualified for those jobs. In order to take the next step up the ladder at Holiday Magic, you were required to attend Holiday Magic's one-week school to learn personal growth and ways to sponsor and inspire your troops. This training provided a substantial source of income for me, since I had a reputation for being an excellent trainer, and each distributor could choose where he or she wanted to take the schooling. My training background in the cookware and insurance businesses had well prepared me for this particular assignment. As a result, people came from all over the country to attend my classes, which were always filled. I was able to stay extremely busy. The maximum number of people in each class was twenty, and the enrollment fee was two hundred dollars. In 1966 that four thousand dollars was a substantial sum of money.

Business was good but I was spending most of the money I made on foolish endeavors. During the weeks that I was not teaching the class, I made a number of needless trips to work through other organizations with Holiday Magic to "show off my talents." In addition, we took one trip from Columbia, South Carolina, to Mississippi, flying first class with our children, and that represented a pretty good chunk of change. Tie that to my expenditures on clothes, restaurants, and other things that until then I had never been able to afford, and it all added up to foolish spending.

At that time at Holiday Magic there was a huge contest going on, and the grand prize was a Rolls-Royce. Second prize was a new Lincoln Continental. It was quite a contest. The winner would be the one who brought in the most business through his or her organization, including all of the new people they had sponsored into the business through the multilevel system. My partner and I felt certain that we had won it and were quite surprised and disappointed when the grand prize went to someone else. I demanded—and was granted—an audience with the president of Holiday Magic, along with several members of the staff.

If memory serves me correctly, I challenged them on twenty-two specific instances where I felt fair play was not the order of the day. All I had to do was win one of the twenty-two, and the decision would have been reversed in our favor. For the first time I really understood the power of politics and how important it was to be good friends with the man in charge. It was an area to which I had paid no attention, and I suffered from it. I lost all twenty-two decisions. The thing that was so frustrating was the fact that there were two cases absolutely identical in nature—zero difference between the two—and yet two entirely different and opposing decisions were made.

The problem came about because sometimes in multilevel there was an honest difference of opinion as to exactly who invited a person to a meeting and had that individual join the company. The one who brought him or her into the business was, in virtually every case, the one who invited him or her to the meeting, but on occasion they would meet a smooth talker who was building a big organization. In many cases the guest was a stranger to the one who had invited him or her so they bypassed the person who invited them and signed up under the person whose name they had heard bandied about as building a big organization.

However, in many of the cases the proselytizing was overt, and the one who was building the organization literally stole the new recruit who had been invited by someone else. In some cases they issued a new agreement and put an earlier date on the contract than when it had actually taken place. There were twenty-two of these decisions that were in question. I lost all twenty-two decisions because the winner, who incidentally later served time in prison (having nothing to do with the Holiday Magic business but rather crimes he apparently committed at a later date), was a close friend of the president of the company, and the president was the one who made the final decision.

I don't need to tell you I was upset by that and years later learned from people in accounting at the company that I had been absolutely right, that we really had won the Rolls-Royce. However, at that time, I was making so much money I swallowed the irony and unfairness and continued to work.

Then a new decision was made from on high. Holiday Magic was now going to stop paying us on our reorder business and pay us only on initial orders. The thing that upset me about this was the fact that previously we were to get not only the override on the initial business, but also an override for all of the business the new recruit did on a reorder basis down the road. At that point I thought that was a significant amount. This change in commissions was devastating to the morale of almost everyone in the organization, and it completely removed the incentive to service existing customers.

Holiday Magic was encouraging me to go into New York and Chicago, as well as Los Angeles, to conduct the mass recruiting meetings. When they urged me to go to New York, I was reluctant; I told them that as far as I was concerned, the Indians knew what they were doing when they saw the Dutchmen coming with twenty-four bucks to buy Manhattan Island. The president of the company looked me in the eye and said, "Well, Zig, you can say what you want to, but we're doing over ninety percent of our business in the major metropolitan areas."

Combine my distaste for having to work in New York and Los Angeles with the revelation that management felt it was no big deal not to pay us royalties on the reorders in our business, because over 90 percent of our business was new orders, and you can appreciate why my enthusiasm for the company began to subside. It became obvious to me that the only thing management cared about selling was the initial inventory, which loaded up lots of closets and garages with makeup and skin-care products that would never be distributed or sold to retail customers. When I put those two things together, despite the fact that I had two instructor general classes filled and already sold and stood to make a significant amount of money from them, I resigned my position. Something was not right with the way these people were doing business. I realized that the only people who were making money were those who were very capable as salespeople but who had no interest in building an ongoing, thriving business. They were loading distributors up on inventory and not following through by helping them sell it. The product they sold was good; it simply was not being retailed to customers, which is now required by law. That was quite a lesson for me to learn. I was shocked and disappointed in the company and its management.

Not long after that a man in the Holiday Magic organization with whom I had become friends, Zan Campbell, came to me with an idea that would put us in a unique position. He had found an unusual product used primarily by middle-aged and older women that had to do with controlled coloring of patterns in cloth. The people behind the sales plan had parties with potential customers in homes and were doing quite well. Zan and I were certain that with the right promotion they could do even better. We got excited about it and designed a plan of action for a company called Chem Dry. They bought into the idea, and for a brief period of time we were going great guns. Then, for whatever reason, they decided they wanted to abandon our successful plan and return to their original sales program. They offered me a position as a trainer where I would travel around the country. They paid me a flat salary and no commissions for doing this. After three months of trying to perform under the changed circumstances, I decided that the income and lifestyle limitations were too severe, and once again I jumped ship.

However, my misadventures were mostly short-term, and I always had the growing speaking business and the cookware sales in place as a backup to provide the family a dependable income. To this day I am still amazed that my whole family didn't rebel at my erratic behavior and leave me. My job and its duties changed nearly every day of the week and they didn't know for certain from one minute to the next what I was doing for a living. But they did know that I was honest and was doing the best I could, working hard all the time.

Special Effort

Because I traveled a great deal, I made a special effort to seek out my children individually and spend time with them. I spent our time together in a variety of unusual ways. For example, I was working in the cookware business when Suzan was born, and when she was five years old I was traveling South Carolina, parts of North Carolina, and Tennessee. On several occasions, when she was old enough to go with me, she stayed with the family of the field manager while he and I worked with customers and made sales calls. When we came in late at night, Suzan would be asleep, exhausted from playing with the field manager's children. I would pick her up, still sleeping, and take her to the hotel, put her to bed, and the next morning she was delighted to have breakfast with her daddy. These were special times for just the two of us to be together, and Suzan talked about them for many years afterward. As the other girls grew old enough to travel with me, my situation had changed dramatically, but I still did special things with them, taking them to the store, bringing them little gifts when I would return from a trip, and always telling them how much I loved them. Many times all of my children have commented on the fact that even though I was busy, I always took time to talk with them, play with them, and shower them with affection.

We also took family vacations. The Redhead and I took the children with us on several sun-and-fun vacations to Myrtle Beach, South Carolina. And there were two Saladmaster conventions that stand out in all of our minds for the good times had by all. One was held at the Western Hills Inn in Oklahoma and offered more activities than the children could attend. They went on hayrides, horseback rides, and learned how to water-ski. They participated in contests for prizes like baby dolls and board games, and in spite of the sprained ankle Julie got trying to water-ski and the extremely bad ear infection Suzan came down with, all the girls ranked the Oklahoma trip as one of their favorites.

The second Saladmaster convention we all remember was held at the Fontainebleau Hotel in Miami Beach, Florida. The girls were excited about the hotel's indoor skating rink and, on the other hand, horrified that the hotel pool was filled with salt water that burned their eyes. The best part of that trip was that my brother, Judge, was also there with all of his family, so the girls got to play with their cousins.

The children weren't the only ones I needed to spend quality time with after an extended period of time on the road. The Redhead did a marvelous job of managing the day-to-day affairs of running a household and raising children, but she needed a break by the time I arrived home. I learned to plan ahead for her R&R. I would arrange for a baby-sitter, and I'd take the Redhead to our favorite quiet, romantic restaurant where we could visit and share the details of our week. After a couple hours of quiet conversation and companionship, both of us would return home feeling reconnected and relaxed.

Now I'm not blaming that particular romantic restaurant, but nine and a half years after the birth of our third daughter, Julie, an amazing thing happened. On February 1, 1964, we joyfully welcomed our son, John Thomas, into the family. When we learned of his pending arrival, I was elated, and the Redhead was shocked. She likes to say that God sent Tom—He sent all three of the girls, too—but at least she had asked for them. Sixteen-year-old Suzan was so embarrassed she could hardly show her face at school. Unlike today, when some women plan to have babies in their late thirties and even into their forties, in those days thirty-six-year-old pregnant women were by far the exception to the rule.

Cindy and Julie seemed unaffected by the new baby news, and their lives went on as usual until we learned that the Redhead needed strict bed rest to maintain the pregnancy. At that point Suzan had to take over preparing family meals, and the younger girls pitched in to help with setting the dining table and cleaning up after dinner. Everyone was a little inconvenienced by the new arrangement, and there was an audible sigh of relief when Tom arrived safe and sound. Only little Julie had any aftereffects, an upset tummy related to having her position as the baby of the family usurped. With the passage of some time she recovered nicely and eventually agreed that she liked her little brother.

Spiritual Matters

I regret to say that during the 1960s I was remiss about attending church. I'm glad I lived far enough away from my mama that she didn't know I wasn't going. The speech she would have given me was one I was glad to miss. Besides, I had a good excuse—one you've probably heard before. Since I usually arrived home from a week of selling on Friday evening and I often left again on Sunday evening, I really didn't want to spend my precious free time in church on Sunday morning.

The Redhead had other ideas, though, and occasionally would convince me that we really did need to take our children to church. We'd rush around getting the children dressed, and I'd be so relieved when we finally sat down on a church pew. Then I'd spend the entire hour of the service planning my work schedule for the week. Since I'd grown up going to church every time the doors opened, I figured I knew everything the preacher might say anyway. I was just more interested in how to make a living at that time in my life than I was in what somebody said two thousand years ago. I didn't know what I was missing, and I was so busy trying to do everything under my own power that I wasn't going to find out what I was missing for some years to come.

PART FOUR

A Whole New Life

Dallas, 1968

In 1968, a relatively new company in Dallas, Automotive Performance, offered me a vice presidency and training director's job. They would pay our moving expenses, and I could keep the entire enrollment fee from the training class I would teach for one week each month. They agreed to pay me enough to live on, and I could spend the rest of my time building my speaking career. Because of the unique offer, and the size and central location of Dallas, which would be advantageous for building my speaking career, I agreed to accept their offer, and we moved to Dallas.

A New House

When we first arrived in Dallas, we stayed in a hotel for several weeks—not ideal circumstances, especially with a pregnant dog that needed to be walked every ten minutes, but we were looking for a house to buy. As I was focusing my efforts on my new training responsibilities, the Redhead was appointed the official family house hunter. In truth she looked at only two houses, and the second one was the decision maker. She was excited, loved it, pointed out all of its remarkable features, and explained in detail how we could use each room. She also very delightedly pointed out the large lot where we could build the arrow-shaped (the arrow aiming up, of course!) swimming pool I had dreamed of ever since I was kicked out of the country club pool in Yazoo City, Mississippi, as a small boy.

The Redhead and I had previously agreed on the price that we could afford. She posed the question, "Suppose we found the dream house? How much more could we go?" We discussed it, trying to keep our enthusiasm in check and not overspend. Finally we decided that under dream house principles, we could go as much as twenty thousand dollars more than we originally agreed upon. Now I realize that in the year 2002 that doesn't sound like a lot of money, but in 1968 that would buy two thousand more square feet of quality construction.

We looked the house over with the Redhead as the guide, and she persuasively pointed out where I could have my office, where I could have the bookshelves I would need for all of my books, and where I would have a closet big enough—even as messy as I was—to put all of my clothes and incidentals. She also pointed out where I could build my swimming pool, where I could have the circular drive I'd always wanted.

She gave me ownership of the house on the tour, even pointing out that the bedroom was so large that not only could we have our morning cup of coffee in the quiet of our own room before the children awoke, but we would need a riding vacuum cleaner to keep it properly clean! The Redhead did a number on me. The problem was that in addition to the twenty thousand "extra" dollars (which I already thought was prohibitive), this house cost yet another eighteen thousand. I protested there was no way we could do it. She then said, "Well, don't worry about it, honey. You know, we don't know anything about real estate in Dallas, and I just wanted you to see what was available."

We went back to our hotel and slept on it. The next morning as I was brushing my teeth she walked in and asked how long I thought we would live in Dallas. I garbled through my toothbrush, "A hundred years." She said, "How long did you say?" I repeated myself with the toothbrush removed. "One hundred years." She said, "No, I mean seriously." I said, "I'm serious, sweetheart. I love Dallas, it's convenient for my travels, and I want to stay here the rest of my life." She said, "Do you really think we'll be here at least thirty more years?" I said, "Why, of course! But why do you ask?"

She said, "Well, I was just thinking. Thirty years. How much does that eighteen thousand dollars figure out per year?" Somehow or another she neglected to mention the original price, the twenty thousand we had already talked about, the cost of insurance, taxes, upkeep, and all the other things that go with home ownership. I said, "Well, that would come out to about six hundred a year." She said, "How much is that a month?" I said, "Well, that's fifty dollars a month." She said, "How much is that a day?" At that point I was just casually (but not evidently) irritated and said, "Now come on, sweetheart. You know that figures out to be about a dollar and seventy cents a day. But why do you ask these questions?" Then she said, "Well, honey, could I ask you one more question?"

Somehow I felt as she stood there, all five feet one and a half inches of her, with a twinkle in her eye and a "Look out, honey" grin on her face, that I was in the process of being had, but there was nothing I could do about it. I said, "Why sure." With a smile on her face she said, "Honey, would you give another dollar and seventy cents a day to have a happy wife instead of just a wife?" The Redhead had used my own tools of the trade to convince me. I don't need to tell you . . . we bought the house!

I shouldn't have worried about the extra expense of buying a nicer house. As it developed, I was the missing link to my new company's puzzle and almost immediately they needed me to teach the training program for two weeks out of the month, then three and finally four. Life was good. I was excited and making considerable sums of money.

Dreams Do Come True—But Sometimes There's a Price

Our move to Dallas precipitated more of my childhood dreams coming to fruition than any other event in my life. One of my childhood dreams stemmed from watching movies in which men attending fancy dances and dinner parties wore what they sarcastically called monkey suits. I thought they looked awfully nice, and I imagined the day I would buy and wear my own tuxedo. That day came to pass in Dallas.

The swimming pool I angrily promised myself when I was a humiliated child was built to my specifications in our backyard in Dallas—right where the Redhead had said I could build it when she was selling me on her dream house. By design, I made it a full two feet longer than the old country club pool I had been kicked out of, and, believe me, I thoroughly enjoyed every dip I ever took in it! My swimming pool dream had come true.

I joined my first country club in Dallas as well. And sweet as it was, it was only the beginning of several country club memberships we've enjoyed over time as residents of Dallas. First we joined Brookhaven Country Club, later we moved to Prestonwood Country Club, and then we built a new home on the golf course, which we have occupied since 1985, and became members at Glen Eagles Country Club. Our move to Dallas marked the turning point in my career and our family's fortunes. Yet another dream had come true.

But I must tell you that the move to Dallas came with a price. It was extremely difficult on Cindy and Julie, who were fifteen and thirteen at the time. Friends are nearly everything to young teenagers as they are just learning adult skills and attitudes. Having close peers who know them well and accept them is very important to their sense of security and self-worth. The events leading to our Dallas move happened so quickly that Cindy and Julie had little time to adjust to the idea of moving and leaving their friends and schools. Cindy had had her driver's license in South Carolina for over a year when we moved, and she had to turn it in because sixteen was the minimum age for drivers in Texas. That loss of independence made her like Dallas even less than she had expected to. She cried herself to sleep many a night that first year, and she avoided socializing with the rest of the family. Her depression and anger made her somewhat of a loner, so much so that she even refused to have her picture made for the high school annual. Then she met a boy, and Dallas didn't seem so bad anymore.

Julie didn't sulk about the move as much as Cindy, but she had to leave her old horse behind, and that broke her heart. We bought her another horse, and it helped her get over her grief to a degree, but Julie didn't fit in in Texas like she had in South Carolina. She had difficulty making friends, was ridiculed for her clothes and her accent, and was called a hick. Eventually she was invited to join a group of kids who weren't the best sort and she made bad choices as a result. Through all of this she understandably developed a deep dislike for the social aspect of school and got on the fast track to graduate early. Truth is she just got on the fast track period. She couldn't wait to be grown up and started working when she was fourteen. That way she didn't have to explain why she didn't have many girlfriends—between riding her horse and working she always had somewhere to go and something to do.

Our daughter Suzan had married her high school sweetheart shortly before he was to leave to fight the war in Vietnam, and he had been gone only a few weeks when we moved to Dallas. Suzan decided to move with us. Over the next few months we learned how unhappy she was in the marriage. Because she and her husband lived together only about three weeks before he was sent to basic training and then on to Officers Candidate

School, the judge in Dallas granted her an annulment. So Suzan found herself over a thousand miles from her friends, dealing with a failed marriage, with no new friends in sight.

Have you ever lived in a house with three extremely unhappy girls between the ages of thirteen and nineteen? It's a very good thing that I spent the extra money on the house to have a happy wife! At least four-year-old Tom didn't mind moving to Dallas. But seriously, I would not handle the move the same way today. It was too wrenching for the girls at that time in their lives. I wouldn't have any qualms at all about moving children under the age of thirteen, but if the children were already established in middle, junior, or high school, I'd show a lot more empathy, get some feedback from them, take their feelings into consideration, and carefully talk it over with them. Sometimes the opportunities a move can open up are just too great to pass up, as it was with my opportunity in Dallas. But if I'd been more considerate of the feelings of everyone in the family, the transition to Dallas would have been much smoother for all of us. Isn't hindsight marvelous for honing wisdom?

Possibly the most frightening experience I've ever had happened only a few days after we moved into the Redhead's dream house in Dallas. We were still unpacking boxes when we suddenly realized that Tom was nowhere to be found. Each of us went searching for him in a different direction. One of our daughters checked the Tennis Club pool behind our house; another started looking in the alley. I went running down the street, knocking on doors, asking neighbors if they had seen our little four-year-old boy. They had not. Then I got into my car and circled the block, looking for him. He was not in sight.

We called the police, and they sent a patrol car out immediately. Then the neighborhood security patrol got in on the action. To add to our distress and anxiety, the security guard exercised extraordinarily poor judgment and bad taste when he tried to sell me his services while I was desperately looking for my little boy. Well, the bottom line is that Suzan's friend Margaret Hill, who was visiting from South Carolina to help with the move, ran up and down the alley calling Tom's name, and Tom heard her, calling out that he was there, at another house nearby. What had happened was very simple: A little girl invited Tom into her house, and the elderly baby-sitter asked no questions about where he came from or whether or not his mother knew where he was, she simply welcomed him to the home to play. When I finally got my arms around my son, I wept in a way that only a similarly terrified, but totally relieved, parent can appreciate and understand.

Regardless of our joy and relief at finding little Tom, I don't recommend that particular method to meet your new neighbors for the first time. The method of introduction stuck with us like an ID badge. We were known as "the people who lost their little boy" for quite some time after that.

All That Shines Is Not . . .

We were living in an unaccustomed state of financial ease, and life was good. Our family life had achieved a degree of security and predictability we had not known before. And we were wise enough, had been through enough, to appreciate all the good things that had come to pass for us. However, life never stands still, and after just two years things changed. The product my company sold was a unit to be installed in a car's engine to increase gasoline mileage, reduce wear and tear on the engine, and enable the car to perform better. It was a water-spray system that worked beautifully when it was properly installed and serviced. The problem was that it was difficult to find enough service stations with employees who had the skill and know-how to do the job properly to keep up with the business we were bringing in. As a result, we had some customer service problems and bottlenecks in the business. Then some internal changes took place in the company. Management felt they needed a different marketing program for the health of the business, so they got involved in a number of new products that didn't require the technical expertise to install. But the new products didn't catch on, and the company began to lose ground. The sad result for all of us was the company ended in bankruptcy.

With the demise of Automotive Performance, our financial status changed suddenly and drastically. Shocked and dismayed, we ended up struggling to keep our dream home and our newfound financial peace. We hadn't held out enough tax money for the IRS, and when the bottom fell out of Automotive Performance, we were unable to pay our income taxes. The embarrassment and humiliation our family felt when the IRS pasted a notice on our front door announcing a tax lien on our home is indescribable. We felt foolish and irresponsible for what had happened, panicky over our lack of resources to turn the situation around, and helpless in the face of our own mistakes combined with bad luck. To have worked so hard and come so far only to lose it all overnight was almost too much. We are eternally grateful to a generous and compassionate friend who stepped in to help us out. Because of him, we were able to hold on to the house until our finances improved.

Life as a Full-Time Speaker

With the loss of the Automotive Performance income, in early 1970 I was thrust prematurely into the speaking career I had wanted for so long, but for which I'd had very little time to prepare and build a clientele. I'd had the good fortune (or was it another one of those coincidences?) to have met some Mary Kay Cosmetics directors, key people in the direct marketing organization. They asked me to come to speak to one of their Monday-morning meetings in the corporate headquarters. I gladly accepted the invitation, hoping something would come from it because I was not offered, nor did I expect, any kind of fee for the engagement.

Little did I realize as I was speaking that around the corner, comfortably seated in a chair, was Mary Kay Ash herself, listening to what I had to say. Apparently, she liked it, because she sent for me when I finished speaking and said she wanted to visit with me. We had quite a delightful interchange and discovered we had many things in common. As a result of our visit, she invited me—and encouraged her directors around the country to invite me—to come in and do sales training and motivational seminars for them.

During the following two years, this was my principal source of income. I did numerous six-hour seminars for Mary Kay Cosmetics directors, most of the seminars spread out over two days, with meetings generally held in the evenings. I told the Mary Kay reps how to get motivated and how to stay motivated. I taught them recruiting procedures and sales techniques, like how to set their sales appointments and how to close their sales. I shared with them goal-setting and goal-reaching procedures as well as personal-growth processes for a balanced life. I recorded the Mary Kay sessions and made a series of customized tapes exclusively for Mary Kay Cosmetics. The tapes were a huge hit, primarily because Mary Kay recorded the introduction for me. She also said some nice things about my work that led the consultants and directors to buy considerable numbers of the tapes, which obviously produced results because they kept buying them. Mary Kay also invited me to speak to two or three of her national conventions. Had it not been for that arrangement with her, my speaking career would probably have been derailed in the beginning for lack of support. The impact Mary Kay Ash had on me and my career is still evident to this day, both to me and those who know me well.

Faith Made the Difference

Making headway in the speaking business wasn't easy. It was truly tough sledding for the next couple of years. Although I was beginning to make progress, it was a very slow process. In 1972 I had been doing some training with a small direct-sales company. Our national convention was in Nashville, Tennessee. During the sessions I'd had with this small company, people kept talking about how remarkable Ann Anderson, their top producer, was. When I finally met Ann herself, she immediately started talking about Sister Jessie, an elderly black lady who had taught her many things and to whose wisdom she felt she owed most of her success. On Sunday afternoon of the convention we had some free time, so the Redhead and I drove to Tullahoma, Tennessee, with Ann. We met and visited with Sister Jessie, who said a few things that impressed me and stuck with me. Then we went back to Nashville, finished the convention, and returned to Dallas. When I got home, the things Sister Jessie had said were still on my mind. I called Ann and asked her to bring Sister Jessie to our home for the Fourth of July weekend to spend some time with us. I sent them tickets, and they came to Dallas.

I Gave My Life to Christ

That weekend Sister Jessie walked into our home talking about Jesus Christ, and for nearly three days that is all she talked about. She spoke of His love and mercy for all of mankind as the Son of God and of the great sacrifice He made on the cross to save us from sin and death. To be brief, she made a very convincing and persuasive case for me to give my life to

Him. I listened intently as her words washed over me and was profoundly moved. The truth of what she said found fertile soil in my heart and turned my life around. There was grace in our home that weekend. God was present and leading us. We went to bed reasonably late that Saturday night, and I had still not made my commitment to accept Christ as my personal Lord and Savior, but what Sister Jessie said was weighing heavily on my mind. The next morning when I awakened, I realized with awe and surprise that I was actually now a different person. There were no bells or whistles, no flashes of light or crashing of thunder. But there was a new peace about me, and I knew that I would never be the same old Zig Ziglar again.

That beautiful, clear, July 4 night as I lay out in my swimming pool, I looked up into the heavens and, praising God more than praying, said, "Lord, I know you put this big, beautiful universe together, and I know that one day you will take it all down." At that precise instant I saw a star fall and leave a small sparkling trail in the night sky. God impressed in my own mind that he was saying, in so many words, "That's right, boy, and don't you ever forget it!" And I never have. On July 4, 1972, Christ asked me to come to Him, and I did. And when I made the commitment to Christ I became a new and better person. I left the old me and my former way of approaching life behind. I wanted to be like Christ, to follow Christ, and introduce others to Him just as dear Sister Jessie did for me that weekend.

A year later, again on the night of July 4, my son and I were sitting out by the pool; suddenly I looked up and said, "Look, son, there goes another falling star." And, as only a nine-year-old could, he said, "No, Dad, it was a Roman candle." I protested and said, "No, son, it was a falling star. I saw it!" He said, "Dad, I was looking, too, and I'm telling you it was a Roman candle." I said, "Okay, boy, your eyes are much younger than mine, and I'll take your word for it that it was a Roman candle, but it certainly looked like a falling star to me."

For the next few seconds there was silence. Then Tom said to me, "You know, Dad, a year ago, when you were in the pool looking up at the sky and you saw that falling star, that star had probably been moving for many, many years. But God knew you would have a need at that very moment, and He sent you that star so you would know that He was in control."

Now, as I frequently have said in my talks, I have a smart son, but he's not that smart! I believe that God impressed upon him to say exactly what he said so that I could once again be reminded that He truly is in control of all things. My heart is awed at the distance God goes to show me how intimate and personal my relationship with Him truly is. God is into details, and I believe He allowed me to struggle for so many years in my business, and in my finances, so that I would know without a doubt that He is the one who is responsible for any and all of the success I have had or ever will have.

I Wanted to Glorify Him by Not Drinking

Interestingly, one of the first things I realized as a new Christian was that drinking doesn't glorify God. The Bible says that our bodies are temples for the Holy Spirit, and I knew putting alcohol in the temple wasn't pleasing to God. I determined that I would stop drinking for that reason. My drinking history was fairly short and sporadic, but as I recalled my brushes with alcohol in the past I knew my decision was the right one.

For example, at one point in my life I was traveling to work in Atlanta, then going back to Columbia, South Carolina, on a regular basis. As I drove home one Friday night I suddenly realized every night that week I had been in a bar, taken one drink, and then left. But the truth is, until then I had never had anything to drink even two nights in a row. My mind wandered back to a childhood memory that I sincerely believe helped influence my decision to stop drinking while I was ahead.

The first home we lived in when we moved to Yazoo City was on Grand Avenue, and the next-door neighbor moved his grocery store from a location three blocks away and built it between our house and his. This store became a gathering place for friends of the owners, who consumed large quantities of beer. One of the regular visitors was an elderly dentist who was an alcoholic. Many times toward the latter part of the evening, which in those days was around nine o'clock, when our kerosene lamps and single lightbulb did not provide enough light for us to do much other than go to bed, we would be sitting on our front steps when this dentist would emerge from the building. Then he would be sick on the side of the store next to our house. The heaving and obvious pain and distress brought on by an alcohol-induced upset stomach were not pretty to either see or hear. In retrospect, I believe I instinctively decided then that I would never become an alcoholic, and it remained in the back of my mind through the years. This was one occasion when a horrible example worked to my benefit.

I had also seen the devastating impact alcohol could have on lives when my older sister married an alcoholic who abused her. Another red flag went up for me when I realized that I enjoyed both the feeling alcohol gave me and the way it tasted. It would be all too easy for me to fall into the habit of taking drinks to relax and socialize, which then put me in danger of abusing alcohol. I decided it was not for me and chose to have nothing more to drink. For several months I maintained that commitment.

Then, as I started my career of speaking and flying around the country, I accumulated quite a number of little miniature, cocktail-size bottles of liquor from my plane trips. Every time I boarded an airplane, a flight attendant offered me a drink or two of those little bottles. I still maintained control, and drank very, very little, no more than three or four times a month. Yet when I became a Christian I realized that if I continued to drink on occasion, I would be taking a risk of not being a good witness for my faith. The morning after I had sorted all of this out, I dumped all of my booze down the drain and said I would never again take a drink.

I maintained that position until November 26 of that year, when the Redhead and I celebrated our anniversary at her hairdresser's newly opened German restaurant. To honor us, he brought us each a glass of wine. I remembered my commitment, knew I should not drink it, but I did not know how to graciously refuse the wine without offending my host. I drank the glass of wine.

Incredible, isn't it? I was willing to abandon my commitment to my Lord because I was unwilling to offend my host. Bad choice.

When I got home that evening after dinner, my seven-year-old son (and he had never asked me this before) looked at me and asked, "Dad, did you have anything to drink tonight?" I said, "Yes, son, I did." That seven-year-old boy looked me in the eye, dropped his head, and said, "Dad, I can't begin to tell you how disappointed I am in you." Where in his limited experience did this rebuke come from? Something or Someone had to have inspired him. And I've got to tell you, it really got to me. I said to Tom, "Well, son, if you will forgive me tonight, I can promise you never again as long as I live will I knowingly take a drink of alcohol." That was November 26, 1972, and from that day until this I have maintained that vow.

I've had only one slipup, but purely out of ignorance of what I had been offered. Once on a plane the attendant handed me what I thought was orange juice. I took one sip, realized there was something besides orange juice in it, and returned the drink. From that day until this I've not had a sip of alcohol. No, I don't believe a drink of alcohol is going to kill me, but I've seen so many instances where people started drinking casually and it eventually became a serious problem for them and everyone around them. Actually, according to the man who is, in my opinion, the top authority on drugs in this country, Dr. Forest Tennant, one out of nine social drinkers will end up with a serious drinking problem. I'm not that kind of gambler. I've kept my commitment.

A Confirming Coincidence

As I am generally inclined to do, when I make a commitment it is all out, no holds barred. There was no exception when I made my commitment to Christ on July 4, 1972.

Soon after I committed my life to Christ we joined First Baptist Church in Dallas, Texas, and learned that the Bible says we should give 10 percent of our income to our church. Despite the fact that our finances were limited, we immediately started doing exactly that. However, right after my commitment to Christ, in a bizarre kind of timing, we were suddenly hit with a whopping six-hundred-dollar-a-week bill that had to be paid each Monday morning without fail. Money was already tight for us, and this unexpected burden put us once again in a struggle for survival. Incredibly, still another unexpected development, with perfect timing, saved the day. I got a letter from General Mills, for whom I had already spoken three or four times, asking to book me for a long series of engagements. For their accounting purposes they wanted to get it in that year's budget and asked if I would be willing to accept all of the money in advance.

Well, because I'm such a kind and considerate fellow, I agreed to their terms. It truly was a miracle, because not once before or since has anything like that happened. Out of the blue the problem was solved. Our needs were met and I started moving full speed ahead.

Not long after this crisis, American Salesmasters really took off, and I was invited to speak all over the country with them. This, too, was a huge boost in my career. Then, as Salesmasters was shifting gears, the Success

Unlimited Positive Mental Attitude Rallies, created by Mr. W. Clement Stone of insurance fame, were getting started, and they invited me to participate by speaking and giving presentations. This, too, represented a huge boost to my career, because I was privileged to share the platform with Paul Harvey, Dr. Norman Vincent Peale, Ira Hayes, Cavett Robert, Heartsell Wilson, Don Hutson, memory expert Billy Burden, Bill Gove, and other outstanding speakers. Some stardust rubbed off on me from my association with these outstanding people. Demand for my speaking services continued to grow.

It wasn't lost on me that when I got my life in line with what God wanted, started living for Him and making Him my first priority, everything else seemed to fall into place. I believe that one of the reasons God let me struggle for forty-five years with only patches of success and accomplishments was so that my ego would not take control of my behavior. I also believe that when good things did start to happen in my life, God wanted to be sure I knew Who was responsible and that I would never be confused about their source. And truthfully, I never have been confused. Today, when I teach my advanced course in math to my Sunday school class—namely that "You plus God equals enough"—I know that I am primarily talking to me.

A Church Home

I learned early in my Christian walk that belonging to a church and associating with other believers is a biblical principle. I'm so glad that I found First Baptist Church in downtown Dallas. Dr. and Mrs. W. A. Criswell taught me the importance of daily Bible study and the significance of clearly understanding that the Bible is the inerrant Word of God. When I started teaching—not preaching—biblical principles in my public and corporate seminars, every facet of my life exploded. First, my relationship with the Lord dramatically improved my relationship with my entire family. Our family relationships were always good. To the best of my ability, humanly speaking, I loved my wife and children as much as a man can love his family. But particularly in the case of my wife, I did not know what real love was until I learned to love her through Him. Patient, kind, forbearing, enduring. What an enrichment that has been to me and to our family.

Many people have asked me what difference my commitment to Christ made in our marriage and what the Redhead thought about it. She was obviously elated with my new life in Christ and said she felt she had gotten a brand-new husband. Today, I laughingly tell people that she loved her first husband, but she's really crazy about the new one!

She said what she said because prior to my daily walk with Jesus I was considerably less sensitive to her needs and less appreciative of the wise input that she has had in my life for these last thirty years. While I was still looking out for number one, me, that is, I made arbitrary decisions about moving from one job to another, from one city to another; about buying new cars and so forth. I had been raised in the "man as the head of the house" era and had completely misinterpreted what it meant to have the Redhead as an equal partner and to appreciate the fact that her input as a woman could mean better family decisions, better actions, better relationships in every way, and even more fulfilling work. Today, I am far more sensitive to her needs and input and the value of her counsel. This new improved arrangement still recognizes my strengths but includes utilizing hers.

From a business perspective, had I been a conniving individual and sought a lifetime partner who would be a social and business asset, there is no way I could have done as well as I have done in choosing the Redhead. Her people skills are awesome; her public acceptance is unbelievable. We've been privileged to dine with presidents and speak to the homeless. She has been with me at the Harvard Forum, the Christian Coalition, and in corporate America. We have been together in schools, churches, and every imaginable situation all over the world, and in every case, no exception, she has always been an asset. Of course, the reason I like to travel with her and be with her everywhere is because of our love and the fact that she is so much fun. But the major difference in our relationship since I became a Christian has been my appreciation of her as a person and of her role as my wife. I only wish I had started listening to and appreciating her earlier!

Another way being a Christian has had a positive effect on my marriage seems archaic to some, but I promise you it shows my wife the great degree of respect I have for her and for our marriage. Not long after that eventful July 4 weekend when I committed my life to Christ, I heard a pastor ask God to build a wall of fire around a young girl in our church who had been kidnapped. He asked God to bring her safely home as she was before she was kidnapped, and God did exactly that. A wall of fire is a powerful image, and I was impressed that I should ask God to build a wall of fire around me, not only to protect me from sin but also to protect me from temptation. I promised Him that if He would do that so that I would not have to use my energy to fight temptation, I would use that energy to serve Him. God heard my request and answered my prayer. I can honestly say that I have not been seriously tempted sexually, financially, or morally from that day until this.

Along with that prayer, I asked God to give me eyes only for my wife. To be completely honest, I borrowed a page from Billy Graham's life and follow the same procedures he does on this subject; that is, I never allow myself to be in a situation that could be misconstrued. I avoid any possibility of misunderstanding or giving the wrong impression by scrupulously watching who I am with, and how and when.

Several years ago during an interview for a magazine article I mentioned that I was especially careful to avoid situations in which my integrity might be compromised and referred to the fact that I did not take my secretary to lunch. The interviewer appeared shocked at my revelation and asked that I elaborate. I said, "Well, first of all, she's a very bright lady. She wouldn't go. Second, if I took her once I might enjoy it so much that I'd take her again. That's the way so many men and women lose their marriages and families, as well as their self-respect. Number three, she and I have nothing to talk about that we cannot more effectively discuss in my office or hers with the doors wide open. Number four, I don't want the Redhead going out to lunch with one of her male acquaintances. And I don't believe in double standards."

This has far more to do with ordinary weaknesses in human nature than lack of love and/or trust in a relationship. Something like 50 percent of all divorces take place because the man or woman met someone in the marketplace and a seemingly harmless relationship developed into something it was never intended to be. Before they knew it, a casual friendship had turned into a romance. Sixty percent of these relationships occurred between people who worked in close proximity with each other, validating the old adage "Familiarity breeds attempt." In addition to all of that, at this point in our lives, I would not do anything that would cause the Redhead one minute's concern. Other policies I follow are insisting that a lone woman not pick me up at the airport or hotel, not sitting with a lone female for a cup of coffee in a private setting, and not having a meal with one woman. When I schedule speaking or book tours, I request either a male escort or two females. Please don't misunderstand. At age seventy-five there are not a whole bunch of lecherous women waiting to pounce on me, but the Bible says that we are to avoid even the appearance of evil.

Speaking of temptation, one of the ways my son benefited by my becoming a Christian was that I made it a point to have "the talk" with him. When Tom was sixteen and headed for his third date with the same young lady, I knew it was time for us to have an extended father-son talk (we had already had my little talk). Evidence was solid that our son was growing up. (If you see evidence of this when your child is eleven—talk to him or her then. It's never too early, but it's often too late.) When the phone rang at our house, it took only two steps—and those in rapid succession—for him to reach it. When he shaved, he made absolutely certain he got all three of the hairs on his face. Yes, he was growing up, and he was interested in girls. So off for an extended weekend in South Texas we went.

We played golf both days, but in between rounds we had meals late into the evening and did a lot of talking. First I explained to my son that he and his girlfriend were at the height of their sexual excitement at that moment in their lives, and so it was imperative that he understand the true meaning and purpose of the gift God has given man. I told him that the Bible is very clear that any sex outside of husband and wife in marriage is a sin. That's really all I had to say about what God had to say. The rest of our conversation centered on the commonsense benefits of abstinence.

I told Tom that if he and his girlfriend got involved sexually, he would never really get to know her. It might sound strange, but young people courting who get involved in sex spend every waking moment planning how they can get off by themselves again. They become deceivers extraordinaire. They mislead their parents by fabricating excuses of why and where they want to go, and the important element of trust is betrayed. "On the other hand," I told Tom, "if you abstain at this point of the greatest temptation, later when you are separated by travel or when your wife is ill, in the last stages of pregnancy, or soon after the baby is born, you will be able to turn down outside temptations when they occur."

I mentioned the possibility of pregnancy resulting from premarital sex and that regardless of the outcome, heartbreak is involved. We believe that abortion is out of the question. The Bible is crystal clear on this issue. Exodus 21:22–23 states that if two men are fighting and accidentally hit a pregnant woman, causing the unborn child to die, the guilty party pays for it with his life.

"If a baby results from premarital sexual relations," I told Tom, "you are faced with two very difficult choices: Give the baby up for adoption or raise the baby yourself. Either way, your life will be changed forever. First, if you give the baby up, on that birth date for the rest of your life you will wonder where and how your son or daughter is. If you elect to raise the baby, the responsibility will put you in an uncomfortable social and financial position. It is a situation that can be resolved successfully, but it imposes some extremely difficult limitations for you if you want a college education."

I also pointed out that, even more important, if they determined to abstain when they were at the height of their sexual passions and they did not eventually marry each other, the young lady would always be able to say, "Tom Ziglar was my first boyfriend. He treated me with respect and showed geniune concern for me." In short, I said, "Son, you can walk away with a clear conscience."

Research is conclusive from numerous studies that young men and women who marry without having indulged in premarital sex have by far the best and happiest sexual relationships after marriage. Research has also determined that odds are twice as great that couples who live together before marriage will end up divorced. I did my best to convince Tom that the benefits of abstinence are absolutely overwhelming.

It was quite a weekend for us. We spent several hours discussing the subject of intimacy, and the last thing Tom said to me as we got ready to leave the hotel to catch our flight back to Dallas was, "Dad, every November twenty-sixth when I watch you and Mom head off to celebrate your wedding anniversary, it makes me want even more the kind of love you and Mom have. That's what I want for my marriage." I believe that special trip with the special objective of helping my son live God's way is one of the reasons my son and I have always enjoyed such an open and very close relationship.

Since the day I accepted Christ as my personal savior, my career has been greatly strengthened. I'm grateful to be able to say that for over thirty years I've never had to solicit another speaking engagement. The phone has rung, and we've simply filled requests. God's grace and goodness have been the reasons for my bookings, and He showed me that very clearly on one occasion I'll never forget.

I was giving a talk in Los Angeles to a very large, highly motivated, very enthusiastic audience. It was one of those occasions when I opened with a bang, the audience responded with considerable enthusiasm, and I thought to myself, Man alive, I've got a live crowd today and I'm really on! In a few minutes I dropped another little gem and the audience again responded wildly; I congratulated myself to myself and said, "Yeah, Zig, you've got 'em now!"

And then a rather fascinating, unexpected thing happened. My tongue got tangled up and wouldn't work properly. As a Christian, I believe God interceded in the situation to teach me a lesson about who was really in charge there. To my embarrassment and dismay, I caught myself saying things backward, or in very peculiar ways. One time I intended to say, "I was going to . . ." and it came out, "I to going was . . ." When that happened the second time, I realized what was going on and I prayed silently. "Lord, I got the message. If you will forgive me and straighten me out, I won't be confused again as to Who is in control."

And that's exactly what happened. He answered my prayer. It was a powerful, very simple, and beautiful reminder of where my gifts and abilities came from and who controlled my use of them. Chances are good there weren't three people in the audience who realized what had happened, but I knew, and I made a permanent promise to myself that never again would I labor under the illusion that I was running things. God does have a way of humbling us when we are tuned in to Him.

As a matter of fact, God can even use us when it seems we're not tuned in to anything, let alone Him. He certainly used my mama that way. My sister Turah took Mama into her home and cared for her until the day she died. During the last three years of my mother's life she was bedridden and her mind was in a state of confusion. I often wondered why the Lord was allowing my mama to linger so long when she'd made it abundantly clear that she was ready and wanted to go home to heaven. Time told the story. The Lord kept Mama here until each and every one of her children was His.

Once when Mama appeared to be on her deathbed Turah called the family together. We rushed to Yazoo City, hoping to arrive at the hospital in time to see her before she died. We arrived to find Mama sitting up in bed telling everyone, "The next time that man in white comes for me, you let me go!" Turah told me later that Mama's heart had stopped, and the doctor had done CPR to bring her back. We can only assume that Mama had a glimpse of what awaited her on the other side and that made having to be earthbound even less desirable to her. The scene was a dramatic testimony to the reality behind her faith. On that occasion I had an opportunity to witness about Christ to another brother, and he accepted Jesus as the Lord of his life.

Turah called everyone once again on February 27, 1975, but this time it was to say that Mama had died peacefully in her sleep. We went home to celebrate her eighty-seven years of godly living and the fact that all of us would one day be with her again in heaven. There isn't anything finer than attending the funeral of someone who has lived life well. I praise God and thank Him for my wonderful mother.

Not only did she raise us and teach us to love God, she also provided the bridge we needed as adults to draw closer as a family. After all those years of seeing one another only during our annual Christmas visits, it was wonderful to come back together and see our extended family during Mother's final illness. Life and our own immediate family responsibilities had made family visits too infrequent. Our coming together for Mama's home going started large annual Ziglar family reunions that continue to this day.

In retrospect there are a few things I wish Mama had lived long enough to see. First, I have been incredibly blessed to have received three different honorary doctorate degrees. In 1985 I received the honorary doctor of law from the Chriswell Center for Biblical Studies. In 1995 I received the honorary doctor of humanities from the Oklahoma Christian University of Science and Arts. And in December 1998 I received the honorary doctor of letters degree for Contribution of Literature on Human Potential from Southern Nazarene University. All three of these doctorate degrees speak volumes about the changes that occurred in my life after I became a Christian on July 4, 1972. What I am most thrilled about is that I've lived my Christian life in such a way that three different church denominations were comfortable in honoring me with those degrees. The second thing that would have made my mother proud is that I was elected to serve as the vice president of the Southern Baptist Convention (SBC). Those of you who have any interest at all in the religious community know that for a number of years we Southern Baptists have been doing some internal squabbling, which has been on many occasions "politely vicious." As a history student I am a firm believer in the authenticity of the Bible, and I believe the entire Bible is the inspired Word of God. I have received incredible personal, family, and professional benefits from the commonsense and everyday wisdom I learned from the Bible, so I was very concerned about what was going on in the Southern Baptist Convention.

Historically, Christians founded twenty-five of the first twenty-seven universities in America for the express purpose of teaching the Bible and living according to its code and principles. Over a period of time, many of our Baptist colleges and seminaries had gradually become more critical of the authenticity of the biblical texts, until most of them were teaching only certain portions of the Bible as truth. As my pastor at the time, Dr. W. A. Criswell, said, "These people believe that part of the Bible is inspired and part of the Bible is uninspired, and they have been inspired to pick out the uninspired."

One by one, many of our Baptist colleges and seminaries were turning further and further from the truth of the Bible, and the Word of God was being debated and not taught. The change was creating disruption and turmoil in the denomination. As a result of their concerns, Dr. Paige Patterson and Judge Paul Pressler organized an effort to steer the convention back to the teaching of the Bible as God's infallible and inerrant Word.

I had been actively teaching a large Sunday school class at First Baptist Church in Dallas when I was asked to run for vice president of the Southern Baptist Convention in 1984 and was elected. In that capacity I was privileged to read countless letters written by parents of students attending our Baptist institutions who had gone to college with great faith and left college with little or no faith. It was a very disturbing state of affairs. For that reason I became heavily involved in the battle. The war lasted nearly twenty years before the ship was righted, but the results have been outstanding since the SBC has restored their seminaries to their original purpose. I am so honored to have been a part of that effort.

The Cavett Factor

It was around the time I became a Christian in 1972 that Cavett Robert finally persuaded me that I had a message that I should put in writing. His influence on my career was substantial. When I came to know Cavett Robert, I met a truly unique man. He was the driving force behind the foundation of the National Speakers Association and was instrumental in helping more speakers get a start in the profession than anyone I know. After Cavett heard me speak a couple of times, he started encouraging me to write my own book. He said, "Zig, you've got lots to say. People need to read it, and I believe it will boost your career quite a bit."

After much thought and consideration, I started the process of writing my first book. I undertook to do the whole thing myself without the participation of a commercial publisher. To finance the publication I presold it to hundreds of Mary Kay ladies, not realizing at the time that it wasn't exactly kosher, according to the law, to do so. In return for their faith in me, my commitment to them was to have the books at the next Mary Kay Convention in Dallas, where I would personally deliver them. My prepublication price was just five dollars. As a first-time author/publisher I ran into some unexpected surprises and delays. Writing a book was more involved than I'd thought it would be. I had to hustle to make my deadline and keep my promise to the Mary Kay ladies. Just when the pressure was really on, my gallbladder ruptured.

For four days I experienced excruciating pain, but the doctors could not come up with the source or a diagnosis. Since innumerable tests and X rays did not reveal the problem, the doctors ordered exploratory surgery. They discovered the ruptured gallbladder but couldn't remove it immediately because an abscess had formed under my liver. In their opinion I was in no condition to handle the full operation, which was radically different from what it is today, so they filled me with antibiotics, sewed me up, and said, "We'll see you later."

Three weeks later I was in better shape and back in the hospital. The operation went well. Oddly, in the long run, though I had originally thought the episode would spell disaster for my publication deadline, the reverse happened. Before my gallbladder slowed me down, while I was writing the book, I was furiously trying to keep up with the rest of my busy schedule at the same time. I was overcommitted, overextended, and stretched to the limit. Had I not had the ruptured gallbladder, I would not have been forced to stay home to finish the book. In that event, I would not have had the books to deliver at the Mary Kay Convention. As it was, the printer had to ship the books by bus from their warehouse in East Tennessee in order to get them to me in time for the convention. I can only guess, with a little horror thrown in, what would have happened to my Mary Kay business had I not delivered those books as promised. I fear it would not have been good. At any rate, it happened. Everything came together in the end. I delivered the books and everybody lived happily—if not ever after, at least for the next few months.

The original title of the book was *Biscuits, Fleas and Pump Handles,* at the insistence of the Redhead and Dan Bellus, vice president of our company at that time. Deep down I knew the choice of title was a marketing mistake, but that was the title of the speech I had been making for several years, and because of its uniqueness we were hopeful—even optimistic— that it would sell. After the first printing, even though we were successful in selling the initial twenty-five thousand copies entirely because I was selling them during my speaking engagements, I knew that I had to change the title.

I sent out a questionnaire to people around the country, asking for suggestions for a new title. A gentleman from Arkansas wrote back to me and said, "There can be only one title. It's *See You at the Top.*" He came to this conclusion through a thorough understanding of my message and a familiarity with my speaking presentations. I was closing all of my talks by saying, "If you'll do these things, I will see you at the top!" I closed my talks that way because the Redhead encouraged me to do so, and people had started identifying me with the phrase.

I had self-published the book because no publisher thought it would sell. That was the best thing that could have happened to me from a financial point of view. After the third printing a small publisher decided it would sell and wanted to put it in bookstores. I was able to negotiate a much better financial arrangement with them because I had a proven seller and their investment up to that point was zero. It's an arrangement that has worked out well for everyone concerned, and even today, after over twenty-five years on the market, *See You at the Top* still sells thirty to fifty thousand copies a year and gives every indication of continuing to sell, especially since I updated and revised it in 2000 to celebrate the twenty-fifth anniversary of its publication.

When I was writing my book *See You at the Top,* it hit me that my weighing well over two hundred pounds was not a good example of following the advice I was giving my readers. I was a new Christian at that time, and it had also occurred to me that I needed to be an example of God's grace. Those considerations, combined with the fact that I did not want to look like a forty-five-year-old "fat cat from Dallas," spurred me into action.

I had been on the weight roller coaster for many years, losing and regaining the pounds time and time again. I recognized that my lack of commitment and personal discipline were the prime problems. I also realized that I was not a medical or nutritional expert, and I decided for the first time that instead of doing it on my own I would seek help. (I had tried the thirty-day diet and lost a month, and I had dieted religiously—meaning I quit eating in church.)

The obvious person to consult, and one whom I knew personally, was Dr. Kenneth Cooper of aerobics fame. He is the author of many books on the subject and the one who started the country jogging. While there was some skepticism in the medical community about what he was doing, it all made perfect sense to me. Besides, he had the documentation to prove that his exercise approach was sound and that it was working. (My idea of exercise before I met Dr. Cooper was to fill the tub, take a bath, pull the plug, and fight the current.)

I went to the Cooper Clinic, took the physical, and followed the advice I was given, which included an exercise program and a well-balanced diet. Thank goodness I did because after I was fairly well recovered from my second gallbladder surgery, the doctor told me that it had been close and had I not been in such great physical condition I may not have made it. But our Lord is providential. God knew about my gallbladder problem long before I did; He prepared me for that by having me get into shape.

Over the years Dr. Cooper and I have become good friends and he has been an invaluable source of information and encouragement to me. Thanks to following his program through the years, today I am within one pound of the weight I achieved as a result of his original instruction.

———

As I write these pages, I have to admit I am hounded by a desire not to fail to mention or express my gratitude for any of the generous people who have helped me along the way. The personal recollection required of me to write this book has stirred up my sense of indebtedness to all of them. I feel a little anxious about accidentally leaving someone out! I am myself a living example of the many good wishes and deeds of others that contribute to anyone's success. God bless them all.

So many people like Dr. Ken Cooper have played a significant part in my life. I'd love to name them all, but that is virtually impossible given the limited space I have to work with. The people who were there for me in the beginning hold a special place in my heart. One of those people was Mary Crowley. I met Mary early on in my speaking career through my work with American Salesmasters. At the time I didn't realize that one day I'd be her brother in Christ and that we'd even attend the same church. Apparently she saw something in me of value because she invited me as a rookie, inexperienced speaker to address her Home Interiors and Gifts organization. I had the privilege of speaking to these people at both regional and national meetings several times.

My respect for Mary Crowley as a businessperson was huge. I was impressed with everything about her—her calm manner, the obvious love and respect her ladies had for her, her wisdom and her common sense. But Mary's heart was the biggest part of her.

When we moved to Dallas, Mary encouraged me on several occasions to join her at First Baptist Church to hear one of the great preachers in the world (Dr. Criswell), but I was always too busy and declined her invitations. Four years later, when I became a Christian, I took her up on her offer and enjoyed fellowshiping with her in church until her death in 1986.

Mary Crowley encouraged me mightily in my business and in my walk with God. She was among the first to hire me to speak, and it is a rare privilege and a delight to be able to say that I knew her well and loved her very much as a sister in Christ. Her unswerving faith, love, gentle spirit, and generous heart had a profound impact on my life. I suspect that one of the reasons she gave me those early opportunities to speak for her company was to let me see faith in action and watch godly women succeed in all areas of life.

The list of people who helped my speaking career is long, but the people who gave me work when I was still an unproven, unknown entity stand out most in my mind. Dick Gardner, one of the founders of American Salesmasters, eventually started an offshoot called the National Association of Sales Education (NASE), and I was fortunate to be included on many of their seminars.

Don Hutson, who worked with and spoke for NASE, also started his own company and invited me to speak for them. Later, Sam Cooper and John Handick started Positive Thinking Rallies in conjunction with W. Clement Stone of *Success* magazine. Even after Stone dropped out of the picture, Cooper and Handick kept the rallies going for several months. They held a number of very large seminars inviting celebrity speakers such as Art Linkletter, Dr. Norman Vincent Peale, Paul Harvey, Bob Richards, Cavett Robert, and others of that caliber. Sharing the platform with such men was an asset to my career.

Eventually I did a number of seminars with John Handick and my nephew, John Ziglar, and most (but not all) of them were around the South. Some of the more prominent seminar sponsors were John Hammond, Phoenix, Arizona, a brother in Christ and a close friend today; Suanne Sandage from Iowa, a sister in Christ and also a close friend today; and the late Jerry Patt and his wife, Kathy, from Fort Worth. I did many seminars for each of these people, and all of them made significant contributions to my career.

One of my more satisfying experiences was with West Texan Juanell Teague and her People Plus organization. Also, Jerry Bacon and the late John Moniz, from Charleston, South Carolina, working part-time, did a super job with the seminars they conducted.

No business is free of fast-buck Eddies, and public speaking in those days had its fair share. As a professional who had his sights set on a long and respectable career, I learned to be wary of potentially unsavory associations. After a few painful experiences, when some of these ambitious but unqualified people attempted to promote a seminar with limited funds and even more limited experience, I quickly learned not to speak for a seminar sponsor until he or she had already completed two or three successful seminars.

The man who gave me the most exposure was Peter Lowe, a young visionary from Canada who lives in Tampa, Florida. My first seminar with

Peter was in New Orleans, a very exciting event, and Peter and I were the only two speakers. He and his wife, Tamara, managed to sell over twenty-five hundred tickets, which was considered quite a significant number in those days. Soon I was doing more and more seminars with Peter Lowe.

Peter's vision grew, and one day he asked me what time I preferred to do seminars. We had been conducting them on weekday evenings from six-thirty P.M. until ten-thiry P.M., by the end of which I was quite tired. I would generally then eat a big meal and get to bed late. You can well imagine this routine's effect on my health—a weight problem and lack of sleep. I told Peter that I didn't know how it might work, but I would love to speak in the morning. He promptly responded, "Let's do it!" The other seminar sponsors I was working with at the time didn't think a daytime schedule would be successful in attracting enough participants to be worthwhile. However, it proved to be the ideal arrangement, and today most of the big public seminars are conducted during the day. As Peter added celebrities to the seminar roster, people like Presidents Reagan, Ford, and Bush, the crowds grew by the thousands, and the heavy print advertising he did for the seminars gave me additional name recognition.

As a result of the huge success of the Peter Lowe Success Seminars, I made the decision to do public seminars exclusively with Peter and gave my other seminar sponsors a one-year notice. This was truly one of the hardest business decisions I've ever made. There is no way I can adequately express the value I place on the relationships I had, and in virtually every case still have, with the men and women who did such outstanding jobs in the seminars they sponsored with me as one of the speakers. Their support and help was invaluable to me, and I hope and believe my support and contribution to their seminars made ours a win-win relationship.

I wish one of my most trusted mentors and the author of the foreword of this book, Fred Smith, had been around to help me with that difficult decision. Fred came along fourteen years after I had been thrust unexpectedly and unprepared into my full-time speaking career, but his counsel has been so constant over the years that I consider him as having been there for me from the start. Before I ever met Fred Smith, I heard others talking about him—his wisdom, his ability to communicate, and his willingness to teach younger men and women some of the important elements of life. His business background ranged from being the director of industrial relationships for five years and then consulting with Genesco for sixteen years. While he was in charge of labor relations with Powell Valve Company, the company never lost a single day of work due to a strike. For twenty years Fred served as a columnist with *Leadership* magazine, a division of *Christianity Today,* and he also served on *Christianity Today's* board of directors for twenty-three years. The three books he's written and the two honorary doctorate degrees he's received are further testament to his wisdom. So I was more than thrilled when I finally got to meet him in 1982 at Holly Lake Ranch, where we have a house and where he and his wife, Mary Alice, had a home for many years. Our deep and abiding friendship has developed over a period of time. We are close friends as couples, and we enjoy sharing evening meals as often as possible. Fred has been an outstanding example and role model for me. I've called on him to help when I didn't have the answers, and Fred and his close friend Seth Macon worked with our company when we were experiencing difficulties. They spotted some weak links and have continued to provide invaluable advice over the years.

Fred and I speak on the phone every week, sometimes three or four times. Wherever we are, whether he is participating as a speaker at our Born to Win seminars, or teaching my Sunday school class, or just in phone conversations, when I connect in any way with Fred Smith, I have my pen and paper handy because he is always teaching—and what he teaches is very important.

His friendship, support, and encouragement have meant much to me for a long time. I cherish every opportunity to spend time with him, but one of the things I value very highly is that when I am "stuck" with a situation, and don't really know which way I want to go, and there is a moral dilemma or spiritual question involved, I can call on Fred. He may not give me an instant answer, but later in the conversation I can count on the fact that he will have been considering it and he eventually gives me some insights that always prove to be extremely helpful. Yes, he really is an important voice in my life, and I cherish his friendship.

Many talented and inspired people I've never had the opportunity to meet have influenced my life through their books or audiotapes. The first book on the profession that I read as a young salesman was *How I Raised Myself from Failure to Success in Selling* by Frank Bettger. For the first time in my life I heard and understood the value of being enthusiastic about what we do. It was an important lesson for me. Later, I read *The Magic of Thinking Big* by Dr. David J. Schwartz, and his book was my first exposure to the concept of having a well-considered, organized structure for all of one's activities that included goals in every area of life. Until then I thought only in terms of having the goal to make four calls a day or at least twenty sales calls each week. Still later, Dr. Norman Vincent Peale, in his book *The Power of Positive Thinking,* taught me that it's not what happens to you but how you *handle* what happens to you that will make the difference in your life.

Today these three concepts taught by these three authors are commonplace and are accepted by virtually everyone, but at the time they came into my life, they were groundbreaking ideas in the business world. They have proven very important additions to my success arsenal, and I'm certainly grateful that they entered the picture. Much of the material I use in my talks and books today is the result of the seeds planted by these three authors.

Three other books that have had a huge influence on the development of my spiritual life are *The Light and the Glory* by Peter Marshall and David Manuel, *Evidence That Demands a Verdict* by Dr. Josh McDowell, and *Original Intent* by David Barton. Dr. Josh McDowell was an attorney who set out to disprove the deity of Christ. Through years of documented research he discovered just the opposite, and he became one of the clearest voices in Christianity for Christ. *The Light and the Glory,* as well as *Original Intent,* prove beyond any doubt that our nation is a "nation under God," discovered by a Christian (Christopher Columbus), and founded as a Christian nation by Christians. I challenge anyone to read either *The Light and the Glory* or *Original Intent* and come to any other conclusion. *Evidence That Demands a Verdict* brings compelling evidence of the truth of our start as a Christian nation.

My complete list of authors and seminar speakers helpful to me is simply too long to include here. So many people have taught me significant things through their books and tapes that it would be impossible to recognize them all. It's safe to say that without their wisdom and instruction my life would have been substantially different and much poorer.

As far as the help I've gotten from other speakers is concerned, I've already covered how Bob Bales influenced my decision to become a speaker.

Dr. Herb True demonstrated and taught me the way to use humor effectively in my presentations. Bill Gove patiently explained to me the value of telling a story and then extracting the message from the story in a way that people would remember the lesson being taught. Dr. Ken McFarland taught me the importance of varying voice inflection and the correct way to use a microphone in order to make certain points, letting your voice increase in volume on certain occasions, then drop much lower when you want to nail down a point. Charlie Cullen taught me the value of closing a talk by reminding the audience of what I had covered. Bob Richards showed me the importance of putting everything you had into a talk. His example of being pleasant and kind to autograph seekers taught me the value of getting to know your audience and letting them know you appreciate them.

Because so many people have given their time and attention to help me be all that I can be, one of the toughest things I ever have to do is say no. I get many requests to do a lot of things, spend a few minutes in an interview here, counsel an individual there, speak at a church or youth group, endorse a book or recorded program, contribute to worthwhile charities and benevolent causes.

Perhaps the most difficult thing for me is to say no to a first-time author who has struggled desperately to complete his or her manuscript, and who believes my endorsement will guarantee the book will be a best-seller. I receive an average of nearly a book every day of the year from someone wanting an endorsement, and it's humanly impossible to read a book every single day and at the same time do the reading and research necessary to keep my material fresh and bring up-to-date encouragement to my audiences. And endorsing a book I haven't read would be dishonest. So, of necessity, in the overwhelming majority of cases, I have to say no. I hate to do that because when I was a first-time author I was fortunate enough to obtain endorsements from some very prominent people, including Dr. Norman Vincent Peale, and I've always felt that was a big help to me. But over the years, I have experienced a couple of disasters by recommending some books, and nearly recommending another, that were in direct contradiction to the things I believe and teach, so it is critical that I be very careful about what I endorse.

Family and Travel

Being together as a family has always been one of my top priorities, but the travel required by my speaking career imposed some tough limitations on the time I could spend at home. Early on I learned out of necessity to combine family time with travel to carve out the time we needed to be together to nourish one another, grow closer, and just enjoy one another's company. Before long, family travel became one of our favorite ways of just being together. We were able to combine the joy of one another's presence with the fun and excitement of visiting new places.

In my travels I've experienced some incredible highs, including flying on the Concorde. At sixty thousand feet you can see the curvature of the Earth. That's exciting. My son and I climbed to the tip of Cape Point, the southernmost point in South Africa. Straight ahead we could see the green of the Indian Ocean as it came together to meet the blue of the Atlantic Ocean, creating one of God's most beautiful sights. Looking to the left, we could see the magnificent mountains; to the right, the beauty of the Atlantic. It was awesome.

The Redhead and I have been able to maintain a good marriage relationship in spite of my heavy travel schedule and the many trips she was unable to make with me. I once was away for a ten-day tour, and neither one of us liked that lengthy separation. Since then, if I'm going to be gone three days or longer, the Redhead travels with me. The Redhead and I have seen Sugar Loaf Mountain in Rio de Janeiro. We've seen the Eiffel Tower, the Washington Monument, Number Ten Downing Street, and Buckingham Palace. We've seen the Berlin Wall and have been awed by the traditional tomb of Christ near Jerusalem. We boarded a cruise ship and enjoyed the Inner Passage to Alaska where we saw amazing icebergs and glaciers.

Another destination that thrilled the Redhead and me, because of its historical magnitude, was the Panama Canal. I was conducting a seminar in Panama, and our host was able to set up a tour for us. Everyone on the boat treated us as visiting dignitaries, and I was even permitted to push the levers that flooded the locks so we could make our passage through the canal. It was like putting my hand on history! What a thrill for me.

One of our other top travel experiences was our trip to tour England,

the Mother Country, when Tom was seventeen. I had three speaking engagements while I was there, so it became a working vacation. We arrived
in London, stayed at one of the relatively new hotels, conducted the seminar, and engaged a car and driver.

Since the Redhead's ancestors came from Scotland, and since there is
a town called Abernathy (her maiden name), we made a side trip to go
through it. Interestingly enough, in the telephone book there was only one
Abernathy family and, according to the Redhead, they spelled their name
wrong! It had an "e" instead of an "a." Nevertheless, it was a delightful little village, and we enjoyed seeing its sights.

As a history major in college, I was thrilled to see the historical sights
in the United Kingdom. The highlight of the trip, however, for Tom and me
was the round of golf we played at the old course, Saint Andrews. The experience still holds special memories for us.

One of our most memorable journeys was our trip to South Africa,
where I was speaking for Holiday Inns. Our hosts had access to the
Londolozi Private Game Reserve and were good friends with the owners
and managers of the camp; they arranged a safari for us. It was three days
of hunting wild animals with our camera. One night on the safari we came
across a rhinoceros that had just lost a battle for a mate—and he had lost
big-time! We saw and marveled at many different game animals, birds, and
just about every creature that Africa has to offer.

Possibly our most delightful and humorous experiences in Africa occurred when we went to an ostrich farm in Oudtshoorn. Since ostriches
can be ridden, I wanted to give it a try. Some natives demonstrated to me
how it could be done. In a matter of minutes with a huge assist from one
of the guides, I found myself astride an ostrich. Suddenly it hit me how
ridiculous it was for a grown man to ride a bird. I got tickled and could not
stop laughing until after I had dismounted. One of my great regrets was
that our camera quit working, and I did not get a single picture of that mo-
mentous experience. How I wish my grandchildren could have seen their
granddaddy astride a big bird—even if it wasn't the yellow Big Bird they
have seen on television!

The most amazing weather event I've seen took place on top of Table
Rock Mountain in Africa. When we arrived on our side of the mountain it
was a beautiful sunshiny day, and when we went inside to have lunch in the

resort that had a 180-degree view, I immediately noticed that it was raining cats and dogs on the other side of the mountain. At that very moment, the rain shifted to the side of the mountain on which we had arrived. Our sunshine was then replaced by a huge downpour. We spent about an hour in the dining room and, as we were getting ready to leave, the rain shifted yet again to the backside of the mountain, and the side at which we had first arrived was again clear and sunny. I found it fascinating that the "local" weather would shift so frequently and completely. Africa was truly a land full of wonder.

However, the most moving, and by far the most inspirational, trip we've ever taken together was our trip to the Holy Land. In 1986 the Redhead and I went to Israel. We landed in Amman, Jordan, and went first to Petra, the site of ancient ruins, and enjoyed the experience very much.

Then our tour bus took us to Israel. The checkpoint at the border was very strict, but we got through without any difficulty. It just happened that our tour guide was a member of the Israeli Armed Forces and was a no-nonsense yet friendly individual. As we visited with him it was obvious that some of his answers were quite guarded, but he knew his history, and he knew the Old Testament quite well. Ben Glosson, a pastor from Hazlehurst, Georgia, was on the trip with us and became quite friendly with our guide, sharing with him the New Testament and what Christ had done for all of us. Ben learned on a later trip to Israel that our guide had met the Messiah. Ben was truly thrilled to hear the good news.

Most of our time was spent around the Sea of Galilee, where much of Christ's ministry took place. I was privileged to serve the Lord's Supper in the Garden of Gethsemane. I was asked to read the Sermon on the Mount in the place where it is believed Christ voiced that sermon. We spent some time on the Sea of Galilee, which they tell me can be calm one minute and an hour later have huge waves and violent winds. In a local restaurant we ate the fish they told us dated back to biblical times, over two thousand years ago. (Actually, the species was two thousand years old. The fish we ate was fresh.) We walked through the marketplaces and were fascinated by all of the things being sold and the incredible displays of foods.

On our trip to the Holy Land the most moving experience for me took place on a Sunday morning in Jerusalem. I will have to admit that the circumstances were such that I was quite involved emotionally. Seeing the sights, including the site where many people believe Christ was entombed, and going into Bethlehem, close to where they say He was born, made for an incredibly stirring experience. On that Sunday morning, Pastor Ben Glosson preached a powerful sermon of faith and hope, and in the midst of his sermon he broke out singing "How Great Thou Art" in his beautiful voice. As he sang, tears ran down my cheeks. I was deeply moved to fully comprehend that God was actually in me, with me, and for me, and was addressing me. It was a once-in-a-lifetime moment, extraordinarily profound and spiritual.

What I experienced was truly unique for me. For several years I had been telling people that I couldn't understand how the Redhead, who had been my wife for nearly forty years, was more beautiful to me than she was on the day we were married. Somehow, it seemed illogical that a grandmother would be more beautiful than an eighteen-year-old bride. Yet she was to me—and still is! It really baffled me because in my logical mind it simply did not compute.

That Sunday morning in Jerusalem, God spoke to me in my spirit and said, "Let me tell you why your wife is more beautiful to you today than she was on your wedding day. I'm letting you look at her through my eyes now, and in my eyes I see perfection. She is forgiven." I'll never forget the experience and how profoundly it affected me—and affects me to this day. Wouldn't it be wonderful if all of us could see all people through God's eyes all the time?

I'm just grateful that God's eyes are always on me. In April 1996, as part of our Pacific Rim Tour, I conducted a seminar in Manila in the Philippines. The Redhead and I were staying in a beautiful, modern, up-to-date hotel. Interestingly enough, the hotel was located close to the low-rent district. My first morning there I was out for my walk and was staying close to the hotel where there was a fair amount of pedestrian traffic. I had been walking for about thirty minutes when suddenly at my side was a small Philippino man who appeared to be about forty years old. He asked if he could walk with me, and I responded very enthusiastically, "Of course!"

I'm a fast walker, and after a block or so he said, "You sure do walk fast." I said, "Yes, I do." He said, "But I have such short legs. It doesn't seem fair that your legs are so much longer than mine." I said, "Perhaps not, but God generally balances things out, and your youth gives you an advantage in that department." After a moment of silence he said, "Are you a great man in America?" I laughingly said, "Well, my wife and children—hopefully—think that I am!" "No, I mean seriously, are you in the government or do you fill an important position?" I responded that I was not in the government, but that I had the privilege of writing and speaking and as a result had been allowed to touch some lives. He said, "You are a great man." I protested (admittedly, only mildly), reiterating that God had blessed me with a beautiful wife, marvelous children, and many friends.

At about this point we had been walking for some fifteen minutes, and I turned to go a certain direction. He said, "I work down this way. Why don't you walk on with me?" I responded, "No, I need to be headed back to get ready for my seminar." He then asked if I would be walking the next morning, and I said, "No, I'll be speaking at this time tomorrow." As he made his departure I had one of the strangest feelings I have ever had and just a few minutes later wished I had walked with him toward the building in which he said he worked.

Later I told a friend of mine about the strange feeling, that I had reflected on it several times since then, and that I felt he might well have been an angel. My friend responded, "Well, I don't know if you knew it or not, but in that area of town Americans are particularly disliked and frequently the locals seek them out to mug them." He then asked if anything had happened on the walk with the stranger. I responded nothing of particular significance occurred, but then I recalled that as we crossed one busy street a car turning from the left was headed toward me, though not at a fast rate of speed, and I had not thought anything about it. The stranger had reached out and put his arm in front of me, indicating that I should stop.

Later, as I pondered this incident, I was pretty strongly impressed, based on what I had just learned, that my walking companion was an angel and he was there to protect me.

As I've reflected on it in the months since then, I have become more convinced than ever. After all, God did provide an angel the night I fell asleep driving home from a cookware demonstration. He also sent twenty-six people throughout my lifetime to guide and protect me at special times, and He prevented me from boarding an elevator that malfunctioned, so why would He not have placed another angel at my side in Manila?

Yes, I've been blessed to see so many magnificent wonders around the world, but I'm content these days to opt for more time at home whenever possible. For several years my trips have primarily been out one day and back the next, or out on Monday, speak in two or three cities, and return on Thursday. The Redhead simply does not enjoy that kind of schedule. However, in virtually every case when I am gone, whether it's for one or three days, I am on the phone with her from two to as many as six times a day. Most of the time she is the first person I talk to in the morning and the last one I speak with at night, with time zones being the determining factor in those cases. In addition, I periodically write her notes and letters expressing my love and affection for her. My verbal expressions of love and gratitude for all she has meant to me have been frequent and many. It takes a little extra effort to stay close from a distance, but I promise you, staying connected emotionally with the Redhead is the best investment of my time that I'll ever make!

I have encouraged the Redhead to spend more time with me on the golf course, but I have to agree—the weather in Texas just doesn't fit the Redhead's idea of "perfect for golfing" very many days of the year. (Of all the recreational activities in which I involve myself, golf is head and shoulders above all the others.) My favorite way of relaxing is a quiet evening with the Redhead—or, for that matter, a quiet morning or breakfast or lunch or dinner! This includes those times when we have nothing in mind except being together.

My favorite place is our home at Holly Lake Ranch, 110 miles east of Dallas. We get down there periodically to enjoy the sights and sounds of nature, the hills, and each other without outside interruption. Because Holly Lake is so peaceful, I accomplish a large percentage of my writing there.

Since I love to read, a priceless gift I was given by my sixth-grade teacher, Mrs. J. K. Worley, my time at the lake includes a significant amount of reading. Because I love to walk, it also includes casual walks with the Redhead and Taffy, our little Welsh corgi, and some serious up-and down-hill walking by myself. We generally like to stay three or four days and love it there whether it's winter, spring, summer, or fall. It is so nice and quiet that sometimes we can't resist the urge to just pick up and go spend the night and come on home the next day.

There are three family events I look forward to each year. Every year on

Memorial Day weekend I make up for lost time with my daughters by taking them to Gatlinburg, Tennessee, with the Redhead and me. We spend three days "overdosing" on good, Southern Gospel music presented by Bill Gaither and his entourage of committed, talented people. We just have an incredibly good time and stay to see the sights and visit nearby towns for four days after the concert is over. We go for long walks by the river that runs through the town, enjoy the scenery, drive through the mountains, and have a ball together.

One early morning in Gatlinburg Cindy was doing her Bible study and I was doing mine. We were enjoying a cup of coffee and each other's company from a distance of about twenty feet when I looked up and saw her. Overwhelmed by a sense of God's goodness, I said to Cindy, "Sweetnin', there is nothing that moves me any more than sharing this time with you, seeing you as a godly woman and wife, studying God's Word." It's a precious moment when you realize your adult children are in the kind of relationship you'd prayed they'd have with their heavenly Father. I would never have witnessed it for myself if we didn't travel together . . . at least not in that light.

When we're in Gatlinburg we especially enjoy visiting with old friends we know from the National Speakers Association who also regularly attend the Gaither concerts. As comrades and fellow believers, we share our profession and our faith—a combination that doubles our enjoyment of one another. Yes, our annual trip to Gatlinburg is an occasion that we start looking forward to on our way home. We just can't wait to get back and do it again.

Yet another annual occasion at which I get to spend time with family is when my son, Tom, and I participate in the Texas Golf Association's Father/Son Golf Tournament. We enjoy four days of time together playing the game both of us love, and he's quite good. My optimism always tells me that my next game will be the best I've ever played, but it's like I told a group I was playing with recently, "You know, I can play lots better than this—I just never have!" Despite that, I really do believe my next game will be my best one.

Our wives go with us and, of course, Tom and Chachis's daughter Alexandra is part of the group. The girls have a good time sight-seeing, shopping, and entertaining one another while we are playing the tournament. It's always fun.

And, finally, the third favorite occasion that takes place every year is when we go to the Ziglar family reunion in Yazoo City, Mississippi. We have aunts, uncles, cousins, nephews, nieces-in-law, sons-in-law, daughters-in-law, and a host of other people in attendance. Because of the wonderful cooks in our family, we don't eat until we're full—we eat until we are tired! The average weight gain, because of the number of little children who don't eat much, is just 3.8 pounds. Over the meal we share good-natured ribbing, serious testimony of God's grace, much laughter, and even a few joyful tears. It's always good to get back together with family, and it truly is a memorable occasion.

The Darkest Day

We had suspected that our oldest daughter, Suzan, was not in good health for several years, but none of our best efforts convinced her to go to the doctor to find out what the problem might be. She had a persistent cough, tired easily, and seemed very short of breath. In December 1993 Suzan was trying to do her Christmas shopping when she realized she couldn't walk more than four or five minutes without needing to sit down and rest. A friend suggested that she might be having heart problems, and she finally went to the doctor after the first of the year.

The diagnosis was pulmonary fibrosis, a disease that causes the lungs to become stiff and unable to expand or contract fully, making for a poor exchange of oxygen to the blood. The doctor told her she would ultimately need a lung transplant, but that probably wouldn't be necessary for another two to three years. We all breathed a sigh of relief that there was no immediate danger of losing her, assumed a degree of denial that allowed us to function, and went on about our lives.

Several months before Suzan's death and long before we realized the seriousness of her illness, she cautioned me in one of our conversations, saying, "Dad, I know how strong your faith is and how optimistic you are about everything. I know that in all probability you will tell Katherine that you know God is going to heal her mother." She went on, "Dad, we don't know that. God is sovereign. If it's in His plans, the healing will take place; if not, it won't, and I don't want my daughter mad at God because she, like her grandfather, believed that God would heal her mother."

Ignorance truly is bliss, and I now believe that denial was playing an incredibly large part in our mind-set. As a family, we were all so unprepared for the turn of events that forever changed all of our lives. A little more than a year after Suzan's diagnosis, as she was preparing to take a trip to St. Louis to be evaluated for a lung transplant, her disease suddenly hit full force. Her husband, Chad, rushed her to the hospital and by the next morning she was in the intensive care unit.

It, of course, developed that Suzan was 100 percent right—I did want to tell Katherine that God would heal her mother. At that stage, there was no doubt in my mind that God would heal Suzan. It was very difficult for me to resist reassuring Katherine that her mother would be healed because I believed it strongly. My optimism knew no bounds in regard to Suzan's recovery because I knew that the prayers that were being raised in our daughter's behalf numbered in the thousands and were being uttered from all parts of the world. Though it was incredibly difficult, I honored my daughter's request. I'm so grateful that I did. My beautiful daughter, Suzan Ziglar Witmeyer, taught me real faith in the face of her impending death. Her mother and I taught her how to live—she taught us how to die.

At nine forty-five A.M. on May 13, 1995, the nurse quietly said to our family, "She's gone." Our firstborn daughter had gone home to be with the Lord only three days after her forty-sixth birthday.

No adequate words exist to describe the grief, the sense of loss, the sensation that something we would never fully understand had taken place. It was one of those incredible moments forever burned into the memory of each of our family members. My son-in-law, Jim Norman, had an especially close friendship with Suzan, and he was the first to break the stunned silence. With a shaky voice and tear-filled eyes, he thanked God for Suzan and asked for His blessings on our family. It was a heart-felt prayer we all desperately needed to hear.

Even though we had known for the past couple of weeks that the odds were against her, and in the preceding forty-eight hours we had accepted the reality that she would soon step into eternity, Suzan's leaving was an incredibly devastating shock. At that exact moment, each one of us was so exhausted and overcome that the enormity and sadness of the moment overwhelmed us.

That she would be welcomed into heaven by her Lord and Savior, Jesus

Christ, was the knowledge that ultimately gave all of us the strength we needed to withstand the grief. We knew that her salvation was secure, that never again would she have difficulty breathing, that never again would there be a sad moment for her. Yes, we understood those things. And we rested in the knowledge that the God Who can never lie had assured us that we would see her again.

After collecting our thoughts, the Redhead and I made plans with Suzan's husband, Chad, and his parents Don and Babe Witmeyer, to go to the funeral home to make all of the necessary arrangements. We met there a couple of hours later. The experience was very difficult. All of us were exhausted; I had not had my shoes off in well over twenty-four hours, and it seemed as if the arrangements for the funeral, the burial plot, and all the intricacies that go with it dragged on and on and on. Finally, after several hours, they were complete and we all went home.

We had many things to do—numerous phone calls to let people know that our Suzan was with her Lord and that the funeral arrangements had been completed. Those hours were a blur, and finally at about ten o'clock that night I went to bed. As I have written in *Confessions of a Grieving Christian,* it was an extraordinarily difficult night. I tried to pray and couldn't. Tried to sleep and couldn't. Tried to read my Bible and couldn't. I finally got up and placed a Gaither Gospel video in the VCR, and lay down on the floor. Almost immediately, while listening to God's Word sung so beautifully by Vestal Goodman, I mercifully drifted into a very sound sleep.

I slept on the floor for two hours, got up, went upstairs, slept another two hours, arose at about seven o'clock, had a light breakfast, and took the walk that brought the peace I so desperately needed. I walked nearly an hour, praying and crying every step of the way, and as I turned toward home God impressed these words on my mind so clearly that it was almost in an audible voice, "Suzan is fine. She's with me. And you're going to be fine, too. I'm all you need. I want you to just keep walking, keep weeping, keep praying."

Even as I was accepting and believing, completely trusting Christ for His promises, I was pondering how anybody deals with the loss of a loved one, but most especially the loss of a child, if they do not have that complete assurance that this loved one (as we did about Suzan) would spend eternity with Him and that we would see her again. Without this undeniable assurance I'm certain that my misery would have extended into every day of my life. The grief is such that I know we will never get over it, but knowing that she's fine and that I will see her again brings incredible comfort to me and to my family.

The next days and weeks were somewhat of a blur. I'll never forget one lady who, in an effort to be encouraging and helpful to me, said, "I know exactly how you feel—I just lost my mother." My response to her was, "Ma'am, with all due respect, you don't have a clue as to what it is to lose a child. I'm from a large family. Out of twelve children, only three of us are still here. I've buried both mother and father, as well as brothers and sisters, but nothing comes close to the grief that accompanies the loss of a child." Suzan was supposed to come to my funeral—I should not have gone to hers. Losing a child is not in the natural order of things.

At a board meeting a couple of years after Suzan's death, I gave each of the board members a copy of my book *Confessions of a Grieving Christian.* The following December I received a letter and videotape by special delivery from board member Kris Friedrich who, with his family, was also a close friend of ours. Kris's letter elaborated on the video, which showed Kris, his wife, and two children in their swimming pool.

He explained how he had read the book on his flight back to California from Dallas, weeping all the way. Then he said he went into his office and read *Confessions of a Happy Christian,* which I had given him a couple of years earlier and he had dutifully placed in his bookcase. However, Kris said what really opened his eyes was when I wrote about the Redhead and me being in Washington just a few weeks after Suzan's death, and how as we walked toward the elevator in our hotel I blurted out, "I wonder where Suzan is and what she's doing." I then immediately said to the Redhead, "Oh, I know exactly where she is and I know exactly what she's doing. She's with our Lord and she's praising and worshiping Him." I followed with the comment that, of all of our four children, she was the only one I could say with absolute certainty as to where she was.

Kris said that when he read that it really hit him and that's when he got it. In addition, God in His mercy had put together Kris's daughter in a friendship with the son of the pastor of a church and, as a result, Kris, his wife, and two children talked with that pastor, committed their lives to Christ, and were baptized in their swimming pool.

While nothing can replace our child, or completely eliminate our grief, a considerable amount of satisfaction and joy comes from knowing that through Suzan's death, the Friedrich family and many others will spend eternity with Christ, one another, and our daughter. That's significant and means a great deal to us.

One of the more comforting benefits of knowing Christ is knowing that the Bible is the inspired Word of God. This knowledge gives one a lot of peace and prevents false or misplaced guilt. Psalms 139:16 clearly states that our days are measured before we are born. In plain English it simply means that our death date is determined even before our birth date. We gave our daughter as much love—and repeatedly told her of our love—as I believe any family can give. Suzan knew she was loved. We provided the best medical care that was available and, thanks to the Internet and the contacts I have with so many organizations where I've spoken, prayers were being uttered for her all around the world. Our whole family was in constant and incessant prayer, pleading for Suzan's life, but her death date long ago had been determined by a loving and all-knowing God. Knowing that the timing of her death was out of our hands removes guilt. So far as I know, none of us has ever said, "Maybe we should have . . ." or "If only we had . . ." or "You know, we could have . . ." Those things simply were never said or, to my knowledge, even contemplated by anyone in our family.

Isaiah 57:1–2 says, "The godly die young and the world knows not why, but God sees the trouble that lies ahead. The godly rest in peace." We're so grateful that our daughter did not have to go through an extended period of illness and suffering. God called her to where she now enjoys perfect health and perfect peace.

We have received more than our share of well-meaning advice from loving friends and acquaintances, things like, "You need to be brave, you need to be strong." That simply is not true. God Himself encourages us to weep on numerous occasions throughout the Bible. Christ Himself set the example when He wept over the death of Lazarus, even though He knew He would raise Lazarus from death in just a matter of moments. On occasion well-meaning friends are inclined to say things like, "Get a life"; "Put it behind you"; "Three years is long enough; get over it"; "You still have three children"; and a host of other things. But you never get over it. It's true that God places other things in your mind and life, but then those occasions arise to remind you of your lost loved one. Even last Sunday when a pretty little girl came forward in church, committing her life to Christ, I saw my Suzan standing there and became teary-eyed as a result.

As I wrote in *Confessions of a Grieving Christian,* for the Christian, death and grieving are like going through a long, mountain tunnel. You know the end is there, you know daylight will come. But you simply do not know when or how. Yet you continue moving forward in that hope. Not in your own strength, but in the strength and promises of Christ. Then when you burst into the bright sunlight as you emerge from that tunnel, you will be standing in the presence of Christ; you will see your loved one there. At that moment, grieving stops and your eternal rejoicing begins.

It's impossible to lose someone you love intensely and completely, the way I loved Suzan, and not learn some valuable lessons. For some time before Suzan died I had made it a point to call her more often and just drop by her house to say hello. I guess a part of me knew our time was limited, and when I think back on those occasions I am always so grateful that I did make time to talk to and be with Suzan.

As a result, I now make what I have coined "airport calls." Not long after we lost Suzan, I returned to Dallas late one evening and couldn't find my car in the airport parking garage. I believe my grief exhausted me, and though I appeared to be functioning well, even to myself, grief was taking its toll. To help reduce any extra stress for me we decided that I should use a limo service to and from the airport.

I never realized how freeing it would be for someone else to do the driving! Neither did I realize what a wonderful window of opportunity it would open for me to call my loved ones and visit with them uninterrupted for the forty-minute drive. Before I started making my airport calls my children found it impossible to keep up with where I was. Now when they hear my voice they ask, "Where are you headed this time, Dad?" Or if I'm returning they'll ask how my talk went and if I had a good audience. I leave town telling them I love them and I arrive telling them I love them. Of course I call them just to say hello when I am in town too, but the airport calls are extra special to all of us.

Second Chances

In the summer of 1998, just three years after Suzan's death, my oldest sister, Turah Allen, became deathly ill and was rushed to the hospital in Jackson, Mississippi. When we arrived and I saw her, I honestly believed that I was seeing her for the last time. She was critically ill, appeared to be on her deathbed, and was completely out of it. I don't recall ever praying any harder than I did for her, and part of it, to be candid, was guilt-induced.

I had fairly well neglected my attention to my older sister. I didn't call her very often, saw her only once or twice a year, wrote seldom. I asked God if He would spare her life, restore her to a semblance of health, and give me an opportunity to make it up to my sister. God graciously responded and put His healing hand on Turah; I kept my promise to her. I still didn't get to see her as often as I would have liked, but I did call her regularly, and we had nice visits on the telephone. I'm so grateful for the additional three years that I did get to spend with my precious sister. She went home to be with the Lord September 18, 2001.

These days I regularly call my only living sibling, Evia Jane, and visit her every chance I get. I regret that so many of my siblings smoked cigarettes, and though I clearly believe Psalms 139:16, I still find it fascinating to know that the nonsmoking members of our family lived an average of over twenty years longer than those who smoked. That's a lot of life to give up for the initial pleasure of a habit that inevitably turns into an expensive and fatal addiction.

Though the doctors say the disease Suzan had, pulmonary fibrosis, presents itself 50 percent of the time in nonsmokers, we know Suzan's cigarette habit only complicated the situation. She was able to kick the habit three years before she died, and I know that had to have improved the quality of those three years immensely.

Keeping a Positive Attitude When Times Are Tough

Suzan's death has impacted me more profoundly than anything since the day I accepted Christ as my Lord and Savior. In spite of the grief, I appreciate the many positives that have come as a result. People have asked me how someone as positive as I was dealing with something as devastating as the loss of my daughter. I can tell you that God walked and is still walking me through the experience. But overall my usual reply to the question of my being positive all the time still applies.

I make it a point to do the things that will make my attitude a positive one. I'm a prolific reader; I have read an average of three hours a day for many years. I always read the daily paper and the Bible. That way I know what both sides are up to! I also read powerful books, excellent magazines, and numerous minipublications, which give me a great deal of hope, help, and encouragement. I firmly believe that you are what you are and where you are because of what has gone into your mind, so I make absolutely certain on a daily basis that good, clean, pure, powerful, positive information goes into my mind. I'm also an avid student of Automobile University. Most of the time when I sit down in my car, I plug in an inspirational, educational tape or CD that encourages, inspires, and informs me in what I'm doing. When disappointments occur—and they do—or, on occasion, even disasters, my faith is my constant companion. Romans 8:28 says, "And we know that all things work together for good to those who love God, to them who are called according to His purpose." This does not say that every individual thing is good, but it does say that God takes all of it and makes it good.

I also keep my spirits up by having and using my sense of humor. I believe that a sense of humor is about as important for family members to have as almost any other quality. Families who have fun together invariably get along better and enjoy life a lot more. I'm grateful that not only do I enjoy a good sense of humor, I also married a woman who has as good a sense of humor as I have. That doesn't necessarily mean you have to be able to tell jokes to have that sense of humor. In all the years we've been married, the Redhead has probably told less than a dozen jokes, and invariably she missed the punch line on most of them. But oh, she loves to laugh, and I love to hear her. Her laughter is one of the most beautiful sounds in my world. The Redhead appreciates humor as few people do. We are delighted that each of our children inherited that same sense of humor. I guess it's catching!

One of the little things I always got considerable enjoyment from was teaching our children to say big words (for them) that they didn't understand. For example, when Suzan was about two or three years old, I taught her to explain to people what sleet was—"frozen precipitation caused by atmospheric conditions." Needless to say, those words were slightly beyond a child of that age, but people were amused and would laugh, and she would smile broadly. It was part of her personality development.

At the table when the kids were small, either at restaurants or for that matter, when we were at home, on a regular basis I would distract one of the children, take his or her dessert saucer, and set it on my knee. The little one would turn back and look bewildered, then start searching all around to see what happened to the dessert plate. This sleight of hand worked only once per child! However, when we had company, I would frequently maneuver to be seated next to the visiting child, and I would pull the same thing on him or her. Invariably he or she would look around in the same bewilderment and I would feign innocence while watching out of the corner of my eye. Sometimes one would say, "What happened to my dessert?," or one of our children would start laughing. Then I would produce the dessert and everyone had a good chuckle.

A couple of years ago, when the Redhead and I, along with daughter Cindy, went to see the Redhead's sister, Eurie Abernathy, who is in a nursing home in Shreveport, Louisiana, we stopped by TCBY for some yogurt. I had finished mine and managed to point out something on the street to Cindy and when she turned around to look, I reached over and was taking a dip out of her yogurt cup (which she still had her hand on) and she felt it. She turned around and, for whatever reason, both of us thought that was the funniest thing either of us had ever experienced! Needless to say, it wasn't, and even as I write this I'll concede that it really wasn't *that* funny, but it's one of those situational things where parent and child were so caught up in the absurdity of it that the two of us, along with the Redhead, thought it was hilarious. As a matter of fact, we still laugh about it on occasion, and I believe we are closer as a result of it.

Years ago I learned that as a speaker, if I could get my audience laughing early in my presentation, invariably their minds would spring open and their receptiveness to what I had to say would increase. It's hard to laugh with someone and then not be more receptive to what that person has to say when he or she gets serious. For that reason, I start every talk I make with something that will get people laughing almost immediately. And when we get together at family reunions, it frequently is a case of who's got the latest joke and who can tell it best. Ziglars do love to laugh.

Times were so difficult for my mother, who had to work so hard, and yet on occasion she would get tickled at some of the shenanigans of her children. When we would visit my brother Huie, the preacher, who had a great sense of humor, he always entertained us with his stories. Humor was a part of my fiber from my earliest childhood memories, and I'm so glad it has always been a part of my life.

Staying up *all* of the time isn't possible; there will always be sobering moments. But one incredible discovery I made after Suzan died was that though I grieved for her with every fiber of my being, I still experienced joy in the midst of my grief. I could laugh at a joke or enjoy the company of others. Those bright rays of lightheartedness somehow broke through the dark veil of grief and gave me a moment's reprieve when I needed it most. God's grace is an incredible blessing.

Incredible Highlights

Having looked at the lowest point of my life, the loss of Suzan, I think it's appropriate to turn my attention to some of the high points. One of the highlights of my life was the invitation to speak to the Republican National Committee on July 25, 1998, in New York. It was truly a marvelous trip and experience. The Plaza Hotel is absolutely beautiful and is located across the street from Central Park, where I enjoyed several walks during the five days we were there. We were treated graciously, and met many important people in the Republican Party, and the response to my presentation was very encouraging. As a matter of fact, it was so well received that one of the principals sent President George Bush a communication about the talk, saying it was one of those occasions when he really enjoyed what the speaker had to say.

President Bush received that message and on August 4 of that year, he and Mrs. Bush were appearing on the Success Seminar in Kansas City. I spoke early that day and was signing books at the product center when a member of the security team came up and said the president would like to see me at twelve o'clock. I don't need to tell you that I cleared the calendar and accepted with considerable enthusiasm! When I walked in, much to my surprise and delight, the president showed me the communication from his associate and invited me to have lunch with him and Mrs. Bush. I was both stunned and delighted, and I was awestruck at the thought of being invited to a private lunch with a couple whom I admired so greatly and who had served their country so long and well. They are just as kind and gracious in person as they have always appeared to be. I could not help but play in my mind, even as we were eating lunch, how neat it would have been had America been able to see him in the same setting in which I was privileged to see him.

Since then the Redhead and I have had dinner with them and I have spoken many times with Barbara (and she always insists that I call her Barbara) and have had an opportunity to visit with them on other occasions. But that meeting, with just the three of us, I'll have to tell you, made this ol' boy from Yazoo City shake his head in awe at his circumstances. It was one of the most meaningful events of my life. Somebody asked me what was on the menu. I don't have a clue! I remember it was good and I was hungry and I did eat, but that really is all I remember about the food. The conversation was pleasant. We talked a little about politics, but mostly about family.

One other highlight of my life took place the day I sat in on the impeachment process. It gave me the chance to witness the good, the bad, and the ugly in American politics. What a tragedy it was to hear the proceedings, realizing that perhaps the brightest man to occupy the Oval Office since Thomas Jefferson had so badly abused that prestigious position, damaging his opportunity to make a real difference in the lives of so many people in the world.

I heard the accusations, I heard the charges, and I heard the senators speak out against the error of his ways. I heard them voice their disgust with him, verbalize how they could not understand how or why he had done what he was accused of doing—having a sexual relationship with an aide young enough to be his daughter; lying to his friends, family, staff, and Cabinet—roundly condemning him for all of these things. Yet, incredibly, they still refused to vote him out of office, even though he had perjured himself, desecrated the office of the president, and cost the American tax payers $45 million in the process.

It was American politics at its worst. Some senators justified their position by saying he was "so good for the economy" and it was "a personal matter," ignoring the fact that there is no doubt that our personal lives strongly influence our public lives and careers. They gave Clinton credit for the good economy, and part of it can be attributed to him, but the reality is that he inherited a rising economy and, after his time in office, left a declining one.

Sitting in on the impeachment hearings was amazing to me in more than one way. I actually had one of those incidents that readers of *American Heritage Magazine* know would make a nice "My Brush with History" article. The day I sat in on the impeachment proceedings I had the privilege of having the famous bean soup in the Senate Dining Room with one of the staff members from my nephew Jim Ziglar's office. At the time Jim was the sergeant-at-arms of the U.S. Senate (he is now commissioner of the Immigration and Naturalization Service). As the staff member and I walked back toward the Senate to watch the continuation of the trial, we were stopped in the hallway outside the entrance to the Senate by another staff member who pushed us to the side and said, "Stop right here." About three seconds later Chief Justice Rehnquist emerged. The staff member stepped in front of him and said, "Justice Rehnquist, this is Zig Ziglar." She introduced me as if I were somebody he surely knew, though there was no way he had a clue as to who I was. He warmly shook my hand and invited me to walk into the Senate proceedings with him. As we walked down the hallway a battery of photographers, reminiscent of what you see in Hollywood movies, were stationed in front and to the left of us. There had to be at least thirty of them. Flashbulbs were popping like crazy. It was all I could do to keep from looking at them and grinning, but I played it cool, if I do say so myself, and kept my eyes straight ahead. About twenty minutes later my nephew started receiving phone calls, asking, "Who is that with Chief Justice Rehnquist?" Not only were they surprised, so was I! One of my proudest possessions is the photograph I received, autographed by Chief Justice Rehnquist in which we are both clearly identifiable. Just a brief encounter, but it was a significant one for me.

You might say that the last few years have been an extremely interesting time for me, politically speaking. Between the Republican National Committee, the Clinton impeachment hearing, and the walk with Judge Rehnquist, I felt as if I'd been living a part of history. But nothing in my political experience tops the thrill of being present to see George W. Bush sworn in as the forty-third president of the United States of America.

Inauguration Day

January 20, 2001, the Redhead and I were at the Inauguration Ceremony in Washington when President George W. Bush, along with Vice President Dick Cheney, took the oath of office. It was an exhilarating experience.

Jim Ziglar was able to get us choice seats for the inauguration. We were about fourteen feet up and about fifty feet to the left of the president. Governors from the states were seated behind us; senators and congressmen sat to the right of us; the wives of the Supreme Court justices were about four rows behind us; and virtually every dignitary imaginable was present in that audience. As Mama would have said, "We were in high cotton."

We were seated an hour before the ceremony began and a light drizzle made the cold air even more chilling. We were cold but not miserable. Most of us elected to wear the thin, plastic rain covers provided for the occasion. I'll be the first to admit that the folks who watched the event on television saw and heard more, but the historical significance of the moment was breathtaking. I watched the changing of the guard and fully understood more than just the changing of the president was taking place. It was a change of philosophies.

Several things in the Inauguration Ceremony itself pointed out the big difference between the outgoing and incoming administrations. The opening prayer delivered by Franklin Graham in the absence of his father, Dr. Billy Graham, whose health would not permit him to be there, was delivered with power and conviction and with the full sense of the significance of the moment. It was truly inspiring and opened the event in a powerful and, in my judgment, appropriate manner. Just as the founding fathers of our country acknowledged Jesus Christ as Lord, so did Franklin Graham conclude his prayer by saying as much. The closing prayer was offered by Pastor John H. Caldwell, and he, too, prayed with heartfelt conviction, challenging all of us, and also concluding in the name of Christ. The return of godly leadership to our country and the prayers that heralded it brought tears of gratitude and relief to my eyes and the eyes of countless others.

The vocalist, U.S. Army Staff Sergeant Alec Maly, had one of the most beautiful voices I've ever heard—crystal clear, sensitive, sentimental, powerful, but not overpowering. I was touched most deeply when he sang "The Star-Spangled Banner." The words were beautifully sung, his voice marvelous, and as he sang the words, "Our flag was still there," my eyes were drawn to our flag, flying strong and straight in the blowing wind. I don't believe there was a dry eye in the audience of forty thousand people watching the program live.

I Had a Lot of Help

Over the years I've "fussed" a lot about the fact that the media is predominantly liberal and, by and large, does not portray the conservative side fairly. However, in all candor, I must admit that, for the most part, the media has been more than fair and even kind to me and, as a result, has enhanced my career significantly.

Early on I got some media publicity when there really was no reason for getting it. I was scarcely known out of my own backyard and yet, somehow, in September 1979, *Esquire* magazine did an article on me of considerable depth, most of it quite favorable. They took many pictures and, overall, definitely boosted my career. For this I am grateful.

Perhaps most amazing, delightful and surprising to me was the treatment that *20/20* gave me. They spent over four days with our team and me when we were conducting what was then our Richer Life Course (today it's the Born to Win Seminar). They interviewed and filmed many of the participants at the beginning of the course and again as the course was ending, giving the participants an opportunity to explain what they took away from the experience. Most of them reported significant growth and absolute delight with the course. When that show aired on July 7, 1980, gratitude filled my bucket because I was just a guy at the beginning of a new career, struggling to get started, and this was truly a break.

60 Minutes featured me just five months later in December 1980, and again I was overwhelmed at the breaks I was getting so early in my career. Never will I forget one specific incident that was quite convincing to the often skeptical press. One morning I was pulling into the parking lot of our office building with Morley Safer, the correspondent for *60 Minutes,* and as we stepped out of the car a young man was getting out of a taxi on the far side of the parking lot. When he saw me, he came rushing over and treated me like the typical fan would treat a rock star. He was beside himself with excitement; he had no earthly idea who Morley Safer was, or that he was affiliated with *60 Minutes,* but he was jumping up and down, pumping my hand, saying, "You changed my life! You changed my life! You are the greatest."

Well, he waxed pretty enthusiastically for a couple of minutes, and finally Morley interrupted him and asked if he would be willing to do that with the cameras on. The young man said yes, he would be happy to do so. When the camera crew arrived and set up, the young man reenacted his behavior of an hour or so earlier, pumping my hand, telling me, "You changed my life!" He enthusiastically said that behind God and his family, I was the one who made the difference. With microphone in hand, Morley then asked me if this was a typical fan. I said, "Morley, there is nothing typical about this guy! He is motivated out of his gourd!" With that, Morley Safer responded, "Well, where do you think this is going to take him? Is this normal, or is this dangerous in some way?"

I said, "Well, Morley, I don't think so. Let me remind you that he said God was first, his family was second, and I was third. Now, as long as he keeps it in that order, he's going to be fine." Interestingly enough, the same young man approached me in a West Texas town in July 1999, almost twenty years after our first meeting, and asked if I remembered the occasion. Obviously I did. He then proceeded to tell me that he now owned three businesses and was doing phenomenally well. He clearly attributed his success in no small measure to the instruction he received from our inspirational course, books, and cassette tapes.

A few weeks later Morley Safer was at the National Speakers Association annual convention in San Antonio where he again interviewed me at some length. I told him at that time about the young man and asked if Morley remembered it. He acknowledged that he did, and I said, "Well, if you want the rest of the story, he's been quite successful since then, so apparently he still has his priorities in order." I was hoping they would go out to West Texas and interview the man again, but for whatever reason, they chose not to do so. The bottom line is that as a result of this publicity, my career was greatly enhanced, and when the 60 Minutes segment aired, our book and tape sales exploded. A similar thing happened when I appeared on the Phil Donahue Show with one of my favorite people, Mary Kay Ash.

I have only had one TV show that was unfair to me, but the following two stories about reporters being grossly unfair involve two men who, I'm convinced, were so skeptical that they would demand a bacteria count on the milk of human kindness, and were so cynical they still believe somebody pushed Humpty Dumpty! Perhaps each was raised in a little town I heard about that wanted to start a Pessimists Club, but the vote was 37–0 against it because nobody thought it would work. At any rate, here are the stories.

One newspaper article was highly critical, and one magazine article was ridiculous. I won't identify either cities or names, but I was a speaker in a large contingent several years ago, and when the article covering the seminar came out in the paper, the journalist who had written it was highly critical of all of us, but he centered on me. (Incredibly enough, he was even critical of Dr. Norman Vincent Peale.) I was not happy with the article, nor were the sponsors of the seminar, but the following Sunday after his article appeared, an entire page was consumed by letters to the editor crying foul, and, of all the rebuttals I've ever seen, they were astonishing. The gist of the letters was, "That guy went to a different seminar from the one I attended!" The folks in the city thought the seminar was great. A little investigation revealed that not only had the young man not even talked with me but neither had he talked to any of the people in attendance. Apparently, he had some personal ax to grind, but I was grateful for the publicity because not only were the defending letters satisfying, they were very productive for my business as well.

The other unflattering article was published in a magazine. I had spent an hour and a half on the phone in the interview because the journalist had positioned himself as a big fan and firm believer in my philosophy. He had the same name as a man who had meant a great deal to me, which I found disarming, and I treated him like a friend, assuming he would at least be fair. Not only was he not fair, the article contained twenty-seven factual errors.

However, as I mentioned earlier, my treatment by the media has been overwhelmingly positive, generous in most cases and fair in the others. My career would have been nowhere close to what it is today had it not been for the print media, as well as for TV and radio.

Oftentimes when I have been interviewed, the journalist will go out of his or her way to thank me for the interview and I always say, "No, I want to thank you, because I learned long ago that you could do quite well without me, but that you were extremely important to me. And I want to thank you for the opportunity to share some of my thoughts and beliefs with you and the audience you enable me to reach."

Because of my speaking career, my professional contacts and networking have centered on my developing relationships with people who can teach me things that will make me a better speaker and writer. I'm truly grateful that I can call on recognized authorities in the fields of psychology, theology, and physiology and seek their guidance. I am grateful for their friendship because it allows me to validate the information I share. I do this because we are physical, mental, and spiritual beings, and if we don't deal with all of who we are, we won't be able to receive or accomplish all life has to offer. I mention this here because I could not have achieved the recognition I've gotten without their help.

In 1994 I received the Wilbur M. McFeely Award through the National Management Council. This award was particularly important to me because so many people thought of me as a speaker and salesperson without being aware of the roles I have played in the development of leadership and management courses. I am so strongly associated with positive thinking, attitude adjusting, goal setting, and learning to live a balanced life—all the things I speak about—that people often don't realize how much time I've spent developing material to help people in business be better leaders and managers.

Also in 1994, I was elected to the Advisory Council of the Boy Scouts of America and still actively serve in that role. This position really honored me because of the scouts' teaching of moral, ethical, and faith values, as well as goal setting and leadership—all topics dear to my heart. On the whole, Boy Scouts enjoy a much higher than average success rate in our society. That's why I'm happy to report that membership, camp attendance, traditional units and registered adult leaders were all up in 2001 and the National Scout Jamboree had over forty thousand in attendance—the largest in over thirty years. I'm grateful that more and more Americans recognize the importance of teaching our kids moral values. Being involved with such an outstanding organization is truly an honor.

In September 1998 I received a particularly meaningful award. I was recognized by the Sales and Marketing Executives as one of the top one hundred marketers in the twentieth century when I received their Marketing

Leadership Award. The very scope of this award gave me special delight because I have supported their endeavors to raise the level of professionalism in sales and marketing.

Receiving the coveted Toastmasters International Golden Gavel Award in 1999 was also a proud moment. The competition internationally for this award is intense. For years I've encouraged people to join Toastmasters because it's fantastic basic training for those who want to succeed and who aspire to be more effective in their speaking presentation.

The Big Week

In my seventy-five years I've certainly enjoyed some big days, big weeks, big months, and big years. But without a doubt the week of August 9, 1999, has been the biggest week—thus far—in my life, as far as recognition, rewards, and pure love are concerned.

The National Speakers Association Annual Convention in San Antonio, Texas (which just happens to be one of my favorite cities in the whole world!), took place from August 6–10, 1999. The Redhead and I were there, enjoying every moment of it, seeing many of our fellow speakers and friends whom we have come to know over the years.

For me, the real highlight of the convention was when I was honored with the Masters of Influence Award. Everyone loves recognition, but we particularly appreciate recognition from our peers. Since in the history of the National Speakers Association I am among fewer than ten people to receive this award, I was genuinely humbled and appreciative.

The National Speakers Association is a remarkable organization, assisting speakers in building their careers and teaching us to accept the awesome responsibility we have when we stand in front of audiences. Whether there be five or five thousand in attendance, we're on display and we have a responsibility to keep our commitment to deliver something of value to that audience. The emphasis on integrity is high, and most people who have joined the association have been high-caliber, good people with talent and a sincere desire to help others. Perhaps the most amazing thing is the willingness the members have to share their "secrets" and procedures to help other speakers do better. The upgrading of the association is a continuing effort, and the sincerity of the speakers has to impress any visitor who looks in on one of the meetings.

To be recognized and honored by this group, which includes people from every walk of life—men and women of considerable ability, high-profile public officials as well as rookies who are just getting their feet wet in the profession—was certainly one of the highlights of my life.

A Night to Remember

On the night of August 11, 1999, at the Adam's Mark Hotel in Dallas, Texas, over a thousand people gathered in the ballroom to accord me the greatest honor I've received in my life. Juanell Teague, a remarkable lady, otherwise known as "the speaker's coach," is a former seminar sponsor, and now a professional consultant who teaches speakers how to build a speaking career. She credits reading my book *See You at the Top* to changing her life, and she decided she wanted to do something special for me. In 1997 she started organizing a tribute for me. Her motive, she said, was simply to give me the recognition she felt I deserved while I was alive to observe it. That's what brought this crowd together. Never have I seen one individual do so much to honor and recognize someone else—certainly not me.

The tribute was an incredible experience. When word got out about what she was doing, many people contacted Juanell asking to be included and submitted their own stories about how the philosophy I've shared over the years has changed their lives. Scores of those who submitted their stories for Juanell's book *The Zig Ziglar Difference* which she wrote with the help of Mike Yorkey, were there in person to greet and share with me.

I'm going to list here some of those who were there August 11, 1999, honoring me with their live, printed, and recorded comments because I want to recognize them. Without them *I* wouldn't be recognizable: Barbara Bush, Mary Kay Ash, Bernie Lofchick, Dr. Jack Graham, Lou Holtz, Hal Krause, Peter Lowe, John Hammond, Paul Sides, George Bell, Bob Lightner, Jim and Naomi Rhode, Nido Qubein, Dennis Parker, Dave Hurley, the Larry Carpenter family, Mike Frank, Pam Lontos, Vincent Cerny, Rod Castle, Barry Cohen. Other contributors were Jan McBarron, Janelle Hail, Ed Hearn, Linda Warner, Clint Lewis, Kim Whitham, Trent Gaines, Carolyn Ward, Christopher Doyle, Gina Lopez, Chris Leto, Teresa Helgeson, Joe Schoenig, John Criswell, Sandy Berardi, and Peter Chantilis (who died just before the tribute).

All of my immediate family were there, and the Redhead even took to the stage to share her experience about spending her life with me. She delighted me more than she can possibly know. Before the program began, my daughter Julie slipped me an envelope saying she wanted to recognize me, too, and to read it later. At home that night I read it and wept. The accolades of a child who knows you are humbling. With her permission and encouragement I share what she wrote:

August 11, 1999
Dearest Daddy,
Tonight is the big tribute. I have been praying that you will not be embarrassed—that the tribute will be tasteful—and that you will enjoy it immensely. I find it a little scary that my humble, shy daddy is going to sit through a night of accolades just for him. I know how you KNOW God is responsible for all you have achieved. And that's just one of the aspects of you that I admire and respect.

I also feel a little anxiety because your gentle heart is so easily moved by gratitude. I fully expect an entire box of Kleenex to disappear off our table—because when you cry—we ALL cry! Daddy, nothing touches my heart more than to see you weep. Going to church with you is extra special because God's spirit moves you so strongly—in song and in witnessing others giving their life to Him. When someone chooses to ask Jesus to be his or her Savior your reaction is as if you have personally been praying for that individual's salvation for years. I love the happiness I see in your tears when you get a new brother or sister in Christ. You cannot imagine the witness your spiritual joy is to others. I am so proud that you are not a proud man. I am so blessed that you have always been open with your emotions and that you are so bold in the way you proclaim Christ as your Savior.

I have also been shored up by the way you have grieved Suzan. Your love for her is so sweet, so total—and your desire to see her again is so intense. Your total faith in that day when you join her is a reminder to me that all is well—that this life really is just an instant in respect to what has been promised to us. Somehow, Suzan's already being with God makes the idea of you and Mom going home more acceptable. I have learned from Suz that I can survive the devastating loss of someone I have indescribable love for. I have learned from you and Mom that grief is grief and it's OK because it is not the end by any means. But when I see you cry for Suz, Dad, it just makes me love you so much. Thank you for being a crier.

Thank you for sharing the joy Mom brings you. I love it so much when you tell me something that transpired between you two and you get so tickled telling me what Mom did. I can tell how much she entertains you just by being who she is. It makes me happy to know she makes you so happy. You must be a pretty good husband because I've never heard Mama complaining about your "husbanding"!

Thank you for always going on and on in your books about your family. I know I edit most of it out (only in the acknowledgments and when you've OBVIOUSLY gone way overboard in the text), but that's just for the poor reader's benefit—I do tell Tom and Cindy or Chachis and Rich and Jim when I have deleted nice things you have written about them in your books. I am glad you are so proud of us—"your family." I just think it's asking a little much for us to have to live up to all of your accolades. You know what I mean, Dad? People read that stuff and then they EXPECT us to REALLY be like that!

Just kidding. For the most part I believe you have a clear vision of who your children are. You took the time to teach us right from wrong and that has served all of us very well. You took the time to share your faith—and your faith has strengthened ours. You took the time to teach us manners, thoughtfulness, kindness, compassion, honesty, character and the qualities of love that make a person lovable. Because of your influence I believe you have very sweet, tenacious, secure children. All of us rank high on tests that measure "opinionated" because you can't teach children absolutes without having them become opinionated. We stand tall, strong and firm on just about every single thing you have ever taught us. I certainly am glad you led us in the "right" way and that you were willing to admit when you had led us astray and then went to work to put us back on the right path. It is easy to want to follow a man who has his eyes wide open. Children feel the darkness of un-admitted wrongs that parents commit, regardless of whether they were intentional or unintentional wrongs. When a father walks in the light of the Lord, his children have no fear. Thank you, Dad, for leading us in the light of Christ.

I have watched you and your company and I know God is using you for His kingdom. I have seen how He has worked through your business and how He has blessed so many things and so many of the people in your life. At the gym the other day a guy asked me what you attributed your success to and without any hesitation I said, "God." A lady was on the treadmill—(we had just finished watching your interview on "Good Morning Texas" or one of those shows)—and she said, "That's right! I've been listening to Zig Ziglar on Christian radio for years and that's why he's so successful."

I had listened to the tape you gave me by Dr. Bruce Wilkinson the day before and had prayed on the way to the gym, "Lord, send me somebody who needs to know you," and that lady opened the door for me to share your salvation story and how your life—and your level of success—changed when you gave your life to the Lord. What a proud child I am to have a father I can so openly proclaim as a follower of Christ! Your example of Christian living is so clean and pure, Dad— thank you for taking care of your reputation. And I praise God for protecting you.

And your delightful grandchild—Amanda. I believe in my heart the prayers you and Mom sent up on her behalf all of these years are responsible for the ministry she has today. I don't know why I feel that so strongly, but when she came telling me of her salvation I instinctively knew you had bombarded the heavens with relentless prayers on her behalf. Thank you, thank you, thank you. Can anyone say thank you enough for a gift so great?

I think, however, that the greatest testament that I see on a daily basis of what kind of man—and father—you are, is in the work we do together. How many daddies are able—ever—to take suggestions—and even criticism from a child and give it unbiased consideration? Not many! The respect you show me in regard to my ideas about how to change or improve your work—which is already outstanding—just floors me. You have been successful so long, you have written so much, you are talented beyond belief and yet I, your youngest daughter, can and do have influence in your creative works. Incredible! I guess you must trust the way you raised me! And you must believe that there is a little of you in me. And you must believe that I am smart. And you must think of me as much more than just "your child." And you must think I am talented, too. How affirming it is to get to work with you.

Anybody would be proud to say they do the work I do with you. But I am especially proud because I know your expectations of me are different than they would be of someone you are not related to. And I am proud because there are actually some authors in this world who are so possessive of every word they write that they won't hear of anyone—not anyone—changing a single letter.

That you let me be a part of your work honors me. I feel validated and I take great pleasure in knowing that I help you do God's work. I've done many jobs that I have loved doing—but none of my work delivered the degree of satisfaction that working with you has given me. I know that what I do is important. Before this job I knew that what I did was "necessary," and I am by nature very happy being "of service" to others— but being of service to you has double perks! I can honestly say I have never loved any of my bosses like I love you, Daddy!

I believe this tribute to you is fitting, Daddy. So many people want so much to express their appreciation for you and the difference you have made in their lives. I am glad a forum has been presented for them to do so openly. I won't be taking the mike tonight, which is why I have written you this letter. How could I possibly tell a big crowd what you mean to me? I weep when I just think of what you mean to me. I am grateful to God that He allowed me to be born to you and Mom. I am sure there are plenty of children who believe they have the best father and I think that's good for them to believe. I'm glad they are in the dark about that because I don't believe they would be nearly as happy as they are if they knew what it is possible for a father to be. And Dad, I believe you are all of everything possible God intended earthly fathers to be. Which is, of course, why I know I have the best father in the whole wide world!!!

I love you Daddy. Enjoy your night.
Little One

All in all, it was an extraordinary evening, and the effort that had been expended just to say, as Juanell said, "Thanks a zillion, Zig," was unbelievable.

Most recently I've been awarded the 2001 Cavett Award from the

National Speakers Association. I can't overemphasize the importance of Cavett Robert's advice to me so many years ago to write my first book. The statue the National Speakers Association gave me looks just like Cavett. I had the pleasure of getting to tell Cavett's widow, Trudy, and his daughters, who flew in to attend the ceremony, how very much he meant to me.

I have been recognized twice as Layman of the Year in the Christian community and have been recognized three times in *The Congressional Record* for my work with youth and the drug war.

I can't express the gratitude I have felt in my heart on receiving each and every one of these accolades. The letters I've received from people who have read or heard my material and been helped by it have humbled me time and time again. I always try to remember that I am but a tool in my Master's hand—I give Him all the credit and pray that I never lose sight of Who really makes a difference in peoples lives. I'm a happy man. Need I say more?

But Life Is Not Always So Wonderful

Early in my efforts to become successful in business, during my "wandering generality" years, I became affiliated with two nationally known figures that gave every indication of being "solid gold." Much to my regret, as a result of business experiences with them, I discovered their public images and their private lives were considerably different. I was extraordinarily disappointed.

In one case, for the first time in my life I became completely discouraged and quite negative. I had received a huge financial blow, but, more important, I had experienced a significant loss of trust in someone I had held in high esteem. There is no way to accurately measure the size of such a loss. The big positive that came out of it was that I made myself a promise that if I ever achieved any degree of prominence, I would work extremely hard, doing everything I could, to make certain that the person I appeared to be was the person I actually am. God has enabled me largely to do that, and that's not to imply that I'm claiming perfection—that would be a ridiculous overstatement of reality. But to the best of my ability, with His help, I have managed to keep my appearance in line with the reality of the man I am inside. And when I fall short of my standards for some reason, I am quick to apologize and do what I can to make it right.

Another huge disappointment has been my syndicated newspaper column. For a number of years I tried very hard to get a syndicated newspaper column, and it just simply was not happening. Finally, it did happen, and I contracted for a daily column. Creators Syndicate, an excellent syndicate, took me on. I felt very strongly that what I had to say would be well received by the public, since my books, tapes, and public appearances had been so well received.

However, newspaper publishers are a different breed. Most did not believe that the public was interested in encouraging, inspiring messages, despite the fact that newspaper readership was steadily declining and has been for the last thirty years. Every survey identified the prime cause of reduced readership as too much negative news and not enough positive news in the newspaper. I personally talked with many editors and publishers who agreed that most newspapers are primarily negative, "But not mine."

The effort hasn't been a total loss, however, because even though my columns, which now run once weekly, and are published in only about thirty papers (with just three exceptions they are small papers), they have been compiled to produce two best-seller books, and the third book derived from the columns appears to be headed in that direction as well. So, even though the publishers don't think that people are interested in good news, the public proves otherwise.

From a career point of view, perhaps my biggest disappointment has been our I Can character-building course for schools. We invested a considerable amount of money and enormous amounts of time in developing and marketing a course for schools. It is true that over 3 million students have taken the course and there is seldom a seminar that I conduct today in which somebody doesn't come up and mention how much the course helped them when they were in school. But I Can has lost money every year since its inception. The maintenance and sales costs are high.

Thankfully, all has not been lost and thousands of students are still reaping the benefits of the course today. The I Can Course is distributed by an independent organization, The Alexander Resource Group, headed by Bob Alexander,* a fine gentleman who worked with us several years. The course is being embraced by more and more schools today, primarily be-

*Bob Alexander, Pres., The Alexander Group, 176 Lake View Dr., N., Macon, GA 31210, 877-USA-ICAN, www.yesican.net.

cause the general public is accepting the fact that character really does count. The 911 call on September 11, 2001, awoke many people to the fact that we need to add the teaching of character and values to our school curriculum. We have confirming data that where the course has been taught, drug usage goes down; violence is reduced; attendance increases; grades go up; relationships among parents, teachers, and students improve; and the overall school attitude is definitely better.

I am not an educator, though we called in educators when we developed The I Can Course to make certain the principles were sound and solid. Results have been exceptionally good. In the schools where the course is taught, even the athletic teams do measurably better. Just two outstanding examples: D. W. Rutledge is the coach at Converse-Judson in San Antonio, Texas, a 5A school. He has taken his football team to the state finals seven times since 1988 and has won four state championships. Coach Dennis Parker, who formerly coached with Rutledge in San Antonio, moved to Marshall, Texas, as head coach. The team had not won a playoff game since 1949, when Y. A. Tittle was quarterback. Three years after Coach Parker arrived, the team was in the playoffs, and the fourth year they won the state championship.

My Best Wasn't Nearly Good Enough

In my career as a speaker I've had some incredible highs and also some serious disappointments. Probably the time I was most disappointed in my performance occurred in 1995. I had been approached by one of the principals in the Washington Symphony Orchestra to participate in a musical presentation about what I had accomplished in my life. He said, "We will write a special score, rehearse the orchestra, give you the script, and during the interludes you will speak from the script." What an honor! Boy, I was excited.

I was, however, deeply concerned about how it might go off because I have no sense of musical rhythm, beat, or tone. When we clap in time to the music during our worship at church, I have to watch the choir to know when to clap my hands. Some of you may think that must be the dumbest thing you've ever heard, and perhaps it is. But it is reality for me. I should have known better than to let my ego carry me away, but they were going to use the show as a fund-raiser, so I joyfully agreed.

On June 1, 1995, the Redhead and I with great excitement and anticipation headed to Washington, D.C. The rehearsals went fairly well and included a few little changes in the script and music that typically occur when all the participants in a show finally get together for the first time. I was still nervous about my performance, but more excited than nervous, and I looked forward eagerly to the event, which was held at the DAR Constitution Hall. Several things were stacked against us from the outset. The building was extremely hot on this early summer night, and the crowd was noisy and enthusiastic. When my magic moment arrived to be in the spotlight, I proceeded to drop the ball in every way imaginable.

First, I did not respond on cue from the conductor as I should have, and that was the beginning of what was an all-night series of fiascoes. The sound system was not adjusted properly; the microphone was too far away from me, and I was unable to get as close to it as I needed to, only to learn later that all I would have had to do was put a little pressure on the podium and the microphone would have moved forward the necessary distance to me. My nephew and his wife were in the audience, and they told me they could hear nothing of what I was saying. Before I was finished, the audience was visiting openly among themselves. At least I assume that's what they were doing, because it was obvious they were not mesmerized by what was happening on stage.

I guess much of my disappointment stems from my ego. I was thrilled and honored to be the subject of so grand a spectacle, a show devoted entirely to me. Many talented people had invested much time and effort in preparing for the event. But the fact was I couldn't carry my part of the show. Worse, there I was, falling flat on my face. To say it was sobering and ego-busting would be the understatement of the decade.

Obviously, I survived the humiliation and disappointment. To be honest, until I started this autobiography I had not thought about that evening for several years. I'm not denying or repressing any of it, but I have been so busy with other things and God has blessed me in so many other ways, that the blessings have simply buried the hurt involved at that time.

My other big disappointment in my speaking performance occurred a number of years ago when I was invited to speak for Holiday Inns. I had become friends with two executives of Holiday Inns who had come through our Born to Win Seminar and who had been impressed with what we had to say and present. Later, they invited me to speak at one of their major company meetings in San Francisco. I felt flattered and privileged to have the opportunity to speak before the associates of Holiday Inn and eagerly looked forward to giving them my best. But at last, when the moment came for me to deliver, I don't know where I was, but I wasn't there. I was not on target. As much as I wanted to give them an occasion to remember, I could not, for some reason, summon my customary energy and conviction. The bottom line is that my time at the podium ended in what I considered a miserable failure. I tried awfully hard—as a matter of fact, perhaps that was the problem. I tried too hard—and I didn't have to have anyone tell me that I did not leave there as their favorite speaker.

I was so deeply disappointed in myself that I offered to speak at the next Holiday Inn convention for free. Despite the fact that I had been well received at other engagements by their organization in Germany and South Africa, and had other successes with them as well, speakers are remembered by their last appearance—and that, incidentally, was my last appearance for Holiday Inns.

There have been other occasions when I disappointed myself and my clients, but since they are the same song with a different verse, I prefer to move quickly to the positives that came from the negatives. Life really is a series of peaks and valleys. My friend C. I. Dixon says that you can't climb a smooth mountain, and has written a book by that title. I agree, because on a smooth mountain you have no outcropping of rock or crevice from which to gain a stable foothold to start your climb. Most of us don't enjoy the valley experiences, and I'm no exception, but it's in the valleys that we grow. Fred Smith says we should never miss the good in the bad experiences that sent us to the valley.

I mention all of this because sometimes people think I don't have the difficulties that others have. I just want you to know that, yes, I disappoint myself, and when I do that, it's inevitable that regardless of what the clients might say, I know I must have, to a degree, disappointed them as well.

Another reason I tell these stories at great length here is because I believe they were catalysts for the careful way I do things today. This is the lesson I learned: Be prepared and be sharp. Because I speak primarily to corporate America as well as at public seminars, I prepare and validate my material before I write it, record it, or verbalize it. This procedure, I believe, gives me an added dimension and allows me to speak more convincingly and with more authority than I would otherwise.

Today, even if I'm going to give the same talk I've given dozens—even hundreds—of times before, I will still spend between three and five hours in preparation. I largely rewrite my notes; I visualize the entire presentation; I insert several new examples or illustrations, tie it in to local situations in many cases, and make certain that I get a good night's sleep the night before.

Where it is permitted (many corporate clients want to keep me a secret until I'm introduced), I love to sit in on the first parts of the meetings, pick up the flavor and feel of the crowd, shake as many hands in the lobby or at the back of the room as is possible, and, in general, check the equipment to make certain everything is in place. I look at the seating arrangement because in many cases the speaking platform will be about twenty-five feet from the front row of chairs. This is a huge hurdle to overcome, so I get there before anything happens to make certain that the seating arrangement is advantageous and that everything is in order. I don't take any chances.

As part of my preparation I also ask for information about the client and conduct an extensive telephone interview to learn what their expectations for me are. This approach enables me to customize the program to meet their needs.

People often ask me if I'm nervous before I speak. I can honestly say no, I'm not. But I am very, very excited about making the same talk the five hundredth time, because I realize I've got a different audience in front of me and never again will I have the privilege of speaking to this exact group of people. I make every talk as if it's going to be the last one I'll ever make. I also pray before each talk I make. One of the things I ask God for is to make me the P. C. Merrell in someone else's life and let me influence and enrich his or her life in a positive way. And I also pray for wisdom, energy, and clarity of expression. Then I go out there and I give that talk everything I've got.

I speak with confidence not because of what comes from me, but because of what comes through me. I believe it would be arrogant for me to think I could just stand up and give one of my talks spontaneously, regardless of how many times I had done it before. Not to prepare would be arrogant, and when you're arrogant, that's when Buster Douglas knocks out Mike Tyson or when the inferior team beats the number one team that expected a cakewalk.

The bottom line is that God has blessed my efforts and my preparation, and, as far as I know, it has now been several years since I have completely dropped the ball in one of my presentations.

The Biggest Business Disappointment by Far: The Zig Ziglar Network

For whatever reason, because of my optimistic nature and upbeat attitude, many people are under the illusion that I have had few, if any, serious business problems. Of course, that is not true.

For over thirty years I have been speaking and training in the network marketing industry. I have spoken for a number of different companies, selling a wide range of products. I have seen the good, the bad, and the indifferent in this industry.

For a number of years I dreamed of starting our own network marketing company. In 1996, the timing seemed to be right to make our move. We had assembled all the pieces of the puzzle we thought were necessary to build a successful network marketing company. We consulted carefully with the best legal minds and the recognized experts in the network marketing industry. We prayerfully approached every phase and step of the process. Our prayer was constant: "Lord, if this is not in Your will, stop it. Put the barrier up. We want to please you." The doors kept opening wider and wider. Our excitement grew.

In February 2000 we had our pre launch. Word had already leaked out, and our office was flooded with phone calls, faxes, visitors—you name it, people were eager to be part of the organization. We were overjoyed at the response. We had planned as carefully, I believe, as any company could before opening the business. We thought we had touched all of the bases.

We put a nutritional line together with a great deal of care and, with scientifically validated information, had produced products that worked. We had included in our products none of the forbidden ingredients that created more problems than they solved. Along with the nutritional products, we were marketing our training materials and inspirational materials. We got off to a good start, and excitement was high. But for whatever reason, in spite of our hard work and enthusiasm, our network marketing program never really caught on. People quickly grew discouraged; many were veterans of the industry, while others were newcomers, but results, while exciting early on, did not meet our expectations.

On September 15, 2000, we launched ZigOnline, which was an affiliate program on the Internet that offered segments of my audio materials indexed by subject. We were so enthusiastic about it and knew that it would be an explosive addition to the Zig Ziglar Network. Instead, it proved to be anything but. It ended up a temporary distraction and took away time, attention, and resources that were badly needed in other areas of the company. Part of this was because our enthusiasm for Internet sales was unfounded.

We did not fail because of a lack of effort, but because we misread the market. Regretfully and full of disappointment, in December 2000 we closed the doors on the Zig Ziglar Network. Our decision resulted in the extreme disappointment and frustration—even bitterness—in the hearts of some who felt we had let them down. We had invested over three years in research, a very large sum of money, and were losing a hundred fifty thousand dollars a month when we finally closed the doors. But we had explored every other possibility and found we had no other option.

My disappointment at the failure of the Zig Ziglar Network is profound. And the way we shut it down represents perhaps my biggest mistake in judgment since I've been in the business world. I did not understand fully the heartbreak experienced by many of the people who had considered the Zig Ziglar Network their golden land of opportunity, their source of high hopes. So when we affiliated ZZN with Nikken, a large, well-capitalized Japanese network marketing company, I did not properly present it to our people. I spared them the background and details that would have given them a better explanation of what our real circumstances were. I did not fully empathize with them, apologize properly for the mistakes and failures we'd had in the Zig Ziglar Network, did not let them clearly understand that my heart broke for them and that I was concerned for them. I'd had several months to consider these things, and yet I sprang the disappointing news on them in a single well-publicized conference call. Instead of diplomatically preparing everyone for the announcement, laying the necessary factual groundwork, going to the leadership individually, as courtesy and sensitivity would seem to require, I had assumed they would understand. I had counted on this one communication being sufficient to carry us through the close of the company. Big mistake. Because of this, I offer my ZZN associates my regrets and seek their forgiveness.

The year 2000 ended up being the most financially disastrous year of my career. The question is, How did I survive the emotional stress and handle that particular failure? Those who know me well—that's my family and the staff with whom I work, particularly Laurie Magers, who has been my executive assistant for over twenty-five years—will tell you they could detect very little difference in either my emotions or my attitude. My major concern was the terrible disappointment of the people I had brought into the organization. Though closing the company involved a serious interior struggle, I've got to tell you that my faith is what made the difference and got me through. As always, Romans 8:28 sustains me when I read "all things work together for good to those who love God, who are called to serve according to His purpose." I can give you many examples in history and my personal life proving things that appeared to be disastrous were actually long-range blessings coming in God's providence. Even, or especially, when we cannot see it at the time, God discloses His hidden blessings in His good time.

As I've already said, the biggest problem emotionally for me was the fact that I disappointed so many people who believed, as did I, that ZZN would be an overwhelming success. Obviously, it wasn't. However, out of that failure came an affiliation with Nikken. I am serving as the spokesperson for Nikken USA and as honorary chairman of Nikken International. This affiliation ultimately puts the company in position to fulfill more rapidly our original mission—to be the difference maker in the personal, family, and professional lives of enough people to make a positive difference in the world. Yes, I'm delighted to know that God is in control of this situation, as He is of every situation, and that these developments are working together not only for my good, but for the good of untold numbers of people throughout the world.

If I Had It to Do Over Again

One question frequently asked of me is, If I had my life to live over, what would I change? I heard a lady answer that question a number of years ago, and though I have long since forgotten her name, I will never forget what she said. "I would not change a thing, because if I did I might not have ended up where I am—and I love where I am!" My sentiments, exactly. Don't misunderstand—that doesn't mean I've done everything right or that I've had no problems, because in many ways I feel as if I've had more than my share as I've just reviewed with you. But each event in my life has been a part of shaping my life as it is today, and I wouldn't have it any other way.

I've been more than blessed with an incredible wife who has been my companion for over fifty-five years, four marvelous children, three outstanding sons-in-law, a beautiful daughter-in-law, four remarkable grandchildren (and very soon a great-grandchild), three terrific step-grand-children, and eight remarkable step-great-grandchildren. My cup truly runneth over!

I consider my family my most significant accomplishment in life. My relationship with my wife, outside of my relationship with Christ, is the most important relationship I have. The Redhead personifies love, loyalty, commitment, forgiveness, companionship, partnership, teamwork, and compassion for others. She is my greatest joy. I frequently tell my audiences that had it not been for her, I would not have enjoyed anything approaching the success I have as a speaker and writer. Yet, during all of the years I struggled to find my niche, not once did she ever complain or say, "It'd be nice if we had more financial stability," or "If only we had a little more money . . ." No, instead it was always, "You can do it, honey. Tomorrow's going to be better."

And the two things that rang my bell then and keep it ringing today are hearing her say, "I love you" and "I believe in you." There is no way I can emphasize the importance of having a cheerleader urging me on every day and praying for me every night.

One of the funniest and most revealing incidents about the Redhead took place at the Marriott Hotel in Richmond, Virginia. I have since returned to the same hotel three times over the last fourteen years, and I always see the man I met the first time I was there. His name is J. Ron Fleming; he is no longer a bellboy, he is now the bell captain, the important-looking man out front in the dressy red uniform, greeting the people, and directing some of the operations. He is really a neat guy.

On April 26, 2001, I was back in the hotel conducting the breakfast for the Peter Lowe Success Seminar that was to follow at the Coliseum. He again greeted me warmly, and we recalled our initial meeting, a delightful memory for both of us. It took place roughly fifteen years ago. I checked into the Marriott after midnight, carrying a couple of bags, and headed to the elevator. A woman followed a few steps behind me carrying two or three bags. I spoke to her pleasantly, but she almost didn't speak to me at all. I can understand why because in her mind I may have been a threat to her.

The lady stepped aboard the elevator, as did I. We went up one floor and then the bellman, Ron Fleming, stepped aboard. When he looked up, he recognized me and went almost berserk. He shouted my name, "Zig Ziglar! My hero! The man who changed my life! You're the greatest!" I mean, he really, really was carrying on excitedly. The lady then calmly asked me, in view of all of this praise and gratitude, "What do you do?" Before I could get a word out, Ron interrupted by saying, "He writes books and he makes speeches! He's the greatest of all!" The lady very coolly looked at me and said, "And to whom or to what do you attribute your remarkable success in life?" One tenth of a second elapsed, and Ron Fleming, proving himself a careful student of my work, cried emphatically, "The Redhead!" The reality is, he was far closer to the truth than he realized.

I can say without any fear of error that had it not been for her love, support, belief in, and encouragement of me, the many good things that have happened in my life would never have occurred.

On November 26, 1996, the Redhead and I celebrated our fiftieth wedding anniversary. We wanted the day to be truly special, so the Redhead planned the menu, reserved the ballroom, and sent out the invitations. We had guests from many different states around the nation and, of course, Brother Bern from Winnipeg, Canada. Our daughters got together and arranged to have the occasion videotaped so we could always remember what a grand celebration it was. We had an abundance of food and a nice little dance band so that we could dance to some of the music we enjoyed when we were courting before our marriage.

A highlight of the evening for us was the comments our children made about our marriage relationship, the impact it had on their lives, and how grateful they were that during all their years they never had to wonder whether we were going to make it together. It was a beautiful evening, and at the end we were exhausted but very happy.

One of the side benefits that came from the occasion was that one of our business friends, who hosts a number of conventions each year, decided then and there to quit serving alcohol at his conventions. He was astonished at the fact that everybody at our anniversary party had such a marvelous time despite the fact that no alcohol was served. We believe it was *because* no alcohol was served that everybody had such a marvelous time. He observed that nobody insulted anybody, nobody was embarrassed, he didn't see anybody making a pass at somebody else's mate, there was no vulgar language or any of the other things that generally happen when booze flows freely.

The next day we spent much time with family and friends from around the country, and on the following day we took off for our dream celebration in Bermuda. It was quite unlike our first honeymoon when we rode the bus to Charlotte, North Carolina. This time we had a nice suite at a beautiful hotel with a par-three golf course on the grounds.

One of the things I mentioned at our anniversary celebration was that I could not help but notice that many of our guests were getting on up in years and they needed to take care of themselves because I was now announcing our seventy-fifth wedding anniversary celebration and everybody there that evening would be invited to return.

Not only does that Redhead have great compassion and love, but she is also a very bright lady. She was the fifth smartest in her class of four hundred, which makes us the perfectly balanced couple, because I was in the part of the class that made the top half possible. Today, we are more in love than ever; we do more things together than ever before; we talk more and have more fun than ever. Those are just some of the reasons I frequently tell audiences that if she ever leaves me I'm going with her.

One of the things the Redhead and I wouldn't change is the way we raised our children. When they were young we never tried to be their buddies, because we knew they needed parents, not friends. Now that they are grown we are all very close friends, and one of our delights is getting to enjoy their companionship. Even if they weren't ours, we'd pick them to be our friends.

The fact that all of our children have stayed close to home is very pleasing to the Redhead and me. Julie and her husband, Jim Norman, are the farthest away. Since they love animals, especially horses, they live on acreage only eighty minutes from our home. These days Jim is a business consultant, sharing turnaround procedures for struggling businesses and helping speakers build their career. One of his diversions and hobbies as an entrepreneur is building Huie Ziglar Rocking Chairs, designed by my brother to relieve the pain in his aching back. The majority of his marketing takes place on the Internet, and all of the work Julie and I do on my books and newspaper column is done over the Internet, so Jim and Julie are ecstatic to be able to work from their home. And we still live close enough to one another to have those regular visits that mean so much to all of us.

Tom and Chachis live only ten minutes away from us, and Richard and Cindy are about thirty minutes away, so we are all very close as a result—in more ways than just geographically. We don't get to see our grandchildren as often as we'd like, but most of them live within sixty miles of us.

We are also grateful that not one of our children has ever questioned whether our love for them was total and complete, or whether we loved them all equally.

Cindy, our middle daughter, and I frequently talk on the phone, as well as take walks together. One of my favorite memories is of years ago when I started jogging and was traveling more than I am today. Cindy and her husband, Richard Oates, lived in Sacramento, California. She started jogging, too, so that when I spoke in Sacramento she could run with me. I can't begin to tell you how much that pleased me. Not just because of the fact that we were jogging together, but also because of what it said about how she felt about her daddy.

Cindy is very sensitive to what is going on, knows her daddy and mom extremely well, and has been a source of counsel to us as well as to our granddaughter, Katherine, during some critical stages in Katherine's life, particularly during the first years after the death of her mother. Cindy remains a valued counselor and close spiritual adviser to Katherine as well as to other members of the family.

Cindy loves her church and working out with Henry Alayon, her personal trainer. Her true delight is found in her certified therapy dog, Emmitt. She and Emmitt visit hospitals, and in 1999 Cindy was recognized as Volunteer of the Year for the Baylor Hospital Animal Therapy Division. She is so much fun to be with, and to this date on our walks we have some of the most encouraging and delightful conversations I am privileged to enjoy.

Once on a walk with the sweetnin', I said to her, "I've been pondering a situation. If all of my children were together and disaster struck, and I could not rescue all of them, which would I choose to rescue?" She asked, "What did you decide?" I said, "It was easy, Sweetin'. I decided I would grab the one closest to me." Then I explained, saying, "I cannot imagine the grief I would have if I had chosen one over another and then all of them survived. The others would go through life thinking, 'Dad loved that one more than he loved me.' There's no way I could let that happen."

It is true that in the last few years of her life, Suzan always signed her notes to me YFC—meaning Your Favorite Child. She also made it a point when she called on the phone to say, "This is your favorite child calling." Suzan regularly reminded her siblings that she was, in fact, the favorite child, having been around the longest, being the smartest, brightest, the prettiest, etc. But all four of our children knew it was a family joke, not a family fact. Since Suzan is not here to egg it on anymore, her siblings took up the banner for her, reminding us at every turn that Suzan is still the favorite.

My youngest daughter, Julie, is the editor of my books and newspaper column, and I dearly love working with her. She brings a fresh perspective and is able to help me a great deal. I have been known to be a little dogmatic, and she has the ability to soften the bluntness and round off the edges, making my message more digestible. She is also very good at stopping me in my tracks when I get off on a tangent.

My son, Tom, is the president and CEO of our company, and our relationship is also quite outstanding. I trust him implicitly to make decisions and regard him as a far more astute financial manager and decision maker in the business world than I am. I know his decisions will be ethically and morally sound and that he will act according to the principles of our company philosophy—that is, character does count, and that we only win when we make winners out of those with whom we deal. I have much comfort in that. Just having the pleasure of working with and talking to him every day about our business is a gift.

In many ways, my relationships with my daughter-in-law and our three sons-in-law represent special highlights in my life. I feel very close to each one of them, and I'm grateful for them. Richard Oates our chief operating officer, received a liver transplant on May 22, 2001. Though there have been two serious additional operations since the transplant, Richard's health is being restored. It's been very difficult to watch someone we love go through a decline, as he did before the transplant. He's always been a high energy, get-it-done-now kind of person, and before the transplant he was struggling just to get through the day. His faith, his attitude, and the extremely healthy liver he received have combined to give him the best chance possible for a normal, healthy life.

I believe that God works in mysterious and, sometimes, miraculous ways. Let me share one such experience we had during Richard's illness. Our family started praying for the donor and his family the day we learned that Richard needed a liver transplant. Initially all of us were baffled at how you pray when you know someone else's dying is what makes your loved one's living possible. We prayed that God would comfort the donor's family and surround them with love, and I personally prayed that Richard's donor would be a Christian. That way both the donor family and the recipient would have their lives dramatically enriched, and we could share in our faith and the knowledge that we'd all be reunited with our loved ones in heaven.

I want to recognize Matthew McCord, Richard's liver donor, in this family section of my book. By God's perfect design, Matthew is our brother in Christ, and his family tells us that he had hoped if he ever got to be a donor that his recipient would be a Christian so that he could meet him one day in heaven.

Our family wept when we learned that even before our families knew one another's names, Matthew's mother, father, and wife had been comforted by the book I wrote when I started my own journey through the grief of losing Suzan. *Confessions of a Grieving Christian* has ministered to Matthew's family when they were grieving. God is so incredible in the way He weaves His tapestry of love and puts us together to comfort one another. Matthew McCord's memory will always be nurtured by our family.

I will always be grateful for Jim Norman, Julie's husband, and his willingness to serve as president of our company at a desperate time in our history when we were in serious trouble. He brought his entrepreneurial skills and successful business background to us and bailed us out of the difficulties we were experiencing. He served us effectively and honorably for six years. He is still a great resource to me indirectly. As Julie does her editing work for me out of her home and Jim's office is at home, Julie can call on him for computer tech support when things go awry. Julie also consults with him when we hit a snag in our writing, and his suggestions and con-tributions on books and columns have proven invaluable. The diary Jim kept as our daughter Suzan lay fighting for her life was a significant contri-bution to *Confessions of a Grieving Christian.*

Chad Witmeyer, Suzan's husband, also worked in our corporate struc-ture for a number of years. Over that period of time we grew close, enjoyed golf games together, and during Suzan's life, our family dinners were always a highlight of our lives. Nearly four years after Suzan's death, Chad married Tracey Wilcox, a beautiful woman who brought two more wonderful chil-dren into the family, Jordan and Eric. This beautiful couple met during the time Tracey served as our sales director. It's truly amazing how the family business has shaped all of our lives.

Then there's Chachis, whom I affectionately call Bonita. She's from Campeche, Mexico, and she and Tom met while attending Austin College. We were thrilled when they chose to be married in our home. They are the proud parents of seven year-old Alexandra, our youngest granddaughter, who delights and entertains us all.

We are extremely proud of our two grown granddaughters. Sunshine, Julie's daughter, also chose to be married in our home on December 30, 2000, and today she and her husband, Nathan Fair, are missionaries with YWAM (Youth with a Mission) in Tyler, Texas, and are totally committed to serving the Lord. They are going to make me a great-grandfather yet again in June 2002. Sunshine's real name is Amanda, but for all of her life she has been Sunshine to me.

Katherine, Suzan and Chad's daughter, is my Keeper, because the in-stant I saw her I knew she was a keeper. She is a senior at North Texas State University, and her name regularly graces the Dean's List. When Katherine made a 4.0, her name went on the President's List as well. She's a delight-ful person, full of life and love, and is working hard to get her degree so that she can enter the teaching profession. I strongly believe she will make a great teacher. (And I'd say the same even if I weren't her grandfather!)

Katherine's sister, Elizabeth, is our other granddaughter. I lovingly call her Little Lover, because that's exactly what she is, a beautiful special needs child, having been born mentally disabled. She's a teenager now, and she owns her daddy Chad, lock, stock, and barrel. Elizabeth opened a whole new world to the Ziglar family. Today the Special Olympics thrill our hearts and simple things like a new word or enough words to make a sentence make us exclaim with joy at the wonder of her latest victory. What a delight and joy she is to be around.

In addition, when Julie married Jim Norman, we were blessed with three wonderful step-grandchildren. Cheryl, whom we call Dede, is married to one of the most devoted, family-oriented men I know, Gus Galindo, and they made it possible for the Redhead and me to join the rank of great-grandparents. Their lovely and vivacious children are Kristina, fifteen, Desirée, thirteen, Sam, five, and Robert, two. The twins, Jenni and Jim (we used to call him Little Jim but that no longer applies), are thirty years old this year—amazing!—and they both struck home runs when it came to choosing a mate. Jim married a beautiful, bright, blonde named Stacy, and they have contributed two precious boys to the family, Jake, five, and Parker, two. Jenni married a smart, handsome firefighter, Andrew Haecker, and they decided to save time and get a two-for-one deal. Their darling identical twin girls, Mable and Molly, arrived beautiful and healthy on July 22, 2000.

In case you have forgotten the number I mentioned earlier and were trying to count, that's eight—yes, eight great-grandchildren. And some of our grandchildren haven't made their first contribution yet! When we're all in one room, it's fairly overwhelming to see what the Redhead and I started! God is truly good!

As far as the public is concerned (my "extended family," that is), the way I most enjoy spending time with them is when I'm teaching my Sunday school class at Prestonwood Baptist Church. We call it the Encouragers Class because it is primarily designed to give people a lift and encouragement for the day and week to come. While it is all biblically based, we also deal with everyday subjects, realizing that people have to eat, dress, drive, shop, visit doctors, and do a host of other things that require living in our modern world.

I always start every lesson with a few jokes and/or humorous stories because I recognize that some members of the class might have had little or nothing to laugh about during the week, and since laughter does so much good, I believe everybody needs to have a good dose of it every day. I make certain they get it on Sunday morning. Then I spend about 85 percent of the class time teaching the Bible and applying the principles contained therein on how to build winning relationships, set and reach goals, maintain the right attitude, develop the qualities that lead to balanced success, get up when they've been knocked down, achieve job security in a no-job-security world—subjects that really are everyday topics that need to be dealt with. What makes my Sunday school teaching different from the speaking I do in the corporate world is that I back up my topics with scripture. And because of the large number of visitors we have in the class, I always tell them how to go to heaven. When the class is over, the members not only feel encouraged, but they also have directions for accomplishing their objectives. I laughingly tell the class that I have so much fun teaching them, I'm afraid someday they're going to start charging me for teaching it because nobody should have that much fun without having to pay a little something for it!

After the class is over we all go to "Big Church" to hear one of the great preachers in America and enjoy the beautiful music our choir always presents. Following Big Church, a number of us (forty to sixty) go to lunch together. When you combine these activities, it explains why Sunday is my favorite day of the week.

How Do You Do It?

When people hear about my big family, my Sunday school class, and my busy work schedule, they ask, "How do you do it, Zig? Where does all of that energy come from?" First of all, God blessed me with good health. Second, I eat sensibly and exercise regularly. Third, I've been using natural nutritional supplements for roughly forty years. Fourth, I simply do not worry. I do the best I can, rely on my faith, and I believe that's all any of us can do to take care of our health and, at the same time, increase our energy.

I'm truly grateful for my energy because doctors say I burn more raw energy in an hour's presentation than a workingman does in eight hours of manual labor. So, when I do a three-hour seminar, I've expended a considerable amount of energy. Traditionally, at the big public seminars, I speak at the breakfasts, then speak to the general assembly, then I typically autograph books for roughly one to two hours before I catch a flight either back to Dallas or to my next engagement. When I sit down on the plane, almost always I'm asleep before the plane leaves the ground. I generally sleep about fifteen to twenty minutes, then I work most of the rest of the flight writing, reading, preparing, studying, etc. I can be really tired or exhausted when I get home after a road trip, but a good night's sleep restores me completely, and I'm off to the races again the next day.

No, I wouldn't change a thing, even though during the first twenty-seven years of our marriage things were particularly tough financially. I bought gasoline fifty cents' worth at a time on many occasions. I miscalculated while selecting groceries and had to put items back because I could not pay for them. I have had my electricity turned off and my telephone disconnected. I had to turn a car back in because I could not pay for it, and, if you'll recall, when our first baby was born the hospital bill was sixty-four dollars—and I had to make two cookware sales in order to get her out of the hospital. Once the Internal Revenue Service put a lien on our front door, much to our embarrassment, because I could not pay my taxes. On more than one occasion we teetered on the verge of bankruptcy, but somehow we always managed to avoid filing.

Yes, in those first twenty-seven years of our marriage, it seems that I was always seeking some kind of arrangement that would bring in significant sums of money. Perhaps this was because of my childhood; perhaps it was because I never seemed to have enough money to do the things I really wanted to do. But much of it can be attributed to the fact that I was not very money wise, foolishly trading cars at the drop of a hat when there was no logical reason—and certainly no need—for the new or different car, other than to satisfy an ego trip of the moment.

Today I can honestly say I am not money motivated. I have no need to be filthy rich, but I do have great need not to be poor. I've been there—more than once—didn't like it, and don't want to go there again.

Yes, there were many difficult years and we do still occasionally hit a rough spot. But always, with the help of God, things work out well. I wouldn't change a thing—I love where I am.

Refired

I've made a concerted effort to minimize my travel schedule the last several years so that I can spend more time with the Redhead, my children, and grandchildren, but the reduced travel schedule is in no way indicative of my move toward retirement. I'm writing now more than I ever have, and I'm creating new programs all the time.

As a matter of fact, when the word *retirement* comes up, which it increasingly does as my age escalates, I tell folks that I have no intention of retiring, even though I recently celebrated the fiftieth anniversary of my twenty-fifth birthday. At age seventy-five I have a considerable amount of energy, and though I'm not guaranteed ten more minutes of life, I believe I am at least ten, maybe even fifteen years away from hitting my peak. As a matter of fact, two weeks before my seventy-fifth birthday I stayed on the treadmill at the aerobics center longer than I was able to stay on it when I was forty-five, overweight, and out of shape. My e-mail and snail mail, as well as personal appearances and phone calls, tell me that I'm still having a positive impact on others through my books, tapes, and public appearances.

Since I'm having a marvelous time, why on earth should I consider retirement? Besides, retirement is never mentioned in the Bible. I often tell people who haven't seen me recently and wonder if I have retired, "I'm not retired, I'm refired. I'm not gonna ease up, let up, shut up, or give up until I'm taken up. As a matter of fact, I'm just getting warmed up!" I'm pleased to say that apparently the good Lord agrees with me.

Code Blue

On Friday, February 22, 2002, I was shown my mortality—an event that I am eternally grateful to be able to recount in this work. At 5:20 A.M. I awakened expecting another fun-filled, perfectly normal, healthy, and active day. Instead, my first trip to the bathroom alerted me to the fact that the diverticulitis that had first presented a problem in 1996 was flaring up for the third time. I was stunned and, frankly, frightened, because there was abundant evidence that, unlike the original two episodes, I was experiencing a far more serious loss of blood and needed to seek immediate treatment.

Before I could even inform the Redhead, I experienced a second alarming loss of blood. At that point I alerted her, and she hurriedly dressed and drove me to Medical City Hospital, where I had been treated during my two previous episodes. On the way, at the Redhead's insistence, I called our three children to let them know we were headed for the hospital. My positive attitude kicked in, and not wanting to alarm them or cause undue concern, I assured each of them that it was no big deal, not life threatening in any way, and that we all knew the routine. I'd be admitted for a few days, and when the doctors were sure the bleeding had stopped, I'd go home again, just as I had in the past. I even encouraged them not to rush to the hospital, because it was in no way an emergency. In retrospect, I could not confess the reality of the volume of blood loss I'd already experienced. I was going to hold on to the hope that things weren't as bad as they looked.

Because I feared a recurrence of bleeding after my second incident with diverticulitis, I had asked my examining physician at the time (now retired) to provide me with a letter that would admit me to any hospital anywhere, bypassing the time-consuming and anxiety-producing process of being admitted to an emergency room for treatment. The letter got me immediate attention, and the paperwork was quickly completed.

The only similarity between the first two incidents and the third one was bleeding. This time I passed out when I stood up for X rays, and I threw up as well. Some of my children don't listen to their father very well, and Cindy and Tom arrived shortly after my fainting spell. Son-in-law Richard followed soon after. It appeared that I was stable, so Tom and Richard left to go take care of things at the company, and Cindy and the Redhead waited with me for the inevitable tests.

When two emergency-room staffers came to get me, we assumed they were moving me to a regular room. The Redhead and Cindy almost had to run to keep up, and we were all surprised when we arrived at the Critical Care Unit. Cindy asked one of the staffers why we were in CCU, and he said they were better prepared to monitor me there in case there was another bleed.

Shortly after I got settled in, I needed to use the restroom again, and though my nurse Maria said I should use the bedpan, I insisted on using the potty chair. I had been sitting upright for only a few seconds before I told Maria I felt weak and immediately passed out again.

Cindy tells me that Maria and another nurse who was with me at the time started calling for help. When no help came, Cindy and the Redhead ran down the hall screaming as loudly as they could, "Help, we need help!" Half a dozen people rushed to the little CCU room and got me back into the bed. After all the excitement was over, Maria told Cindy that just about the time she was going to start mouth-to-mouth resuscitation and pound on my chest, I came to.

When the aide arrived to wheel me down to Nuclear Medicine for a bleeding scan, Cindy insisted that she and her mother ride down in the elevator with me and wait just outside the door where the test was to be performed. Cindy tells me that she was standing, peering in on me through the open door, when she got a disapproving look from one of the nurses and decided she'd better sit down in a chair by her mother. Someone closed the door, and in just a matter of seconds the door flew open and several panic-stricken nurses came running out and scattered in all directions. Cindy demanded to know what was going on, if my heart had stopped, and if they were losing me. No one answered as they regrouped and disappeared behind the closed door. Cindy and the Redhead were seeing a Code Blue and I, on the other hand, was experiencing one.

Cindy tells me that she hesitated outside the door for just an instant, then she ran into the room, got as close to me as she could, and yelled, "Daddy, Daddy, angels are all around you and Jesus is here! Hang on!" She said they had one of those breathing bags over my face and were getting ready to put on my chest the paddles that jump-start the heart when she ran back to check on the Redhead, yelling ahead, "Pray, Mama! Pray!"

Sometime during the Code Blue, I saw a man who appeared to be about fifty-five years old seated in a chair. He was wearing a hat and a tan suit, and he looked straight at me, smiled slightly, and gave me a hand signal indicating things were going to be all right. I'm convinced that man was an angel. I had asked God for my life and told him there were things I still wanted to do. The angel gave me the assurance that I would have that extended time to take care of my wife and my family.

I am so grateful that Cindy was there to support her mother and pray for me when I needed it most. It breaks my heart to hear Cindy describe how her mother looked. She said my bride was standing with her fists clenched under her chin and her eyes closed tightly against the nightmare that was unfolding. When they started to pray, the only word that would come out was Jesus. Jesus, Jesus, Jesus. And just as Romans 8:26 promises, Jesus alone was enough.

In James 5:16, the Bible says, "The effectual fervent prayer of a righteous man availeth much." The heavens were bombarded with just such prayers when Cindy and the Redhead pleaded for my life—and much was given. My blood pressure had dropped out of sight, and the scene looked like something out of a movie when the flat line and the continuous tone on the heart monitor replace the peaks, valleys, and beeps of a healthy heartbeat.

Cindy said she and the Redhead prayed that way for a time, and then she went back into the room to check on me. Apparently I had just come around, and the nurse asked how I felt. In what I'm told is my usual form I replied, "I feel fine. How do you feel?" That's when Cindy said she knew her daddy was going to be okay.

I began improving immediately when they started the blood transfusions to replace the six pints of blood I had lost. After all the tests were completed and I was well stabilized, the doctors visited and convinced me that it would be wise to circumvent any chance of an instant replay. Surgery to remove the majority of my diverticuli-ridden colon was scheduled for the next morning. It went extremely well, and after a ten-day stay in the hospital, I returned home. The doctors said my excellent physical condition contributed greatly to the remarkable strides I made in my recovery. I believe the multitudes of prayers that were prayed on my behalf made all the difference.

There is even more to this miracle. When Bernie Lofchick, my best friend of thirty-seven years, learned of my brush with death and that I was in the hospital, he became deeply concerned—or, as he put it, he was downright worried. He called every day to inquire about my progress, and we have talked every day but one since I left the hospital. A few days after the Code Blue, Bernie had a dream that he described so clearly that it was more like a vision. He pointed out that his past dreams had always been "fuzzy," not brilliantly clear like this one.

Bernie dreamed that our daughter Suzan, who died on May 13, 1995, appeared to him dressed in white and wearing a white veil. He commented that she "looked like an angel." Bernie and Suzan had always had a close relationship, and shared mutual admiration for each other. He said in the dream Suzan said to him, "Don't worry, Uncle Bernie, Dad's going to be fine, and he's going to be around a long time." Bernie had been so worried that he had been wrestling with whether he should fly to Dallas to see me. After the dream, however, he knew it would not be necessary, and the worry disappeared.

From my perspective it's extremely important that you not become too focused on this event, or too enamored with this turn of events and revelation from God. I can't be certain as to what it all means; only eternity can determine that. But I don't want you to miss the message or the lessons that God can bring as a result of this revelation. My Bible clearly tells me that Jesus Christ is the same yesterday, today, and forever, and the Bible contains a number of examples where God reveals Himself and teaches through dreams. This particular part of the miracle simply brings another dimension to that miracle. God had assured me through the angel that appeared to me that He was going to extend my life, so Bernie's dream was a validation of what God had already told me, and simply added another dimension. It's my conviction that when God has a message to deliver, He takes pains to remove any questions that we might have. I do worship a great God.

I don't need to tell you that my gratitude bucket is running over because I was spared. I find it more than a little ironic that I am able to thank God for returning me to life twice: once as the nine-day-old infant you read about at the beginning of this book and again as a man in the declining years of his life. It is an awesome feeling to look back and see His hand on me throughout my life and to know He has more for me to do here on Earth. Though I have no fear of dying and meeting my Lord, it is mighty good to still be here.

As I have told those who are especially close to me, "I'm not saying I'm going to be a 'better' husband, father, friend, etc., but I will be because I already am a more grateful, compassionate, committed husband, father, friend, etc., than before." I know, as my friend Lou Holtz says, "what's important now." My priorities and my focus, thanks to God's grace, are more clearly defined than ever, and my faith and resolve are steadfast.

The question many will ask is, "What is next for you, Zig?" This, of course, I do not know, but I'm certain of one thing: I am going to pray without ceasing so that I might stay in the center of God's will, and as long as I am in the center of His will, I know that things are going to be just fine.

And Now, Most Important

The day is coming when you and I will experience a Code Blue from which there is no return. I know where I'll be going when the line goes flat and the rhythmic beeping becomes one continuous melancholy tone. Do you know where you are going? It is my conviction that everybody believes in God to one extent or another. Many who vehemently deny they believe are often the first to blame God when tragedy or disaster strikes in their personal, family, or professional lives, or in the lives of others. This means they really do believe there is a God and that He does have incredible power. With this in mind, doesn't it make sense that this same God also has the power to do some marvelous and wonderful, loving things for them? After all, for hundreds of years His book, the Holy Bible, has been the world's number one best-seller, and millions of people have testified to His grace and goodness.

Now I would like to take you on a short trip to introduce you to the God Who made every aspect of my life better and more meaningful, and Who has guaranteed that I will spend eternity with my loved ones, including many friends and associates.

The Bible is crystal clear on what we must do to spend eternity in heaven with Christ. Step one, recognize that you are a sinner, because all have sinned and fallen short of the glory of God (Romans 3:23), and simply ask God to forgive you of those sins. The bad news and the good news both figure here. The good news is there is nothing you can do that is bad enough to keep you out of heaven; the bad news is there is nothing you can do that is good enough to get you into heaven. The best news: It is not what you do, but what He did on the cross, that guarantees your eternity. Step two, Romans 10:9 clearly says that if you will confess with your mouth that Jesus is Lord, and believe in your heart that God raised Him from death, you will be saved.

So what do you have to do? Nothing but believe. You don't even have to do any work on your own. Ephesians 2:8 says, "For it is by grace, through faith, you are saved, that not of yourself, lest any man should boast."

You mean all I've got to do is accept my salvation as a gift? Absolutely. John 6:29 says, "The work of God is this—to believe in the One He has sent." Some people, letting their pride stand in the way, insist that they must do *something* to earn a place in eternity with Christ. The answer is clear. The thief on the cross, a convicted felon, was promised by the God Who cannot lie that that very day He would see him in paradise. Quite obviously, the thief could do no good deed, encourage no one to live a good life, do any work at all between the cross and heaven. Doesn't it make sense that the same God Who can take the thief, a convicted felon, from the cross straight to heaven can take you from wherever you are into eternity with Him? I hope you will pray this simple sinner's prayer:

"Oh, Lord, I confess that I am a sinner. I ask you to forgive me of my sins. I confess with my mouth that Jesus is Lord and believe in my heart that God raised Him from death."

If you have sincerely prayed that simple prayer, I will see you in eternity. If you have questions or would like additional information, I will be more than happy to send you material that elaborates on what I have just shared with you. God bless you as you pray about the most important decision you can or will ever make.

"Zig"
Zig Ziglar Corporation
2009 Chenault Drive
Carrollton, Texas 75006
972-233-9191
lmagers@zigziglar.com